What Othe

CHAD DAYBELL, TH

"It's no surprise Tom Evans was picked for jury duty for one of the most high-profile criminal cases in America. I can tell you unequivocally he's a man of great character, empathy, and integrity. And, as a former Lori Vallow Daybell juror, Tom will give you perspective you simply won't find anywhere else. I loved his first book *Money, Power and Sex, the Lori Vallow Daybell Trial by Juror Number 18*, and look forward to reading about many more fascinating criminal cases. Every true-crime devotee should read Tom Evans."

Joel Waldman
Former Fox News National Correspondent
and Host of *Surviving the Survivor—*
the true crime podcast and book

"Tom Evans delves into the chilling story of Chad Daybell, whose descent into religious fanaticism spiraled into a devastating trail of children's murders. Drawing from his personal experience as Alternate Juror 18 in the Lori Vallow case, Evans explores the dark intersection of faith and violence, exposing the dangerous consequences of unchecked zealotry and idolatry. This thought-provoking narrative is a must-read for those seeking to understand the complexities of belief and manipulation to satisfy basic old fashioned sexual desire in the guise of religious extremism."

Linda Kenney Baden
high-profile trial attorney, EP and
Host of *Justice Served* on Court TV

CHAD DAYBELL

THE ONE MIGHTY AND STRONG

RELIGIOUS ZEALOTRY, MORMON FUNDAMENTALISM, AND MURDER IN IDAHO

Book 2 in The Murder Trials of Chad Daybell and Lori Vallow Daybell Series

TOM EVANS

Juror #18 in the Lori Vallow Daybell Trial

Chad Daybell, The One Mighty and Strong
© 2025 Tom Evans

Photo credits: Lauren Matthias, Kay Woodcock, Melanie Vallow, Ray Hermosillo, Tom Evans, Susan Evans, Jeanine Harrop Hansen

ISBN (paperback): 979-8-9925688-0-6
ISBN (ebook): 979-8-9925688-1-3
ISBN (audiobook): 979-8-9925688-2-0

Published by Tom Evans
Contact the author at tomevansauthor@gmail.com

To Clint Hansen,

a good friend and a good man

who left us too early.

CONTENTS

Introduction...XIII

Part I

The Life and Times of Chad Daybell
1

1 The Charges Against Chad Daybell 3

2 1968, A Year of Trials and Tribulation 7

3 A Child Is Born.................................16

4 The Boy Becomes a Man......................29

5 Mormon Beliefs and Mormon Influence......38

6 Visions of Glory...............................53

7 Other Influences on Chad Daybell............59

8 Lori Needed to Save People and Chad
  Needed People Who Needed to Be Saved 63

9 Chad Meets Lori 70

10 Killing Charles 73

11 Rexburg Police Get a Call....................83

12 Killing Tammy 89

13 Killing Tylee and JJ 103

14 Tylee Ashlyn Ryan
   (September 24, 2002–September 9, 2019) 109

15 Joshua Jaxon Vallow
   (May 25, 2012–September 23, 2019) 121

16 Who Were JJ and Tylee? 128

17 Other Victims 132

18 Diving into Chad's Mind 141

PART II

The Trial of Chad Daybell

147

19 What the Heck Just Happened? 149

20 Courtroom #400, Ada County
   Courthouse, Boise, Idaho 153

   Monday, April 1, 2024 153

   The Defense 157

   The Prosecution 160

21 Back to Court 164

   Monday, April 1, 2024 164

   Tuesday, April 2, 2024, Chad Has No Shame 166

   Wednesday, April 3, 2024, Cheesy Eggs 167

   Thursday, April 4, 2024, Groundhog Day 169

   Monday, April 8, 2024, Peremptory Challenges 170

*Wednesday, April 10, 2024, Opening
Statements and Witnesses for the Prosecution* 172

Thursday, April 11, 2024, Judge Boyce's Gag Order . . . 176

Monday, April 15, 2024, Deputy "K" 180

*Tuesday, April 16, 2024,
"All That Glitters Is Not Gold"* 184

*Wednesday, April 17, 2024,
"May I Approach the Witness?"* 193

*Thursday, April 18, 2024,
Is Melanie Gibb Protected?* 195

Friday, April 19, 2024, Is Melanie Gibb Complicit? 198

*Monday, April 22, 2024, "A Dark
Number Provided the Justification for Killing"* 204

Tuesday, April 23, 2024, The Seven Gatherers 211

*Wednesday, April 24, 2024,
What Really Happened to Tammy?* 221

Thursday, April 25, 2024, More "Priorisms". 225

Friday, April 26, 2024, More Red Flags 226

Saturday, April 27, 2024, Memorial for Tylee and JJ . . 230

*Monday, April 29, 2024,
Who Else Was Alex in Contact With?* 234

Thursday, May 2, 2024, Victims Find Their Voice 235

*Thursday, May 3, 2024,
The Pursuit for Justice Begins* 240

Monday, May 6, 2024, Another Nail in the Coffin 242

Tuesday, May 7, 2024, My Dilemma 245

Wednesday, May 8, 2024, Another Hard Day in Court . . . 248

Thursday, May 9, 2024,
Prior Actually Makes a Solid Point..................253

Friday, May 10, 2024, There Is an
Upstairs in Chad's House 254

Monday, May 13, 2024, Was Alex a Sexual Deviant?...258

Tuesday, May 14, 2024, Prior Missed
an Opportunity..................................260

Wednesday, May 15, 2024, "A Marvelous Plan"........262

22 The Prosecution Rests! 264

23 The Defense 266

Friday, May 17, 2024, John Prior's Turn 266

Monday, May 20, 2024, Prior Puts
His Foot in It...................................270

Tuesday, May 21, 2024, The Professor
Contributes Nothing.............................271

Wednesday, May 22, 2024, "Give Them
Something to Scream About" 271

24 The Defense Rests.............................274

Thursday, May 23, 2024, Outsmarting Mr. Prior 274

25 Closing Arguments 276

Wednesday, May 29, 2024 276

26 More Questions..............................284

Epilogue: My Feelings about It All 291

Who's Who 299

Acknowledgements...............................303

About the Author 305

Family and friends of victims gather at a Boise tavern following the sentencing of Chad Daybell. From left, Jeanine Hansen, Clint Hansen, Sarah Nelson, Lauren Matthias, Kay Woodcock, and Larry Woodcock.

To JJ's grandparents, Kay and Larry, Tammy's aunt Vicki, and all of the family members of the victims and perpetrators of this horrific tragedy. These people could be hiding themselves away somewhere, and who would blame them? Instead, to their great credit, they are exposing themselves to the world. They do it for justice, they do it for honesty, and they do it because they are good human beings who, even more than the rest of us, need answers, because, with answers, maybe we can move forward in a better way and keep others from going down the dark path that Chad and Lori Daybell chose.

I spent a lot of time with the family, police, and prosecutors during the Chad Daybell trial. The most inspiring thing was how members of both families—people who *could* hold animosities toward each other and who could have a lack of trust for each other—cried together, consoled each other, and supported each other.

These are the most anguished, the most tenacious, and the most determined people I have ever had the privilege of being associated with. They have opened their arms and trusted me enough to call me family, and they can never know what an honor that is.

I hope this book is worthy of their trust and of their confidence in me.

Being an author is not something I ever thought I would be, but like Larry Woodcock, JJ's Paw Paw says: "Hold my beer and watch me." When my time as a juror in the Lori Vallow Daybell trial was over, I wrote a book titled *Money, Power and Sex* about my days on the jury in her trial. I knew I had to tell that story. Just as I knew I had to tell the story about Chad Daybell.

This is the second book in the series—about the Chad Daybell trial, from my view in the gallery, not on the jury, this time. I tell the story as the trial unfolds with a first section on background you'll find helpful. You find out when I do what the witnesses say and the verdict, although that's not a secret.

The third book in this series will document Lori Vallow Daybell's trials in Arizona, the first being her trial for the murder of her then husband, Charles Vallow. When that trial is concluded, there will be another one for her role in the attempted murder of her niece's husband, Brandon Boudreaux.

Whether I crash and burn or am successful is beside the point. The point is that this horrendous story *must* be told. No one had the front-row seat, like I did. So here goes.

INTRODUCTION

When I first stepped into the courtroom as a prospective juror in the Lori Vallow Daybell trial in early April 2023, I had no idea how much my life would be affected. In fact, my plan was to serve my time as a juror and get back to the life I had planned for myself as quickly as possible. It sure didn't work out that way.

In fact, the first time I saw Lori in person, my world went dark, and I felt a weight or heaviness that's hard to describe. I have heard others who had the same experience struggle to explain it. They're the only ones who really understand. In that moment, the moment I was first exposed in person, to Lori Vallow Daybell, I knew I had a huge responsibility as a juror, and I began to get the sense that I wasn't going to walk away from this unscathed.

I have never been a particularly spiritual person. I know good and evil exist in the people who inhabit our world, but I never thought of it as something bigger than ourselves. Like the devil or evil forces at work. Not until the day I walked into that courtroom and met Lori Vallow Daybell face-to-face. I was terrified in that moment to suddenly and unexpectedly, fully know that there are most definitely evil forces and that those forces work through people. I would have to rethink my world view.

For now, though, I needed to do my best to put that aside and focus on the task at hand. For the next five weeks I lived my life in one dimension. The depth of the trial consumed me, and I wasn't able to even think about anything else. The case was unbelievably convoluted, with layer over layer of evidence presented to us by the prosecution team. I found myself struggling to understand what was presented in court. I couldn't look anything up or even talk to anyone about the case. I couldn't read or watch anything. I couldn't even take my notes home at night and review what I heard in court.

In spite of all that, by the time the trial was about half over, I had heard enough evidence to convince me that Lori Vallow Daybell was guilty on all counts. There was no doubt in my mind, reasonable or otherwise, that this woman had conspired to murder the wife of her now-husband and her two children. In fact, I felt like she may have done more than just conspire to the murders; she may have participated. That couldn't be proven, so I would have to settle for the charges against her.

The trial and my part in it did, however, leave me with a lot of questions.

Welcome to my book about Chad Daybell. I hope you find it interesting and worthy of your time. This is my second book about the murders of JJ Vallow, Tylee Ryan, and Tammy Daybell in Idaho and the alleged murder of Charles Vallow and the attempted murder of Brandon Boudreaux in Arizona. If you haven't yet read my book *Money, Power and Sex: The Lori Vallow Daybell Trial by Juror Number 18*, I recommend you go back and do that before reading this book. Although it isn't as comprehensive as this book, my account from the jury box gives some background and insight that is not included in this book.

In this book, on the other hand, I do my best to add information and clarification to what I wrote in *Money, Power and*

Sex. I also have some new insight since writing that book. Maybe it's more like an evolution in my thinking, but I have come to some new conclusions. I was a juror in the Lori Vallow Daybell trial, and I attended every day of the Chad Daybell trial one year later.

I think you will find this book to be different from most true crime books. I separate it into two parts. Part I is about Chad Daybell's life and the times he lived in. I try to give a little historical perspective in order to give younger readers an idea of what life was like in the 1960s and 1970s. To have a true understanding of Chad Daybell, it's important to know about the place and time he grew up in and how those events might have influenced him. The influences on Chad that brought him to where he is today—a convicted killer awaiting the fulfillment of his death sentence—started when he was young.

Part I is an attempt to explain what led Chad Daybell to commit the crimes he committed. An explanation of some Mormon history and the fundamentalist Mormon history as well as contemporary fundamentalist Mormonism that Chad and Lori Daybell were involved in. Some of what influenced Chad were books like *Visions of Glory: One Man's Astonishing Account of the Last Days* by John Pontius and *A Greater Tomorrow: My Journey Beyond the Veil* by Julie Rowe.

I listened to a woman named "Anna" on the *Hidden: True Crime* podcast, and she had a lot to say about *Visions of Glory*, Julie Rowe, and many other influences relating to Chad and Lori Daybell. She was a member of AVOW (Another Voice of Warning) for eight years and knows a lot of the key people in this case and was close to Chad and Lori Daybell.

I also interviewed a woman named Julie who was Julie Rowe's friend and follower for nine years. She still believes in concepts like prior probations and visions, but is angry and speaking out about people who use those ideas for personal gain.

Chad Daybell comes off as an extremely uninteresting person. His mannerisms, the slow way he speaks, how he dresses, and his monotonous voice all scream *boring*. And he is boring. His books are boring beyond most people's ability to endure, his speeches are boring, and his beliefs are boring and downright tedious. At this point I have read a lot of his books. Some books can be hard to read because they are too technical or too in depth or hard to follow. Chad's books were hard to read because they are so elementary. Actually, that's too nice a word. They were boring, repetitive, unbelievable, and downright childish. People did seem to like his children's books, although now I bet they are kind of freaked out by them. His and his wife Tammy's children's books do speak of visions and the prophet speaking directly to God and Jesus, but I think they keep to what is considered scripture in the LDS (Church of Jesus Christ of Latter-day Saints, Mormon) religion.

But, with all that being true, why are we so interested in him? Why are so many people digging into his past? Of course, it's because of the heinous crimes he committed. We're looking for answers, the reasons behind his horrific crimes. The crimes Chad Daybell, Lori Vallow, and Alex Cox committed are the most vicious, brutal, and unforgivable crimes against totally innocent human beings that I can imagine. They were committed for bizarre and selfish reasons. It is impossible for any of us to understand why. It is even harder to understand how. How can a mother, a father, a husband, a wife, and an uncle bring themselves to destroy the lives of those closest and most dependent upon them?

Part I is also my story about the horrific events that unfolded between 2018 and 2020 that led to the two trials in 2023 and 2024 and, in turn, led to five life sentences for Lori Vallow Daybell and six death sentences for Chad Daybell.

You should consider both parts to be mostly factual. I do, however, fill in some gaps with my best guess on what actually happened. It is done with a lot of knowledge through hundreds of hours of research. I talked to everyone who would talk to me who had anything to do with Chad and Lori Daybell. I had exclusive access to some of the key people in this story because of the fact that I was a juror in the Lori Vallow Daybell trial.

Unlike other authors who have written about this true crime, only I had the opportunity to interview the whole prosecution team for both trials. I also got to interview in depth Rexburg Lieutenant Ray Hermosillo, the case detective for the investigations and trials. Lt. Hermosillo was closely involved from the very beginning.

I spent a lot of time talking to people on the periphery of Chad Daybell, and that actually provided me with a lot of insight. People who followed the same beliefs as Chad. People who take the LDS faith a little further than what I think the church intends. These are the people with wall tents, rifles, ammo, and ten years of food that will never go bad in their basements. People who really believe that the second coming of Christ is right around the corner and could happen at any moment, and who further believe that the LDS faith and Rexburg, Idaho, will be front and center.

Many other key people talked to me and helped me come to the conclusions I came to. I did try to talk to Chad Daybell and Lori Vallow Daybell, but of course I got no response from either one. Lori is at the Maricopa County jail, and I've tried to contact her there several times. There is an app and I had to deposit $10. Each message costs 25 cents. Guess I'm out $10, but I had to try the off chance that she would finally come clean. I have heard that she does communicate with some people, but she is only willing to talk about her fanatical beliefs. Who would want to hear that from her?

Apparently, someone does, and given Lori's crimes, that baffles me.

Chad is on death row at the Idaho Maximum Security Institution just outside of Kuna, Idaho. His inmate number is 158911. The only way I am allowed to contact Chad is through snail mail, and I have sent him a note asking if he would be willing to talk to me. He shares death row with some infamous people in Idaho: serial killer Thomas Creech (whose failed execution set off a controversy over death chemicals), Robin Row (she murdered her husband and two children), and killer Gerald Pizzuto, to name just three.

Talking to Chad and Lori is the only way to fill in the gaps. They are the only ones left who know everything that happened. I think that was their plan, and they are sticking to it in spite of the results. At some point, I would think they would realize what they have done and ask for forgiveness or at the very least admit to their crimes. It seems, though, that we mere mortals are so far beneath them that it's just not worth their time to explain things to us. Apparently, it will all make sense to us someday, at least to those of us who are worthy enough to survive the coming apocalypse or make it to the celestial kingdom. I say that with some sarcasm, of course, just to give you an idea of how I believe Chad and Lori think.

I have also tried to talk to Chad's close followers and members of his inner circle: Melani Boudreaux, Melanie Gibb, Zulema Pastenes, and Audrey Barattiero, among others. They may have more to lose by talking to me than Lori or Chad Daybell at this point. I tried to talk to everyone I could think of who might be able to give me some insight on Chad Daybell. Unfortunately, most people either have something to hide themselves or don't want to be associated with him.

There is, however, a ton of information out there, and I studied everything I could get my eyes or ears on. I know some people may be willing to talk now that the trial is over, and I will do my best to talk to them. One of the reasons I chose to attend the Chad Daybell trial is that I would have access to family members and others close to the victims and perpetrators. I have gotten close to many of them, and, thankfully, they have opened their hearts and shared their thoughts with me. I was also able to talk to a lot of people who hold some of the same beliefs as Chad and Lori, some of whom know them personally.

So, mostly factual, but some conjecture on my part in an attempt to write a story and not just a timeline of events as they happened. There may be some people who are close to this story who find fault in what I have written, and indeed there may be fault, but this is my best effort.

Part I is also about how I think Chad became who he was. What influenced him to get to the point where he was a liar, con man, adulterer, and murderer. This I think is the most important part of my book, but also probably the hardest part for the reader to get through. I think it will be worth it for you. It will give you some real insight on how someone gets to a point where he is able to murder children. And that's the point, right? I mean, punishing Chad is *a* point, but I think *the* point of the whole thing, the interest in him and the trial, is to find ways to keep it from happening again. People who hold the same beliefs as Chad and Lori are still out there and in fact gaining momentum in spite of the dangers.

It is also my story about *how* it all happened—all of Chad and Lori's weird beliefs and where those beliefs led them. It was the hardest part of the book for me to write and will probably be the hardest for you to read. Not in the way my description of what influenced him is hard, but emotionally hard. Still important though. Through understanding what his crimes were, we learn what the pitfalls of his beliefs and many other people's beliefs are. We see that those kinds of extreme beliefs can take a person to extremes that shock and horrify the rest of us and are so dangerous that they can lead a person or people to commit the most unthinkable crimes against helpless children—children who they are supposed to love, provide for, and protect.

I attended CrimeCon in Nashville the first week of June 2024, with a table to sell my first book. Personal photo.

Part II is about the Chad Daybell triple murder trial. I already knew some of the key players, so attending the trial as an observer gave me an opportunity to speak with them. Judge Boyce was kind enough to reserve a spot for me in the courtroom because I had been a juror in the Lori Vallow Daybell trial, and he knew I was writing about both trials. I have to say that he and his court attorney, Courtney, do everything they can to make jurors aware of how much we are appreciated.

I was in court every day for Chad's trial right up until the day of the verdict. This time not as a juror, but as an ordinary citizen. I wasn't hog-tied by the rules a juror is subjected to. I got to talk to other people as the trial progressed, and I was able to watch the news reports at the end of each day. If something happened on any given day that I didn't fully understand, I was able to research it until I did.

The timing of the verdict was unfortunate for me. I had obligations and was literally on the plane taking off to Crime-Con in Nashville as the verdict was read. (CrimeCon is sort of an annual love fest among true crime addicts, writers, readers, forensic investigators, podcasters, and law enforcement.) I hated to not be in the courtroom for the reading of the verdict, but at CrimeCon I could discuss the case with other crime investigators (and sell my first book—okay, there was a commercial motive as well). It wasn't like a celebration or anything. Who could celebrate the conviction of Chad Daybell? But I would have liked the opportunity to be there to congratulate the police and prosecutors on a job well done. They had over four years into this case by the time Chad's verdict was handed down, and they deserved a pat on the back.

I did get to be live on the *Surviving the Survivor* podcast with Joel Waldman when Chad's sentence was read in court. That was a surreal moment for me. I guess everyone at Crime-Con was listening. A cheer broke out when he was sentenced to death. That made me feel a little uncomfortable, but what is the proper reaction to someone getting sentenced to death? I suppose people were cheering that justice was served, and I do get that aspect of it.

I began writing this book in October 2023. As I began writing, the trial was set to begin on April 1, 2024. I wouldn't finish writing this book until the trial was over because I wanted to include that, so you get to go through that with me. When we get to that part of the book, I will do my best to let you live it with me, to let you know what it feels like inside the courtroom. Yes, unlike Lori's trial, Judge Boyce allowed court cameras to televise the proceedings, so you could have watched it on TV, and I hope you did that, but watching it on the court TV won't show you all of the emotion, the tension, and the tears, the little things said by people in the gallery during a break. The court cameras are prepositioned by the court, and no one else is allowed to video inside the courtroom or even on the fourth floor of the courthouse. I was there, so I share all of that with you that I think is appropriate.

Who am I to tell this story? Before I received the notice to appear at the courthouse to do my civic duty as a juror, I was living my best life designing and building custom homes. With my wife, Susan, we raised our two kids in a small Idaho town. Susan was a teacher, and I served on the school board and coached baseball and basketball. As you will come to find out, this experience changed my life too.

I'm not a journalist, a reporter, or even a writer. I relied on professionals to help me edit and publish my books. When someone has a critical story to tell, the words tumble out. I felt compelled to tell this story.

Sadly, this is the story of the brutal, ritualistic murder of two innocent children at the hands of their mother and Chad Daybell, as well as the murder of Chad Daybell's wife Tammy at the hands of her husband and Lori's brother Alex. It is not a story I tell for entertainment value. I tell this story because we need to know what happened and why. Or, more importantly, how. How does a mother and her sadistic husband allow themselves to do what they did? How does a loving husband of twenty-nine years so callously end the life of his wife and the mother of their five children?

These are questions those of us who have followed these cases are all struggling to answer. I don't think I can answer the question of how they could do it definitively in this book, but my hope is that this book will keep the question alive and cause us to keep digging until we get the answer.

The story is convoluted beyond belief, it's deeper than our ability to comprehend, and it's sad almost beyond our ability to endure, but endure we will.

JJ's grandmother Kay Woodcock (from left), Lauren Matthias of the *Hidden True Crime* podcast, and Tammy's aunt Vicki Hoban take a moment at the courthouse. Photo provided by Lauren Matthias.

Since you are reading this book, I want to welcome you into a community of the strongest, most loving and determined people you will ever encounter. Don't worry if you have not been to the trial or met any of those involved. You are one of us because you care. When the Lori Vallow Daybell trial ended, I did not know this, but I can tell you that the community of people who loved JJ, Tylee, Tammy, and Charles and the people who loved the people who love the ones who loved them pulled me out of my despair and my loss of faith in my fellow human beings.

This diverse group of people of all different colors, religions, occupations, and pasts have come together, united by one thing: love. They have no time for racism, sexism, or any kind of judgment based on anything other than your character and your ability to care. How beautiful is that and how refreshing?

In diving into the horror of the events I recount in this book, you will be rescued by a community of people who know what's really important: you, me, the children, justice, harmony, safety, community, honesty, love, and a common purpose.

THE LIFE AND TIMES OF CHAD DAYBELL

1

THE CHARGES AGAINST CHAD DAYBELL

C had Daybell is facing three counts of murder and three counts of conspiracy to commit murder for the murders of his wife, Tammy Daybell, and his new wife Lori Daybell's children, Tylee Ryan and JJ Vallow. He is also facing two counts of insurance fraud for accepting Tammy's life insurance benefits after murdering her.

The prosecution is pursuing the death penalty in this case. It will be up to the jury to sentence Chad Daybell with death or not to sentence him to death. In death penalty cases, the jury and not the judge determines the sentencing.

Here's how that works in Idaho: Once the trial is over and if a guilty verdict is reached, the trial goes to the sentencing phase. In the sentencing phase Chad will be given the opportunity to plead for his life. John Prior, Chad's defense attorney, will bring witnesses in to help with that. The jury will go back into deliberations, and if all twelve jurors agree, they will sentence him to death. If even one juror does not agree, for any reason, personal or to do with the case, they will have to go back into court and tell Judge Boyce that they were unable to come to a unanimous decision.

At that point, it would go back to Judge Boyce for sentencing, but the death penalty would be off the table. If he is found guilty, though, the two options will be death or life in prison for the three counts of first-degree murder and three counts of conspiracy to commit murder.

I worry about the jurors in this case. I would not want to be confronted with having to sentence someone to death, even someone who I believe is as evil as Chad Daybell. I could do it and I would do it. I'm just saying having to do it will take a toll on those jurors. They will pay a price. Good people, who had nothing to do with this case prior to getting the jury summons in the mail, like I did. I wish them well.

Fortunately, the jury instructions take a little of the responsibility off the jurors. It's not like the jury gets to say, yeah, he's guilty, but we don't want him put to death. They don't have an option for anything like that. If he is guilty and the jury finds that there are aggravating circumstances, according to the instructions, the penalty is death. So, in the sentencing phase, I think if Chad has been found guilty, it will be hard for anyone pleading for his life to change the outcome.

In the Lori Vallow Daybell trial, the jury I was on had the dark cloud of possibly having to be sequestered over our heads. It would not have been fun, especially in a trial that lasted for five weeks of testimony. In the end we did not have to be sequestered. The jurors for the Chad Daybell trial did end up being sequestered for the sentencing phase.

We know that a jury, a jury that I served on, already convicted Lori Daybell of the same charges, and she was sentenced to five life sentences and added years for grand theft by deception.

The reason Lori Daybell did not face a death penalty was that her lawyers, John Thomas and Jim Archibald, were able to get it removed prior to her trial. I think they considered that a win, and I further think they knew they had little chance of getting her anything less than life in prison. The two attorneys did what they could for her, and I don't think they had any chance to do anything more.

Idaho law does not allow for an insanity plea or even using insanity as a defense. John Thomas and Jim Archibald were ordered by Judge Boyce to not bring Lori Vallow Daybell's sanity up in court in front of the jury. Lori Vallow Daybell tied their hands further, not allowing them to blame anything on Chad Daybell.

I think Chad will have even less of a chance of avoiding at least a life sentence. The prosecution will submit all of the same evidence that got Lori convicted and more. I don't know for sure yet what more the prosecution will present, but they promise me that it won't be the same trial. I think they held back some of the evidence in the Lori Vallow Daybell trial, saving it for the Chad Daybell trial.

I have watched and listened to Chad's attorney, John Prior, in all of the many pretrial hearings, and one thing that I can say about him is that he is capable of droning on for a long time to make a simple point. I would go so far as to say he uses that as a strategy. Long after everyone understands what point he is trying to make, he is still talking. He also talks in circles.

Interestingly, John Prior is not a death penalty–certified attorney in Idaho, but he is still representing Chad in this death penalty trial. If the court had appointed an attorney, that attorney would have to have been death penalty–certified, but since Chad chose Prior, he does not have to be death penalty–certified. Further, Judge Boyce offered to appoint a death penalty–certified attorney to the case, not to replace Prior, but to assist, and Prior rejected the offer. Why would he refuse help? He claimed he had a mountain of work to do defending Chad. I think it was simply that he did not want to share the limelight.

John Prior has talked about the fact that he intends to call on a lot of witnesses, and I'm sure he will cross-examine the prosecution's witnesses in depth. Lori Vallow Daybell's attorneys, John Thomas and Jim Archibald, did not call one witness in her trial, and their cross-examinations were brief. The testimony in that trial lasted five weeks, so I'm guessing it's safe to say this one will go longer.

I am writing this story as the Chad Daybell trial progresses. By the time you are done reading, the trial will be over and Chad will have been sentenced. So, read on and I will write about it as we go.

2

1968, A YEAR OF TRIALS AND TRIBULATION

I entered my eleventh year in 1968. A lot of things happened that year. If you were alive in the 1960s, you remember them. If you were born later, you may have heard of some of them. If you were born after 9/11, you may have a flawed view of the history of our country, and you might think you are living in the worst time in our country now, thanks to a mostly deeply dishonest media who doesn't have a clue what the truth even means and couldn't care less, and an educational system that is more concerned with indoctrinating you than educating you.

I now have a lot of friends in the media who have supported me and are honest, hardworking folks. My wife is a retired teacher. I'm not trying to insult anyone in the media or any teachers. It's the institutions that are broken, not necessarily the people who work in them.

Not that I discount the events of the COVID-19 years, the government shutdowns, looting and rioting, school shootings, an at-best questionable election, defunding the police, an open border, and the results of those events. They were severe, and we're going to be feeling the effects for a long time.

I know in the paragraphs above, I ignited some emotions and that you have some opinions of your own, but bear with me and let's go back to 1968, the year Chad Daybell was born. Just one year in the most turbulent, deadly decade of our country. I grew up just as probably almost every American of the time, watching Walter Cronkite report on the Vietnam War on TV every evening. Of course, TV wasn't new, but the amount of reporting and video coverage on TV was unprecedented. For the first time in American history, we could see with our own eyes, the events, tragic or magical, the day or the day after they happened.

The numbers of American soldiers dying in the most expensive year of the war were reported nightly. They were staggering, and we were shown the bodies of our young soldiers lying dead and mutilated in the jungle. I was fortunate to be born just in time to not get drafted. The last draft happened in the US four years later on December 7, 1972.

One thing you could count on, watching the news, is that it would be horrific. Atrocities were committed mostly by the North Vietnamese Army, but sometimes shockingly by our side. Some 5,000 citizens of Hue, Vietnam, were either clubbed to death or buried alive by the North Vietnamese Army. The My Lai Massacre happened in 1968 where American soldiers were later accused of massacring innocent citizens of Vietnam.

I don't have an opinion about these events other than that they are sad. I wasn't there. Those who fought in Vietnam have been affected in ways I can't understand. I know a lot of them and they have all been affected in one way or another, mostly negatively. A lot of them suffer from what we used to call shell shock and now call PTSD. Every one of them, though, is proud of their service to their country, even if they question our motives in that war, and I am proud of them for their service.

America was more divided in 1968 than any time since the Civil War. Our cities seemed to be at war. Protests broke out in the streets resulting in more death, destruction, and violence. Three protestors protesting a Whites-only bowling alley in South Carolina were killed by highway patrolmen. "Sit-ins" started up on college campuses pitting students against the "establishment." Among all of the turmoil women began to burn their bras, deciding it was time for them to finally win the fight for their own rights. Violent protests broke out at the Democratic National Convention in Chicago, Illinois.

On April 4,1968, Martin Luther King Jr., the massively popular, peaceful voice of the Civil Rights Movement, was shot dead on his motel room balcony. At least forty people died in the ensuing riots. On June 5, 1968, the extremely popular presidential hopeful, Robert Kennedy, was shot in the head and died after winning the California Democratic Party presidential primary in Los Angeles, less than five years after his brother and our president, John F. Kennedy, was assassinated. These two events broke the heart of our country.

On top of everything else that was happening, our beloved leaders, leaders who we actually respected and loved, and who deserved our respect and love, were murdered in cold blood right in front of our eyes. No one knew what to think. Why was this happening? Was it a conspiracy? Were we ourselves at fault? How could our country ever recover? How could we move forward without these people who held our hope?

On top of the horrific Vietnam War and the violence it inspired at home, we were in the midst of the Cold War. Cold War sounds harmless, but let me tell you, it was terrifying. We were constantly told that nuclear war with Russia could and most likely would erupt at any moment. We had drills at school where we were taught to get under our desks and put our hands over our heads in case a nuclear bomb was launched. We had watched on TV the fake towns with fake people in the Nevada nuclear test sites and watched all the houses and mannequins disintegrate. By this time, we were also aware of the cancer those close to the test sites died from, so we all knew it was useless to try to survive, but what else could we do?

The Berlin Wall had been standing for about twenty years, and no one knew for sure what was going on on the other side. That whole part of the world was completely isolated from the free world, and nobody could penetrate it and tell us what life was like in that part of communist Eastern Germany.

It would be four more years before President Nixon would go to China. Before that happened, China was almost as isolated to the free world as East Berlin. At that time, we had no trade with China. No American goods were allowed in China. Chinese citizens didn't even know what Coca-Cola and McDonald's were. We knew that Chinese citizens were not free and were mistreated, but our attempts to change that only resulted in heartache and strife at home.

We learned of an American B-52 bomber that had crash landed in the sea by Greenland carrying four nuclear bombs. It's a miracle that they didn't explode. Still, they would have to be safely recovered, and who knew if they might still go off.

The nuclear-powered submarine, the USS *Scorpion*, sank, drowning all hands, ninety-nine men. What would become of its nuclear reactor? Could it explode? Would there be nuclear waste polluting the ocean? We really didn't know the answers.

And we hadn't gotten over the Cuban Missile Crisis that happened in 1962 when the US was forced to stand up to Russia and make them back down from installing nuclear missile sites just miles off the Florida coast. We were literally minutes away from all-out nuclear war when cooler heads prevailed and we were all saved.

The Civil Rights Act was passed by President Lyndon B. Johnson right before he declared that he would not run for reelection. Richard Nixon ended up winning the Republican primary and going on to be elected the thirty-seventh president.

The gold standard was repealed by Congress, meaning that the US dollar would no longer be backed by gold. Up until that time, the United States held an amount of gold, the value of which was equal to the amount of dollars in circulation. It's easy to imagine that once the dollar no longer had to be backed by an equal amount of gold, inflation would become a problem. After all, there could be any number of dollars put into circulation. It would be up to the government to decide how many.

This is one of the most explosive events that happened in 1968, and no one ever even talks about it. It opened the door to out-of-control government spending and where we are with our economy today, out-of-control government spending and an insurmountable deficit and national debt.

Think of it this way: Prior to ending the gold standard and not having a balanced budget amendment, the government had to go to the taxpayers for whatever money they wanted to spend. The taxpayers had the option of saying no. Post-gold standard, they can just inject money into the economy instead of having to raise money through taxes to spend. The more dollars they inject and put into circulation, the less each dollar is worth. It's exactly the same as taking money out of your wallet or bank account without even having to ask you.

Any number of highly intelligent, high-paid economists with PhDs will tell you why I'm wrong, why it's not that simple, but those economists are benefiting from the system we have now, either directly from the federal government or indirectly.

Petula Clark was singing with Harry Belafonte on TV. Petula Clark was an extremely popular White singer, and Harry Belafonte was an extremely popular Black singer. Clark had the audacity to touch Belafonte on the arm on national TV. This kind of familiarity between a White woman and a Black man was not okay with a lot of people in 1968, and it caused a huge uproar. I bring it up just to show where we were in our country back then compared to now.

Thankfully we have come a long way, even though we have some to go. We seem to take two steps forward and one step backward in regard to race, but hopefully we'll get there someday.

Yale University reluctantly admitted its first women in 1968. It was very controversial at the time. Most men were not excited about sharing their smokey study halls and their libraries of knowledge with the fairer half. After all, the fairer half had already burned their bras and proven that they would not adhere to the august unwritten rules of decorum.

We still had a long way to go in terms of workplace safety in 1968. President Nixon wouldn't sign the Occupational Safety and Health Act (OSHA) until 1970. In the Farmington Mine disaster in West Virginia seventy-eight men died. Mining disasters and workplace accidents in general were not uncommon back then. The people who held those kinds of jobs mostly just accepted the risk as part of the job.

1968 was also the year we learned of the Zodiac killer. I lived in the Bay Area of California then, and I think the Zodiac killer was every bit as terrifying as any of the things listed above. He is known to have randomly murdered five people and left two others for dead who ended up surviving. In his cryptic notes to police, he takes credit for thirty-seven other murders. His terrifying and confusing notes were printed on the front page of newspapers and shown on the news on TV. We still don't know who he was, and it's still an open investigation.

And on top of it all, it was the year that HIV first entered the United States. It was a deadly virus, and at the time doctors didn't know for sure how it was transmitted. What they did know was that it was especially viral in gay men. Gay men had been fighting for their rights along with everyone else, and HIV did not help. The public became aware of the virus when it exploded in an epidemic ten or twelve years later and we were forced to come to terms with it. Even though we have at least tamed the virus in the US, it remains extremely deadly in places like Africa where medical care and education barely exist.

Okay, so even though it has even less to do with this story than my ramblings here, who can talk about the 1960s without mentioning the music? The hordes wouldn't show up for Woodstock on Yasgur's farm in upstate New York until 1969, but the music of the '60s was the best, inspired I guess by all the turmoil and drug use. Still, I hold to the idea that we had the coolest music and the coolest cars ever created. Both are still cherished by millions, just turn on FM radio. At least half of the music you hear came from that decade. Okay, I know the only people who listen to FM radio are from the '60s, but the point is still valid.

And the cars. Just pay attention as you drive through town. You will notice a lot of the cars and pickups are still going, mainly because they are so cherished by their owners. I think it's because of their simplicity. I have a 1969 Chevy pickup, and if it breaks, I can fix it. I don't need a computer or anything much more than some basic tools and my own hands and eyes.

Why am I so attracted to that? Why is it important to me to have a vehicle that I can work on myself? I think it gives me a sense of independence, of freedom.

Something else happened in 1968. Something to lift our spirits and take our minds off all of the turmoil. Something to give us hope. In 1962 President Kennedy announced that we would land a man on the moon by the end of the decade. In 1968 we got much closer to that goal and actually started to believe it could happen. Astronauts on Apollo 7 circled the moon, seeing firsthand the back side of the moon for the first time and actually sending pictures back of the sunrise on Earth. This one event was a miracle. It was heavenly, and it was like a message from God telling us we can overcome all of the turmoil back here on Earth.

Southeast Idaho and rural Utah haven't changed as much as the rest of the country since 1968. The population in Rexburg, Idaho, the area where three of the four murders I write about occurred, was about 8,000 in 1968 compared to 41,000 now with a lot of that growth happening since 2019. But 41,000 is still a pretty small town especially for the seat of Madison County and home to Brigham Young University Idaho. It's still mostly a farming community, although small farms have declined in recent years because it's impossible to make a small farm profitable anymore.

If you haven't lived in a small town, it might be hard for you to understand what it's like. Everyone knows everyone, especially since 95 percent of the people there are members of the Mormon Church. People still feel like they have control over their community. It's not hard to put yourself into a position to make change. You can get elected to the school board or city council if you're willing to put in the time. The Chamber of Commerce still runs the downtown. Small mom and pop businesses still exist to some extent, although a lot of them failed during the COVID-19 disaster. Even so, if you live there and go into the local McDonald's, you probably recognize at least some of the people working there.

While small towns in Idaho and Utah in the 1960s maybe didn't have to suffer as much firsthand as the more urban areas of our country, they did still have to send their young men to Vietnam, and national policies have had a negative effect. Still, people are now and always have been more patriotic, family oriented, and Christian. Crime is much lower and homelessness is almost nonexistent. Drugs like meth and fentanyl have definitely taken a toll. These drugs find their way into our small towns and have a huge impact on our young people.

Still, Chad's childhood was pretty idyllic in small-town Utah. He was able to play whatever sports he wanted to play. He was free and safe to roam as much as he wanted. When he learned to ride a bike, he could ride for miles without fear of being abducted. He could walk to and from school with a group of buddies. Unfortunately, he did more to change all of that in his community than any outside influence or government policy.

3

A CHILD IS BORN

Among the many other seemingly insignificant events that occurred in 1968, a child was born. Chad Guy Daybell was born on August 11, 1968, in Provo, Utah. A perfectly normal birth into a perfectly normal family in a perfectly normal community. Or so it seemed.

Provo, Utah, was and still is a highly Mormon community and possibly, to its credit, seemingly immune to most of the problems of the rest of the country. Chad was born into a family that was normally Mormon. A tight-knit, conservative, patriotic, religious family. Church, family, and country came first.

So the question arises: What led Chad Daybell, who was born into a seemingly normal family in a seemingly normal community, to become the force behind the alleged murder of a husband and the murder of two innocent children and his own wife?

That is the question, right? We know he did it. We don't know for sure if he was at the scene of three of the four murders when they happened, but we do know that he was the force that caused the murders. Much like Charles Manson and Ervil LeBaron before him, he called for the murders. But what led him to murder?

It's not an easy question to answer, but I'm going to answer it in this book. I'm going to go through all of the information that is available to us and that information will lead to a conclusion—the conclusion that Chad Guy Daybell is a murderer and a child murderer to boot. In the mind of Chad Daybell these murders were the right thing to do, his way forward.

As I said, Chad Daybell was born into a normal Mormon family. In fact, his grandfather, on his mother's side, who Chad got his middle name from, Guy Oyler, married Flora Chappell in 1943. Guy served in the Navy and saw action in the South Pacific on the USS *Pocomoke* during WW2, having left for the Navy right after marrying Flora. After the war Guy supported his family as a truck driver before moving on to become the owner of a successful painting company. He became a success the old-fashioned way, working hard and keeping his word, much like a lot of the Greatest Generation.

Guy also served as a bishop in his ward and claims to have had a visitation from an angel. So, in Chad's family, the idea that someone besides the prophet of the Mormon Church could have that happen wasn't original to Chad. Guy passed away in 2008, and after his death Chad said his grandfather was busy in the spirit world. That's a very Mormon thing to say. In fact, the first time I heard someone say that firsthand was the first time I heard Lori Daybell speak in person at her sentencing. She claimed she spoke to the people that she and Chad had murdered, and they were happy and busy in the spirit world.

I can't find much information about Chad's grandmother Flora, so I think it's safe to say that she was most likely the supporter of her priestholder husband, doing what good Mormon wives are expected to do to this day, support their husband and his sons and teach the daughters how to do the same.

Pretty much the same story on Chad's father's side. Finity Daybell joined the Mormon Church and moved his family from England to Utah in 1864. Like most Mormon converts of the time, they had to suffer through harsh winters and severe poverty in the early years. The Daybell family eventually thrived, though mostly by farming in the early years, and then moving on to logging. Chad's grandfather, Kieth Daybell survived WW2 even though he was wounded twice and was taken prisoner by the Germans. After coming home from the war, Kieth and brothers Theo and LaVar started the Daybell Lumber Company in the Uinta Mountains of NE Utah.

What do we know about Chad Daybell's childhood? It's surprisingly hard to find any information about it. Maybe not so surprising when you realize that his childhood was pretty much a normal childhood. I mean if you were to look me up and try to find information about my childhood, you wouldn't find anything. Nothing out of the normal or newsworthy. So that's the most important thing to know about Chad Daybell's childhood. The other problem with finding information about Chad's childhood is that people don't want to associate themselves with him. Can't blame them for that.

Most of what I was able to find out came from Chad's sister-in-law, Heather Daybell. She allowed herself to be interviewed by Lauren and Dr. John Matthias on their *Hidden True Crime* podcast. I had the opportunity to meet her, but she is understandably protective of her privacy and declined my request to interview her. Heather is married to Chad's younger brother Matt.

I have also met Matt and had some brief conversations with him. He also wouldn't talk to me about the case. I got the feeling that if I pushed, I may have gotten at least one of the two to talk, but they don't know me, they don't know what

I'm writing, and I respect their privacy. In fact, I think they are brave and sincere just to expose themselves as much as they do.

I'll say here that when it comes to family members of the victims, the approach I take is to just be around. I've watched some people in the media push them for an interview, and I refuse to do that, no matter how important I think the information I might get from them is. I have found that it's better if they get to know me naturally. I let it be known that I have questions for them and what I am doing, and I let them decide if they want to talk to me or not. It may not be the best investigative approach, but it's respectful and I don't hate myself. It's surprising to me how many family members have opened up and trusted me, and I am thankful for that.

Heather grew up close to the Daybell family and knew Chad as a teenager, and she says a lot about Chad's family and his life as a teenager. It's to Heather's husband, Matt Daybell's credit, that he seems to be a normal human being. Is he still a practicing Mormon? Yes, he is, and that says something about the Mormon faith. In spite of all the problems associated with the Mormon Church, I guess Matt still finds it worthy. In spite of all of the crazy offshoots and its fundamentalist history, I guess Matt must think at least that the Mormon Church is headed in the right direction and that it's still worth promoting.

Millions of Americans agree with him. A lot of really good people I became associated with as a prior juror and author agree with him. And, like I said before, Mormon country is mostly immune to a lot of the problems the rest of the country is suffering from.

What else do we know about Chad's childhood? It was very similar to my childhood and most people's childhoods prior to the advent of social media and smartphones. He played sports, rode bikes, and hung out outside with his friends.

Later on, he worked part-time, liked girls, went to school, did his homework, and continued playing sports and hanging out with his friends. He was student council treasurer his senior year of high school. Pretty typical.

The most striking thing to me about Chad Daybell and Lori Vallow Daybell, for that matter, is that they led normal lives all the way up until the time they met. I hear a lot about what a loser Chad was, that he had no ambition of his own, he was just an overweight, unattractive nobody.

I understand why people don't want to say anything positive about him now that we know what he did, but I do have to say that before going down the path he chose and eventually meeting Lori, he was a faithful, hardworking, family-oriented young man. He was ambitious enough to start his own publishing company and author several books of his own.

As I said in the introduction, for the most part, his books about the second coming of Christ and the New World and his visions for faithful Mormons are unsophisticated and downright childish, but he wrote them, he published them, and he had a following. A lot of people loved them. He had worked hard going back and forth between journalism, which was what he was educated in, and being a cemetery sexton, which required a lot of overtime and came with a lot of responsibility.

He got good grades in school, played sports with some success, and was always active in the church. He was awarded an academic scholarship to Brigham Young University. He seemed to be focused and driven to succeed. He wasn't always sure what direction he wanted to go, but at least, according to his autobiography, he put a lot of thought into figuring it out.

In 1987 at the age of nineteen, Chad was sent by the church on his mission to New Jersey. Some of his experiences there seem to contribute to his belief in visions. This is where, according to his autobiography, he says he starts to "work on developing my gift." He goes on further to say that when he and his companion, Elder Hepworth, gave a blessing to a girl named Lina, her wrist was miraculously healed. So now we see Chad believes he is a faith healer.

The only other thing I can see that he believed, or claimed to believe, when he was a young man that was out of the ordinary was that he could *see through the veil.* Seeing through the veil is a Mormon thing. Mormons believe that when you are born, a veil is placed over you to keep you from having knowledge that you are not ready for.

They explain it like this: You lived in heaven before coming to earth, so all the knowledge you had from your life in heaven would have to be hidden from you while you served your time on earth. I wonder why. Why wouldn't we be able to have all the knowledge possible? Wouldn't it be better if we were allowed that knowledge on earth? I suppose our time on earth is a test for some reason. That's why Mormons call our time on earth a probation. I think these are the kinds of questions Mormons are taught not to ask. We aren't meant to understand.

And in Chad's case, he believed that people have a spiritual life or existence before and after life on this earth. Since his veil had been torn, he was able to communicate with other spiritual beings, his ancestors, angels, even Jesus, and this gave him insight and standing that the rest of us don't have.

This is not, however, an uncommon thing for Mormons to believe. Mormon prophets claim to have a direct line to God. They get visions and revelations that direct their actions and, in turn, direct the actions of their followers. In Chad's case, though, he felt that he had knowledge that the rest of us don't have, and that put him above everyone else. He was directed by spirits and angels.

I think this is the idea that led him down a path that brought him to where he is now. Believing he could see through the veil in itself wouldn't have been enough to lead him to murder. Plenty of other Mormons and people in other religions have believed the same thing, but it was the beginning of a path he chose that led him to believe things that opened doors for him to get to where he ended up.

The question is, did he actually believe the voices in his head were spirits, or did he use that idea in order to raise his position in life and get people to follow him? To put himself above everyone else? He seems to believe that he should have been the president of the whole Mormon Church and that would have put him in a position to have millions of followers.

It kind of reminds me of Barney Fife, the bumbling deputy on *The Andy Griffith Show*, or George Costanza. If you don't know who these characters are, you are missing out on some really good comedy. Anyway, George (from the *Seinfeld* show) was contemplating his future one day and considering his options. He thought maybe he could be the manager of the Yankees, like that option might be open for him. Such naivete sometimes allows people to get to a higher position in life than someone who is maybe more realistic about their qualifications. Of course, George didn't get to be the manager of the Yankees, but he did land an executive position with the team. I definitely think Chad had that quality, but of course it didn't work out for him.

So that is a path that Chad chose. Or maybe think of it as a freeway with lots of off-ramps and on-ramps at this point. He would still have plenty of choices or options that would lead him in a good or a bad direction. Early on, it looks like it could have led to a good life with a great family and plenty of success.

Chad didn't publish his autobiography until 2017, so the question arises: Did Chad actually believe he was a faith healer way back in 1987, or did he make it up later to support his idea that he was superior to the rest of us?

When Chad hit his third home run of the game, the crowd, small as it was, went kind of nuts. Even after the cheers died down, Chad could hear people talking about him. He overheard his friend's dad in the stands say he was something special. Even at twelve years old, Chad felt he *was* special, and he was glad to hear someone take notice. He was sure that sometime in the future they would all take notice. This one little baseball game was just the beginning for him. Someday the whole world would recognize the name Chad Daybell. He is the one mighty and strong, and he will be followed and revered by millions.

At least this was an idea he had had in his head for a while now. He wasn't sure why, but he knew he had a connection to the spirit world. He was trying to put it all together. He daydreamed a lot, and when he did, these are the visions he had. When he prayed, and he prayed a lot, he felt a connection to spirits. He felt like Joseph Smith had something to say to him. He felt like his ancestors have something to say to him.

Chad loved to read, especially history and even more especially his own family history. In fourth grade he gave writing a try. He wrote his first novel, *The Murder of Dr. Jay and His Assistant*. His teacher loved it, and he even got a commendation letter from the school superintendent. The interesting thing about that title to me is that it gives me the idea that Chad might have been obsessed with murder, even at that young age. In fact, most of his books are extremely violent.

He had been reading in the temple about his great-great-grandfather on his father's side, Finity Daybell. Finity joined the church and immigrated to Utah from England in 1864. That was only twenty years after Joseph Smith was murdered in Carthage, so Chad knew his roots went all the way back almost to the beginning of the Mormon Church. Finity must have known Brigham Young personally. Chad wondered what that was like, being in the presence of someone so mighty and pure.

Chad spent a lot of time contemplating his future. He knew it would be bright, but he had no idea how he would achieve the greatness he knew was to be his. When he had his first near death experience (NDE) after jumping off a cliff into the Flaming Gorge Reservoir, a whole new world opened up to him, or as he said, "My knowledge of the world expanded beyond what normal people get to see." That's when he knew he had a gift directly from God. God had chosen him.

Chad had been at Flaming Gorge Reservoir in Wyoming with a group of friends. He was nervous about making the jump, but didn't want to seem weak in front of his friends. When he hit the water, he said he felt something snap in his neck. He thought he had broken his neck. He says he realized later that it was his veil tearing that he felt. Under the water he was able to see that he had a connection to the spirit world. The spirits talked to him, saying he had work to do before he would die.

Now he was able to see things that other people did not get to see. He could see that we all have a spiritual being that is much greater than our mortal being. It is everlasting, all knowing, and beautiful. He could see that he had a life before this life on earth and he would have one after. He could also see that he had walked on this earth many times before in past lives or previous probations as he called them. Probations because each existence on earth is like a test or like you are on probation to see if you are worthy.

No one close to Chad remembers him saying anything at the time about a near death experience, so this may be another idea he came up with later.

Because of the teachings of the church, which Chad took very seriously, he knew that as a good Mormon, he was supposed to prepare himself for the second coming of Christ. That is the whole point of our existence on this earth. He felt like he would be fortunate enough to be on this earth when it happens. He thought that was the point of his being able to see through the veil. It must be that in some way he would be the leader of all of the saints, preparing themselves for what was to come.

But what was to come? How would the second coming of Christ happen? He had so many questions, but he had faith that the answers would be shown to him when the time was right, because that is what he was taught. He would have the information he needed when he was developed enough to understand what it meant. He knew he had a long way to go, and he was determined to be the best Mormon he could be and determined to be worthy in the eyes of God.

So Chad studied hard, read the Bible, and the *Book of Mormon* and whatever other religious reading material he could get his hands on. He kept up with his studies at school. He wasn't the best student, not top of his class or anything like that, but he worked hard and did well. His friends and his peers were not as serious as he was. They had no idea and seemed to care less about what was coming.

Chad had friends and a social life, but he always felt separated, apart from everyone else. Sometimes he felt left out, like he didn't fit in, but other times he felt that he was so far above everyone else and so much more special and that was what separated him. Still, he was a typical student. Not standing out and not making any particular impression on anyone. I think, though, that this might give us a clue as to how he can sit in court in front of the police, the families of his victims, the prosecution, and the judge, showing no emotion or any sense of awareness. He has always been apart from us, and he is used to it.

The biggest problem for Chad was that he just kind of quit growing for a while. In the years following his three-home-run game, his teammates outgrew him. Suddenly he was one of the smallest kids on the team, and his friends had moved away from him. As a result, Chad spent more time in the library reading religious books. In his autobiography, *Living on the Edge of Heaven*, he says this is when he first read about reincarnation and past lives. He says he thought it was false at the time, and he quit reading about it. I find that strange because he embraced that idea later.

Chad had become angry by this point. Not uncommon for kids entering puberty. He talks about a day when he just started stomping on bees for no reason. He kept it up until a voice told him to stop. Was it his conscience or a spirit talking to him? He says it was a spirit, and this incident makes me think he actually believed that the voice in his head was a spirit. We all have the voice in our heads, but most of us attribute it to our conscience. This is an important point and one I have pondered a lot. Why did Chad think his conscience was an angel, Jesus, or ancestor speaking to him? He goes on to talk about praying in his room and having a spirit rush into the room. He says this event caused his chest to burn with confirmation about the truthfulness of the *Book of Mormon* and he actually cried.

Thinking about this I just think that some people are so open to the idea of spirits and spirituality. It's in the way our brains work. Some people are realists, sometimes to a fault, and some people are idealists, sometimes to a fault. Chad describing this particular event makes me think he was an idealist to an extreme fault. He believed what he wanted to believe in spite of the facts. I think this idea is supported by the fact that he was a journalist. Journalists and artistic people in general tend to be more idealistic. Scientists, mathematicians, and engineers tend to be more realistic.

Another thing that struck me in Chad's autobiography is when he talks about getting his first patriarchal blessing. He says it was made clear to him in his blessing that he had a long, wonderful life ahead of him. There would be spiritual gifts that would be made known to him later in life and he would bless the lives of others. I should note here that the Mormon Church says that patriarchal blessings are not to be shared with the public. The fact that Chad shares this in his autobiography goes directly against the teachings of the church.

Who can give a patriarchal blessing? In the Mormon Church, a patriarch is called and ordained to give patriarchal blessings. So this person is supposed to have knowledge about your past lives, your lineage, and your future. The Mormon Church says: "The patriarchal blessing contains counsel from the Lord." This is another problematic idea to me. Where does this person get his information? How does he know what the future holds for someone? And, if he can tell you your future, what effect would that have on you?

Okay, so I'm guessing that this patriarch is supposed to keep it general and not be looking into a crystal ball and saying something like: "You're going to die young" or "You will be super rich." Still, if you are an idealist like we know Chad to be, you might be inclined to read into what is said in your patriarchal blessing. Also, the information given in your blessing is supposed to come from God. So apparently this person, this human being living with the rest of us on this earth, has the voice of God in his head? That opens up a lot of possibilities and not all of them are good.

Chad does not say if his patriarchal blessing said he was descended from the tribe of Ephraim. The tribe of Ephraim is specifically given the primary responsibility to lead the latter-day work of the Lord. A person receiving his or her patriarchal blessing is supposed to be told whether they descended from the tribe of Ephraim or the tribe of Jacob. There is a lot more to it than that, but that is the important part to us.

27

If he was told he was descended from the tribe of Ephraim, that would have supported his idea that he was to lead the 144,000 at the time of the second coming of Christ. If he was not told that, if he was told he descended from the tribe of Jacob, then I think we can surmise that Chad just used whatever part of scripture and Mormon belief that would suit his needs and left out those parts that didn't fit his narrative. It's really too bad he left that part out. I think it would tell us a lot about Chad.

Chad goes on to say in his autobiography that this is about the time he started helping out a family in need. There was an elderly man in his neighborhood who could no longer support his own weight. For three years, between the ages of fourteen and seventeen, Chad went twice a day to help this man. This sounds to me like a good Christian young man in a good Christian family doing the Christian thing, helping his neighbor. I think Chad did grow up in a good Christian family, and we know for sure he grew up in a good Christian area. It is a huge commitment for a teenager either way, so I think we can say that, so far, Chad is on the right path in spite of his belief that he was above everyone else.

4

THE BOY
BECOMES A MAN

C had met Tammy Douglas, and they were married in the temple in 1990. It looked like it was meant to be. Tammy had had her eye on Chad, and Chad was totally smitten by her. They were a great match, having the same desires for their lives together, with church, family, and country coming first. She even helped Chad get his job at the cemetery where she worked.

Getting married in the temple is a big deal in the Mormon world. You have to have a certain standing in the church to even be allowed to enter the temple. The ceremony and the rituals were described to me by a woman who was married in the temple. You should read her book *Silenced in the Name of God* by Stephanie Taylor for an account of what she was put through.

The couple worked hard together and built a family of their own, including five children. At the time of their marriage, Chad was still a student at BYU where he was studying journalism and working as a reporter for the *Daily Universe*, the school paper. After graduation, he went on to work as a copyeditor at the Ogden *Standard-Examiner*.

In 1993 Chad and Tammy went on a family vacation to La Jolla, California, where Chad claims to have had his second near death experience (NDE). According to Chad, he was swimming in the ocean when he was overcome by a rogue wave. He eventually made it back to shore and was taken to the hospital for stitches. He had been held underwater by the undertow for several minutes, and this is when he claims to have "died" and seen visions.

However, his brother was there at the time and remembers the incident, but doesn't remember anything about Chad's NDE. He thinks Chad may have come up with this idea later to promote the idea that Chad was a visionary. In his autobiography Chad makes other hard-to-believe claims, one being that he saw the horrific events of September 11, 2001, in Manhattan in a dream he had in 2000.

It wasn't long after this that Chad started claiming he saw the second coming of Christ in his visions and writing about what that would be like. He started out saying his books about this were works of fiction. In fact, in his "Author's Notes," he writes that they are fiction, but he eventually made the claim that it was all actually true. Most of the books that Chad wrote are about this. I won't recount the whole thing here. I just want to give you the idea so you can see where Chad's mind was and how he worked at gaining followers.

I have to say here that I have wondered a lot about Chad and Tammy's five children. They are all adults now, but I wonder how they were influenced by Chad's beliefs. According to Chad's son Garth, he learned at one point that Chad's books were the truth. He had previously been told that they were fiction and were meant more to inspire thought than to predict the future. Garth says that during a time when author Julie Rowe stayed with the Daybell family, he learned from his dad that his books were actually true.

The interesting point of this to me is that when Garth heard the books were true, he believed it. I learned a lot about Garth and his sister Emma during the Chad Daybell trial. They testified for the defense, and I recount their testimony later in this book. Chad's mother also testified, but for the prosecution. I wish any of the people testifying for the defense would have stuck around after they testified, but they all bolted from the courthouse as soon as they were released by Judge Boyce.

According to Chad and his followers, there was to be a great earthquake in the Salt Lake City area followed by floods and plagues. There would be a great gathering of like-minded Mormons in the Rexburg area. In fact, there actually are properties set aside around Rexburg where tent cities are expected to be built. These Mormons who survive are the ones who are prepared spiritually and practically for the second coming. It seems like for someone to be prepared spiritually, they would not only have to be in good standing with the Mormon Church, they would have to have taken it a step further.

Those who would be prepared spiritually would have, in Chad's mind, been members of Another Voice of Warning (AVOW) or Preparing a People (PaP) and would be prepared to lead people through the horrible events that would occur on earth. They would be prepared to gather souls and lead others to Zion. Zion would be in Missouri where the Mormon Church actually has set aside land for this reason. They would be responsible for not only surviving Mormons, but other Christians whom they would convert. They would also have to be prepared to "atone" those who were unconvertible. In this way, by killing them and spilling their blood on the ground, they could save the souls of those who refused to follow.

Blood atonement was an early Mormon doctrine. There is some speculation that Brigham Young used it through his "avenging angels" to thwart his enemies when he was governor of Utah and prophet of the Mormon Church.

Preparing a People was a prepper community that Chad was deeply involved in. It focused on helping people prepare for the second coming of Christ. It was mainly focused on supplies, guns, and whatever one would have to do to be prepared. They would have gatherings or conferences where people like Chad would speak and sell their books. It was also a great opportunity for Chad to mine his followers.

AVOW is the same kind of group, but focuses more on spiritual preparation. It is thought that only the most spiritually prepared people would survive.

To be practically prepared meant that you had all of the equipment, food, and weapons you would need. Preppers who follow people like Chad (and, yes, they are still out there) have basements, storage sheds, or bunkers full of food, wall tents, weapons, and ammunition. There are lists of all the items one should stock away in preparation. The tents are symbolic as well as practical. There would be tent cities put together for survivors, and the survivors would be nomads working their way to Zion.

The trip to Zion was also a symbolic as well as a practical journey. One is supposed to arrive in Zion in rags, having overcome all of the obstacles to get there. One is supposed to learn important lessons on the trip that prepare one for the higher level one would live on in Zion and in preparation for meeting Jesus.

Path to Glory. Just a doodle I did sitting in court listening to testimony showing some of the elements of Chad's (and others') beliefs.

In Chad's books, Jesus seems to show up in different forms. One day he appears godlike, and another day he is working in the fields with everyone else. In the book *Visions of Glory* written by John Pontius, his main character, Spencer, claims to be like Jesus's assistant and works closely with Jesus. This tells us a lot about how these people like the now deceased author Pontius and Chad Daybell think. They are so narcissistic, they think they will be special to Jesus.

So this is the man Tammy is married to. This is the father of her children. As they progress through their marriage, Chad dives deeper and deeper into these beliefs. He believes *he* knows when the second coming of Christ will happen. He believes *he* will be the one to lead the survivors of the events leading up to the second coming. He believes *he* has knowledge beyond what the rest of us are allowed to have because he is a translated being, closer to Christ. He believes he had previous lives on earth, which he calls probations. And he conditions his children to believe these things.

At some point he starts believing that he has the ability to rank people on a scale. If I were to prioritize the things about Chad that are important in terms of calculating his guilt, this scale is on the top of the list. It is the single most important idea that directly points to the fact that it was Chad who called for the murders of Tammy, Tylee, and JJ. Lori seems to have happily followed him in this idea, but it was Chad's idea, Chad's plan. It was Chad's excuse for getting people out of his way. It was a light or dark scale. The higher up you went on the light scale, the closer to Christ you were. The lower down you went on the dark scale, the closer to Satan you were.

Chad took this even further, believing that he was the one who could save a soul from the demons or zombies, as he called them, who inhabited the body of someone on the dark scale. The zombies could be cast out. If you weren't too far down on the dark scale, the zombies could be cast out with a simple ceremony using prayer. The further down on the dark scale one was, the harder it was to cast out these zombies. The body may even need to be destroyed to cast out the zombie and save the soul of the person whose body had been inhabited. But the body had to be killed in specific ways in order to release the soul, so the soul could move on to heaven. In simple terms, it would have to be more brutal. Binding and burning are two of the ways to kill a body and cast out a zombie.

As we know from the Lori Vallow Daybell trial, her adopted son, JJ, was bound with duct tape and plastic, and her daughter, Tylee, was burned. This is an important point in the Chad Daybell trial. I'm not sure how many people caught it, but the point of the trial was to place the blame for the murders on Chad. Chad had the light and dark scale, and Chad was the one who said the bodies of those whose souls he was saving needed to be burned or bound.

In a conversation I recently listened to between Lori and her son, Colby, Lori makes the absurd claim that it was Tylee's wish to be cremated and that is why she had been burned. She also claims that Tylee is somehow responsible for JJ's death. Tylee died two weeks before JJ. Was she saying that Tylee somehow came back from the dead and killed JJ? Whatever she was trying to say, it was infuriating to hear her try to blame JJ's death on Tylee. Lori has absolutely zero remorse and zero consideration for the people she left alive who loved her victims. I am astounded by that every time I hear her speak.

And on December 6, 2024, the judge in Phoenix gave her permission to represent herself in the upcoming trial for the murder of Charles. How much more damage will she do to the people who loved her victims? She will be allowed to cross-examine them and even call them herself as witnesses. I hope the judge controls her closely, because if he doesn't, it will be the Lori show and it will be a mess. I will be there.

So this is the man Chad became. Tammy wasn't a part of any of this. She wasn't involved in the prepper community, and there is no indication that she shared any of these beliefs with Chad, in spite of Chad's daughter Emma's claim while testifying for the defense that Tammy was the one who had these beliefs. In fact, I think this is why Chad felt that he had to murder Tammy. Not only did she not go along with his ideas of the second coming, polygamy, zombies, and Chad's ability to predict when the second coming would happen, she was starting to get in the way of his way forward.

I don't have any direct evidence of this, but I think Chad tried for years to get Tammy to go along with his ideas about plural wives. It must have been terribly sad for her. I think the fact that Chad started saying that Tammy was going to die young and he would have a second life after her is a good indication that she didn't go along with him. I had hoped that after the trial was over, maybe one of the women in Chad's inner circle would open up and talk to me or someone else. That didn't happen.

The really frustrating thing about all of this is that Tammy never did anything but support Chad. She was a faithful wife who worked hard to help support her family. She not only worked to help financially when Chad failed to provide enough income, but she supported his decisions, even if she doubted that they were the best decisions. She worked hard in their publishing business, even though it never brought in much money and took Chad away from other work that would have supported the family better.

Tammy had complications with the birth of their fourth child and was strongly advised to not have any more children. In spite of the fact that they knew it could kill her, they had their fifth child in March of 2000. I wonder if in Chad's mind this event supported the idea that his faith was stronger than physical facts, his faith led to a successful birth of their fifth child, and his faith kept Tammy alive. I think it shows a lack of caring about Tammy on Chad's part. Chad and Tammy both knew she could die giving birth to this child, but they did it anyway.

I do get a sense when I research Chad and Tammy's early life that Chad felt he had some kind of control over who lived or died, who got to fulfill their life on this earth. Nothing said out loud, but there seems to be that undertone. He doesn't say that Tammy is supposed to die young until around 2018, but I think he may have had the idea that he held that power and that would be a clue to where his mind was.

In the world according to Chad, you had an eternal spirit and your life on this earth was just for a short time anyway and pretty insignificant in the whole scheme of things. Life on earth is hard and people suffer. Life as an eternal spirit was always happy, healthful, and busy.

So maybe not so much that he had control, but more like your life on earth was not all that important, which meant that if he decided that you needed to die, maybe he was doing you a favor by killing you. I don't think, though, that he had murder in mind at this point. I think he had some off-ramps and different paths to choose to get to that point. We'll revisit this idea later in this book.

At this point, right before Chad and Lori meet in St. George, Chad and Tammy have five kids, live in a small house in Rexburg, and have a failed publishing business. On the surface, Tammy is still happy and supportive of her husband, but if you live in Mormon country, you learn to put on a good front. Appearances are important. You will work through your problems. You have faith in the priesthood. Put your questions on a shelf is how they say it.

5

MORMON BELIEFS AND MORMON INFLUENCE

What is it about Mormonism that leads to Mormon fundamentalism? The Mormon Church not only does not condone or in any way take responsibility for fundamentalist offshoots, they constantly tell their members not to even consider going down that path. But something in Mormon doctrine leads some people to fanaticism. If we're going to answer the question of why these fundamentalist offshoots exist and even keep arising. We need to look closer at the Mormon Church whether or not the church wants to take any responsibility.

I have to say that I tried to talk to anyone high up in the Mormon Church here in Idaho to prepare for my writing of this chapter. My request went up the ladder, but unfortunately in the end, no one was willing to do that. I was referred to the church website and to the young Mormon missionaries. That was not the counsel I was looking for, and I was disappointed by it.

I understand that the church prefers to distance itself from this story, and I further understand why no one in the church would want to take the risk of talking to me. After all, how do they know I won't twist their words or write something purposely to put the Mormon Church in a bad light? There are people out there doing that. I do wish that we could have bridged that some way because I personally think that until we open up and start talking about what led Chad and Lori Daybell to do what they did, we aren't getting any closer to preventing it from happening again.

Not that I think the Mormon Church is in any way at fault. No one would have thought that Chad and Lori would have done what they did, especially people who knew them, but weren't in their inner circle. Still, there are aspects of the Mormon religion that might contribute to someone like Chad Daybell taking it further than what is intended. My main point in writing these two books is to expose whatever it is that might lead to abusing more innocent or weaker people. Hopefully start a conversation at least.

Let's take a look at Mormon doctrine and list the factors that might differ in Mormon doctrine from other religions. I cite the specific references:

1. **Prophets get visions and revelations from God, angels, and spirits.** (Articles of Faith 7 and 9: *We believe in the gift of tongues, prophecy, revelation, visions, healing, interpretation of tongues, and so forth. We believe all that God has revealed. All that He does now reveal. And we believe that He will yet reveal many great and important things pertaining to the Kingdom of God.*)

2. **You are given a veil that keeps you from having knowledge that you are not ready for.** (This isn't an exclusively Mormon belief, but it seems that the Mormon Church puts more importance on this idea than other churches do.) (Doctrine and Covenants 38: *But the day soon cometh that ye shall see me, and know that I am: for the veil of darkness shall soon be rent. And he that is not purified shall not abide the day.*) (Doctrine and Covenants 110: *The veil was taken from our minds, and the eyes of our understanding were opened.*) (Doctrine and Covenants 67: *The veil shall be rent and you shall see me and know that I am.*)

3. **Men are the priest holders.** (Excerpt from a letter written by President Kimball on June 8, 1978: *all worthy male members of the church may be ordained to the priesthood.*)

4. **Preparing for the second coming of Christ, again not exclusive to the Mormon Church, but the Mormon Church puts more emphasis on it.** (Doctrine and Covenants 133: *The Saints are commanded to prepare for the Second Coming; all men are commanded to flee from Babylon, come to Zion. and prepare for the great day of the Lord.*)

5. **Church hierarchy.** (Doctrine and Covenants 102: *The president of the church, who is also the president of the council, is appointed by revelation, and acknowledged in his administration by the voice of the church.*)

6. **Discernment.** (Doctrine and Covenants 46: *Church leaders are given power to discern the gifts of the Spirit.*)

Now let's take them one at a time:

1. Joseph Smith was the first prophet of the Mormon Church, and he claimed that he was the only one who God would speak to. He had the power to receive revelations and visions directly from God. If Joseph Smith spoke, it was the word of God. If Joseph Smith gave you an order, it was said by him to have come directly from God and you had better obey. The same goes for all of the prophets who came after Joseph Smith. But how does one become a prophet? The only thing I can find that disqualifies you is if you are not a man. What does qualify you is you have to be one of the Quorum of the Twelve Apostles in the Mormon Church and the prophet before you has to have died.

It is said that a true prophet is always chosen by God. This is where it gets sticky to me. I don't believe God speaks to any man, no matter how religious he is or how high up he is in any church. But if you do have that belief, then it seems to open a door for anyone to claim he is speaking to God and he is a prophet. We have seen this over and over in the offshoot fundamentalist churches—Warren Jeffs, for example, and look what that led to. His church, the Fundamentalist Church of Jesus Christ of Latter-day Saints (FLDS), is a polygamist group that claims to follow the original tenets of the Mormon Church. This of course includes polygamy, but child sexual assault has been a huge problem with that church.

I mentioned Ervil LeBaron earlier in this book. His was the Church of the First Born of the Lamb of God. He claimed to be a prophet and to speak directly to God. His beliefs led to many murders of members of his church, rival churches and even family members. It isn't thought that he did any of the murders himself. His followers were so brainwashed that they did the murders for him, and women and children were not excluded.

Again, these churches are in no way associated with the Church of Jesus Christ of Latter-day Saints, commonly known as the Mormon Church. In fact, the leaders of these other churches take from Mormon beliefs only what works for them in order to gain power over others and leave out the parts that don't further their own selfish agendas.

Anyway, we can see that the idea that there can be a prophet and that prophet speaks directly to God can be problematic. The prophet's word is said to be the word of God and God would only have you do things that are good even if it looks bad to us mere mortals. Of course, these people would be said to be false prophets, and obviously they are, but the point is that the idea that any mortal man can be a prophet and speak or get visions directly from God is where the problem lies.

If a man like Chad believed he was getting messages from God and those messages were to commit crimes, he would have to commit those crimes. Also, if Chad only said he got messages from God and others believed him, those others would feel like they had to obey Chad's orders. After all, they came directly from God. I think this is exactly how Chad and Lori influenced Lori's brother, Alex Cox, to murder Lori's husband Charles Vallow, her children Tylee and JJ, and at least assist in the murder of Chad's wife Tammy Daybell.

2. Chad claimed that his veil was torn and that allowed him to see through it and speak to spirits on the other side. This would support his claim that he was special and that he was getting messages directly from God. So if you are Mormon and you believe this can happen, you can believe that someone like Chad is the "chosen one." Chad definitely used this to his advantage. He used his supposed near death experiences to promote himself.

This idea is supported by the fact that near death experiences or NDEs have become an extremely popular talking point in the Mormon world. In recent years many books have been written by Mormon authors and many speeches have been given by Mormon speakers about NDEs, especially in the prepper community. The fact that the Mormon Church has not discounted the book *Visions of Glory* or the person who it is actually written about is problematic. If you haven't read the book (and I don't think you need to), it's all about a man named Spencer who is able to travel through space and time. He recounts his experiences predicting what life will be like for Mormons at the time of the second coming of Christ.

3. Only men are the priest holders. This means that half of the population is subservient to the other half. Mormon women are taught to follow the lead of the men and support them even if supporting them goes against what they think is right. This would put someone like Tammy in a position of following Chad, even if she didn't understand or agree with what he ordered. It would also influence Lori.

This idea was important in the Chad Daybell trial. Prosecutors were faced with a problem. They had already said in Lori Daybell's trial that she was the leader, that she was the force behind the murders. She was manipulative to an extreme, and she used her sexual prowess to influence Chad. Now these same prosecutors are back in court trying to prove that Chad was really the one behind the murders.

Chad's attorney, John Prior, argues that point. How can they say one thing in one trial to one jury and contradict themselves to another jury in another trial? It would be unfair and unethical.

But Chad and Lori are Mormon, and according to the Mormon Church, men are the leaders. So even though Lori may have been the one with the ideas, the responsibility would ultimately be Chad's. I really believe that in Lori's mind Chad was a very powerful prophet with a direct connection to Christ. Of course, they can't put it that way in court.

I wondered if the prosecution would be more likely to pick Mormons for jury duty in this trial. I think that Mormons would be more likely to put the responsibility on a man. Of course, they won't know which potential jurors are Mormon when they interview them in court. I listened for questions coming from the prosecution during jury selection that might lead to an answer from a prospective juror that would give a clue as to whether that prospective juror was Mormon, and I did not hear such a question. Further, having gotten to know the prosecutors, I would say they are above asking such a question or even thinking that religion has anything to do with convicting Chad Daybell. It's all about the law to them, as it should be.

Obviously, the priesthood isn't meant to lead to women following men to the point of committing murder, especially murder of their own children, but if one is susceptible to taking it to that extreme, it certainly doesn't help.

In the Mormon Church men and women both take the priesthood very seriously. Women are taught that men are the ones who hold the key to the celestial kingdom. If you want to reach that glorious existence, you have to follow your priest-holder husband no matter what. He has knowledge that you aren't privy to, his very existence is on a higher level than yours, and so you aren't capable of understanding everything that he understands.

Mormon women are taught to forgive their husbands and fathers for their weaknesses. I mentioned before a woman named Stephanie Taylor. She wrote a book titled *Silenced in the Name of God.* In it she describes how she was molested by her father her whole life. Her father was excused by the Mormon

Church, and Stephanie was expected to forgive him. He was eventually held to account by the court system and sent to prison.

The problem here is obvious. If your husband says your kids are dark, like Chad said to Lori, and that you have had conversations with angels in the spirit world and they say your kids are zombies and you believe he lives on a higher plane than you, you had better just go along with him. I know the rest of us would not have gone down the path Lori did with Chad, but this is exactly what allowed her to in the state of mind she was in.

I'm told that some Mormon Churches are more patriarchal than others and that Chad and Lori's was very patriarchal and this, of course, would serve to fuel the fire.

4. Mormons are taught to prepare for some kind of disaster that would affect their ability to obtain the things we all need to survive. Again, not a bad idea. We should all do what we can to be prepared. We saw what happened to the supply chain during the COVID-19 disaster. What if we couldn't get gas, the power was shut off, and the shelves at the supermarket were empty?

Mormons believe that if they are better prepared, they will be in a good position to thrive and take the lead for the survivors of whatever natural or manmade disaster occurs. So it is the responsibility of each Mormon family to stock up and be ready. That's where "Latter Day" comes in in the Church of Jesus Christ of Latter-day Saints. They are preparing for the second coming of Christ and believe it will not be a peaceful time leading up to it. There will be three and a half years of tribulation followed by three and a half years of extreme tribulation. They even take it one step further, believing that it will be Mormons who run what's left of the world and it will be their responsibility to save souls, living and dead.

There is also a more practical reason behind the Mormon idea of being prepared. It actually started out in the early years when Mormons lived off what they could produce on their farms. They were directed by the church to stock enough grain and supplies to survive for two years. If each family did this, they would be in a stronger position to survive drought or any other natural disaster that might affect their crops. It was their only way of surviving. There was no government assistance or anything or anyone who could bail them out.

Chad believed that Rexburg, Idaho, would be the place where the second coming of Christ would occur. That's the reason he gave for Lori to move there from Arizona. He believed that there would be 144,000 people left and that he would be their leader guiding them in the terrestrial, telestial, and celestial world, the three Mormon degrees or kingdoms of glory attainable in heaven. Terrestrial pertaining to earth, telestial although not a real word (it was made up by Joseph Smith) is meant to describe someone's perfect state after Jesus comes back to earth, and celestial meaning heaven and meant only for those who have lived a righteous life and have accepted the teachings of Jesus Christ. There is a lot more to all of this, but I am far from a Mormon scholar, and we don't need to go too deep into Mormonism to understand what happened with Chad Daybell.

The problem is that some people take this part of Mormon doctrine to an extreme. There are prepper groups that believe it's going to be so chaotic that everyone will be killing each other for their own survival. Now you not only need food and water. You need gas, a bunker, several automatic rifles, and lots and lots of ammunition. You also need your own militia group with an organized system of governing itself. Maybe it can even be run by a prophet who will be able to see into the future.

There are several prepper groups out there that one can join. Some are just social media groups and kind of fun, I guess, but some are a lot more serious. Preparing a People was Chad and Lori's chosen group. They held podcasts and generally used the ideas to promote themselves and sell Chad's books. Another Voice of Warning (AVOW) is another group and is dedicated to preparedness and spiritual insights. There are more, probably many more, but these are the two associated with Chad Daybell and his followers.

Preparing a People flyer.

Preparing a People was never affiliated with the Mormon Church, and in fact the Mormon Church warned its members not to associate themselves with it. Preparing a People also went outside of Mormon doctrine. It has become inactive since Tylee and JJ were found buried in Chad's backyard. Other groups have cropped up to take its place though. Same people, same ideas, just a different name.

AVOW is a community dedicated to preparedness and spiritual insights. The leader of AVOW defended Chad right up until the bodies were found, but immediately denounced him after.

But what does prepping have to do with Chad Daybell and his crimes?

He took the idea further than anyone would have expected him to. The idea that you have to prepare for the second coming of Christ is one thing, but Chad took it further. He claimed to know when that would happen. July 22, 2020, was supposed to be the day a great earthquake would occur along the Wasatch Front in the Salt Lake City area. Chad would be ready for it, and he would be the one to gather the 144,000 worthy survivors beginning on July 23, 2020.

Since he was a prophet or *the* prophet, he was able to predict this based on *his* ability to see beyond the veil. What he needed was to find followers who would take that extra step with him and not only believe with him that the second coming would happen on that day, but also that Chad was meant to be their leader.

If people truly believed him, then what difference would it make if you murdered someone before it happened? After all, according to Chad, it was going to be a terrible time to live through, even if you did live through it. Maybe you would be doing someone a favor by saving them from having to go through that.

It goes way deeper, of course. Some people not only needed to be saved from having to suffer through the end of days, they needed to be saved from themselves or from their weaknesses that allowed the demons to invade their bodies. The problem I have with this particular Mormon idea is they get to decide who is worthy, who lives, and who dies.

5. In the Mormon Church one can work his or her way up the ladder. Only so far for women, of course. The education required for this comes through the church and the good works one accomplishes. I would also think how well one

does socially in the church, not only in one's experiences with the church elders, but also how well one does in general, how liked one is.

This can cause there to be competition and pettiness within the church. If someone has ambitions to move up in the church, that person would have to stand out among his or her peers. I think that in the case of someone like Chad, who had the belief that he was supposed to rise up in the church, it could cause him to do things to get noticed by the elders. Certainly, writing his books, claiming to have communication with spirits, and giving speeches whenever he had the opportunity looks like someone trying to work his way up. And we know that Chad said he thought he should be president of the whole Mormon Church, so certainly he had ambitions, and those ambitions are part of what led him down the paths he chose.

But what about fundamentalist offshoots? Some of them are extreme to say the least. In *Money, Power and Sex* I talk about cults in general and Mormon cults in particular, but what is it about the Mormon Church that inspires or at least allows for these cults? Again, the Mormon Church is in no way affiliated with any of them, and I know these cults are a thorn in the side of the Mormon Church.

Most of the cults I can think of that have LDS in their name claim to adhere to the original doctrine as it was laid out by Joseph Smith. Warren Jeffs's Fundamentalist Church of Jesus Christ of Latter-day Saints and Ervil LeBaron's Church of the Lamb of God, among others, claim that the original doctrine was correct and that the Mormon Church was wrong when it moved away from it. Their belief is that a man has to have multiple wives and many children in order to be worthy of making it to the celestial kingdom. They also believe that blood atonement is the last chance a sinner would have to make it to heaven.

Therefore, members of these churches or cults feel they have the right to multiple wives and the right to murder. In fact, it's more than a right; they claim to believe that they get revelations from God directing them to commit these acts. And, of course, Jeffs and LeBaron have taken it to an extreme using murder and mayhem, rape, kidnapping, and child sexual assault in order for the leaders to get what they want.

It's the original doctrine that causes these problems, not what the Mormon Church is now. And it's usually one maniacal man who will do whatever it takes to get what he wants and who uses the original doctrine to do so.

I think it's fair to at least say that the Mormon Church, because of its history, has created a space, an avenue for maniacal people to use to further their position in life, to absolve themselves from their guilt to do so, and to excuse themselves for murder and all of the other crimes I mention. Further, I think the church puts men like Chad on a pedestal and creates a situation where anyone like Chad feels safe and even entitled enough to do the things he did, just as Ervil LeBaron and Warren Jeffs did.

Okay, not everyone is Chad Daybell, Ervil LeBaron, or Warren Jeffs, but there have been enough of those guys that I think it's time to come to terms with it rather than sweep it under the rug.

When Judge Boyce sentenced Lori Daybell, he told her he didn't believe that any God in any religion would want her to do the things she did. None of us who live in the real world would think that any God in any religion would want her to do the things she did. The problem with Lori and Chad is that they didn't live in the real world. At least not in their minds. They lived in a world where they manipulated scripture and Mormon beliefs into whatever way they needed to get what they wanted.

6. Mormons are taught that the leaders of the church are gifted with what they call discernment. They have the ability to know a person who has come into their consciousness. They can tell if one is good or bad. They know if you are lying to them.

In Chad Daybell's case, the leaders of the church were not able to discern that he was bad or lying to them. The problem with that is that if they had the ability to discern that he was bad and they didn't discern that he was bad, how does that look to people associated with Chad? It would look like he was not bad and so the things he was doing would not be bad. Further, the things he was telling you to do must not be bad. Chad must be right.

I personally find the idea of discernment problematic. It seems manipulative to me. If a person believes that someone can tell when you are going down the wrong path, it might keep that person from going down that wrong path. Sounds good, but who decides for you what paths are right and what paths are wrong? Those with the God-given power of discernment do.

Don't get me wrong. We all need spiritual guidance. We need rules to help guide us.

The problem is things that the psychiatric community have declared to be normal behavior are looked down upon and called sins by the Mormon Church. They consider it to be behavior that should be corrected if you are actively participating in it. This can be damaging to the individual, but further, it can be damaging to a whole following of a church. It can actually cause more of the behavior the church is trying to stop.

Pornography is an obvious example. A 2009 report by Harvard Economics Professor Benjamin Edelman claims Utah is the state with the highest percentage of pornography usage.

Where do you stand on pornography? One hundred percent against it on any level? Soft porn is okay? In a healthy relationship a little porn is okay? Teenagers looking at porn is normal? Porn is awesome?

I know, it's one of those subjects that is controversial and that we as a country are struggling with it. The Mormon Church is clear. It's all bad and anyone participating in watching it needs counseling—counseling provided by the church. Actually, one step further, *counselors* provided by the church. This is automatically problematic. For one to practice as a licensed counselor in Idaho, one must be approved by the Idaho Licensing Board of Professional Counselors and Marriage and Family Therapists. Just like with a surgeon, there are accepted practices that one is required to follow.

Does a counselor follow church doctrine or does a counselor follow best practices as laid out by the Idaho Licensing Board of Professional Counselors and Marriage and Family Therapists (ILBPCMFT)? The two are sometimes in conflict with each other. Counselors are paid by the church if a church member can't afford to pay for it themselves, but these counselors have sworn an oath to follow best practices as laid out by ILBPCMFT. There is an obvious legal conflict here. Is there a flaw in the fact that the church can recommend counseling and offer to pay for counseling and provide a list of church-approved counselors? It just seems to me to be like one of those conflicts that could be avoided if the church didn't try so hard to control its members.

Discernment is a controlling device or at least a way for some in the church to control others. Maybe they are abusing their agency with the church and with God if they use it that way, but at the very least, the door is opened for some to do that.

6

VISIONS OF GLORY

L et's dive deeper into the book *Visions of Glory* written by John Pontius and its influence on Chad and Lori. The book was extremely popular with Mormons prior to the developments with Chad and Lori Daybell. Lori was reading it by the pool in Hawaii when she was served the court order to produce Tylee and JJ. I actually noticed it in court as a juror in Lori Vallow Daybell's trial when we were shown the video. I just thought it was a religious book at the time and that in itself was significant to me, but I had no idea of the real significance. At the time of the murders, the book had not been denounced by the Mormon Church, and it was widely read by its members.

The book claims to be one man's account of his visions that he received during his life and that he wanted to share those visions with his fellow Mormons so they could see what the future held.

What the future held for Mormons was pretty bright, according to Pontius. It had a huge influence on the prepper and the NDE community. As I read the book myself in preparation for writing this book, I was disgusted with the idea that one man would profess to have so much knowledge. Pontius wrote the book as if he were doing a great deed in sharing the experiences of his main character, Spencer. Sharing Spencer's experiences was supposed to give people insight and hope for a bright future. It would guide them in preparing for the second coming of Christ. It would assure them that they were on the right path—or members of the right church at least.

My copy of *Visions of Glory* by John Pontius for reference during the trial and the writing of my books.

While reading the book, I wondered if Chad may have thought he was Spencer. He at least believed or professed to believe in the concepts Spencer believed.

The main thought the book brought into question to me was how many people were involved with Chad Daybell? How many real followers did he have? There is an important connection here between Chad Daybell and the book *Visions of Glory*, and Chad was not a lone participant in his beliefs. Not only did he have followers, but he had people he looked up to and he had peers. Who were they?

Thom Harrison is widely thought to be the real person that the character Spencer in *Visions of Glory* represents. Thom Harrison is a sex therapist and member of the Mormon Church. The church pays Thom Harrison to provide therapy to its members. This goes back to the problem I wrote about in chapter 5 with the differences between church beliefs and accepted practices in the psychology community.

In *Visions of Glory*, Spencer shares his visions of the second coming of Christ. He describes what life will be like on the ground for Mormons as well as his own experiences with his personal relationship with Jesus Christ. His experiences and his relationship with Christ is said in the book to be just what he experiences in his visions. So these are visions and not reality. He had these visions while he was sick in a coma and thought to be on his deathbed. The problem is that even though he says they are visions and he makes no claim that he really experienced these things, they are presented in a way to make people think that these visions are like a crystal ball, as if he really was given a gift of being able to see the future.

And people believe this stuff. Chad and Lori Daybell took *Visions of Glory* as scripture—meaning it is the true word of God. Chad and Lori's followers did too. They not only believed Pontius's account of Spencer's experiences, but they further believed that a human being can have these experiences. A human being like Chad Daybell who also professed to have visions and a personal and not just spiritual relationship with Christ.

We can see the influence the book has on Chad through his own writing. His accounts of what our future holds in his books are extremely similar to those in the Pontius book. I think he just found a way that works, a way to draw people in, a way to gain followers.

Julie Rowe is another person we know was influenced by the book. She at least was influenced enough to use the premise of *Visions of Glory* to promote herself and her own supposed NDEs. Chad Daybell was at one time her friend and the publisher of her book, *A Greater Tomorrow: My Journey Beyond the Veil.*

In her book she claims that she had near death experiences, and her NDEs gave her knowledge from the spiritual world that the rest of us do not have. Her book was very successful and that alone, I think, influenced Chad. He could use his own claims of NDEs to promote himself. It would be another one of those paths he chose, another wrong turn that took him closer to who he became.

There were several people in the inner circle or upper echelon of the prepper group, Preparing a People. They did podcasts, firesides, and events together. A lot of the people in this inner circle were women, and Chad was one of their leaders. We heard some of these women testify in the Lori Daybell trial and in the Chad Daybell trial, and some questions came to my mind that I doubt we'll ever get a solid answer to. Was polygamy what it was really all about? Were these events and firesides just a way for Chad and other male leaders of the group to recruit women?

We know Chad used the line, "We were married in a previous life," on Lori and she fell for it hook, line, and sinker.

Did he use the same line on other women, and did some other women fall for it? I think so. At the very least, we can say that this would have been another path Chad chose that took him in a dangerous direction. He was using his gift of agency to recruit women into the fold. *Agency* in this context is a Mormon term. It means that if you have a certain standing in a particular area, that is your agency, and as a good Mormon man, you should respect that and not use it to your own advantage. You should only use your standing to promote God or the church or entities like that. We can clearly see that Chad was abusing that.

In court in the Lori Vallow Daybell trial, we listened to some of these women testify for the prosecution, and I remember wondering at the time if these women might have had a sexual relationship with Chad. They certainly weren't going to say that in court, but I wonder if sometime in the future, maybe once they aren't afraid of facing some consequences, one or more of them might tell us the rest of the story. I hope so. It would clear up a lot of questions for me.

We know prosecuting attorney Lindsey Blake said in her opening statement in Lori Vallow Daybell's trial that it was all about money, power, and sex, but was Chad only interested in sex with Lori or did it go further than that? Did Chad try to get Tammy to go along with his ideas on polygamy? Did Tammy balk at the idea? Was that one of the reasons Chad had to "do away" with her, or was it just so he could continue with his relationship with Lori?

I'm pretty sure that Chad envisioned a life of multiple wives on earth, and I'm even more sure he envisioned a celestial life with multiple wives. It has been said that you need at least three wives to make it to the celestial kingdom. Read the Mormon Doctrine and Covenants Section 132 in its entirety if you want to learn more about Mormon doctrine. It's actually quite scary stuff, especially for women.

We know Chad had Tammy and Lori, but who was the third? Maybe there were even more. I do think that Chad was satisfied with just being with Lori after meeting her and starting a sexual relationship with her, but as we know, he was a visionary, so my guess is that he was looking to the future and hoping to expand his harem.

7

OTHER INFLUENCES ON CHAD DAYBELL

Trying to be fair, I asked myself this question: Was it just the Mormon Church and its beliefs or religious fundamentalist beliefs that influenced Chad Daybell, or was there more to it? Were there other influences in his family, childhood, schooling, and missionary work?

The answer is, I can't find any.

There seems to be no crazy uncle or anyone in his young life who abused him. He doesn't seem to have been a victim of any kind. Other than his claims of near death experiences, he doesn't seem to have had any profoundly damaging or violent occurrences in his development. Usually, when we get into the minds of criminals who commit horrific crimes, their past is brutal. They have been severely psychologically damaged by some past event or events.

Not with Chad. Chad has no excuse. He was brought up as I described. In a good family, good church, and good community. This, to me, makes his crimes even less excusable and less forgivable. He took advantage of the civilized community he lived in to do the unthinkable. We see that in people's response before Tylee's and JJ's remains were found.

People in the Rexburg area reacted in the most innocent way, believing the kids were somehow lost or hidden away. It didn't cross their minds that the children had been brutally murdered and buried in Chad's backyard. If it had crossed their minds, they would not have shown Chad the support they showed him. They wouldn't have held vigils just feet away from where Tylee and JJ were eventually found buried.

I think this is the reason this case gets so much attention. We just don't have the answer to how Chad and Lori Daybell could have done the things they did. The murders of Tylee and JJ were so horribly brutal. I only bring this up to make my point. The last thing I want to do is relive what I was exposed to in court or make any family, law enforcement, or anyone close to this case have to think about the way Tylee and JJ were murdered. The contrast of the pictures I saw of their exhumed bodies (or in Tylee's case, what was left of her body) to the pictures I saw of Chad and Lori getting married on a beach in Kauai is stunning to say the least.

I struggled to explain it in my first book and I'm struggling to explain it now, but I wanted to make these points:

1. The murders were vicious and brutal beyond comparison.
2. Chad and Lori Daybell to this day show absolutely zero remorse and take no responsibility. In fact, they put us all through these trials even when they must have known they had no hope of winning.

3. Chad and Lori Daybell had other options if they didn't want to raise Tylee and JJ. They could have divorced their spouses and moved on together. That would have been frowned upon in their Mormon world, but it would not have been a crime.

Why did they so brutally murder the children? JJ was bound with duct tape and plastic. They wrapped him up until he suffocated. Tylee was dismembered and burned. Her body was literally hacked into pieces. I would expect the perpetrators of such unspeakable murders to be monsters. I would expect that the world they lived in must have been hellish. I would think they must have been subjected to horror their whole lives.

But no. Chad and Lori Vallow Daybell lived relatively good lives. Other than some abuse of Lori by the hand of one and possibly two of her five husbands, both of their lives really couldn't have been more idyllic.

Is that the problem? Were they suffocating in Mormon-ville? Were they so stifled by the perfect yards with white plastic fences, the stamped-out houses, and the clean-cut neighbors that it drove them crazy? Did they lose their value of life because everyone was the same, every house, everything people wore, everything people said?

It's kind of like spoiling a kid. We call it *spoiling* for a reason. If you give a kid every toy he could ever want, those toys hold no value. If a kid is raised poor and has only a few toys, he will covet them. Of course, it goes further than that. The rich kid, even though he doesn't value the toys given to him, will become more demanding of even more toys, and of course, these toys still end up holding no value.

The community Chad grew up in is rich in security, safety, and human kindness. Could he have been spoiled with that to the point that he didn't value it? I'm going leave it at that for now. I think I will pose this idea to Dr. John, the podcaster, and see what he thinks.

I do think that all of these books, all of the people who claim to have NDEs and visions, and all the people who claim to communicate with Jesus or God or dead relatives, feed off each other. Some people want to believe so badly that they are special, that when they hear someone else say they have had these experiences, it shores up the idea in their own minds that the voice they hear in their head is actually something more than just their own conscience. I further think that some people use the ideas just to promote themselves and gain standing. Chad saw Julie Rowe benefit financially and otherwise using her claims.

Is Chad a psychopath? This is a really interesting question. I think that in a legal sense, Chad is not psychotic. But one would have to be crazy to believe the things Chad believes and to do the acts Chad did. He believes in things that are not real. Okay, so crazy. But he also was able to know to lie and try to hide his crimes from the rest of us. When I think of a crazy person, I think of someone who is so out of touch, they wouldn't know right from wrong. Chad did know right from wrong in spite of his horrible crimes. In that sense, in a legal sense, he is not a psychopath. He is capable of understanding he is committing crimes.

8

LORI NEEDED TO SAVE PEOPLE, AND CHAD NEEDED PEOPLE WHO NEEDED TO BE SAVED

Prior to marrying Chad Daybell, Lori had been married four times. Her first marriage was at seventeen years old and didn't last long. She married the man she married against her family's wishes. He was not Mormon and in fact was nothing more than a drug dealer with no future.

Lori did what Lori wanted to do. She was not afraid of what her family thought of any of the things she did. She always had that quality, or maybe it's more of a fault. Her second husband, also not Mormon, wasn't much better.

Adam Cox, Lori's brother who grew up very close to Lori, thinks the reason she married these losers was in order to save them. He thinks she had a need to save people. More than that, she needed to be needed by people. If they needed saving, they needed Lori and she needed that. That explains her attraction to someone like Chad, who, as we know, was beneath her in the looks department. He needed her and he worshipped her.

Chad, on the other hand, needed people who needed to be saved. Sounds like the same concept, but it's not. Chad didn't need to be glamorous or have a close relationship with someone who worshipped him. He needed numbers. He needed everyone to follow him to the Promised Land. He was the prophet. He was the one who spoke to God. He was the one who could see through the veil.

Whether it be for the sake of selling books, for the sake of his moral standing, to strengthen his idea that he was immortal or whatever, crowds of people following him is what he needed. And it seems like he was frustrated in this way.

He did have a small following. Some people loved his books and loved to listen to him speak. They would invite him to their homes to have fireside chats with a group of like-minded people. He had even been invited to speak at conferences with bigger crowds. But these groups and conferences were outside of the church, and I don't think that was enough for him. I think that he couldn't make it inside the Mormon Church and really wanted that to the point where he thought he had earned it. But still, he was somewhat shunned by the mainstream Mormon Church.

Shortly before Chad and Tammy moved to Rexburg, the church they attended in Utah needed a new bishop. Chad thought he should be considered. Someone else was appointed bishop. Did that come into Chad's decision to move to Rexburg?

He thought he should have been picked. He thought he had earned it. He needed it.

The prepper crowd, though, the NDE crowd, these people not only accepted him, but looked up to him. They gave him a platform, and he took full advantage of it to the point that I think, in his mind, he became the true leader of Mormons. He thought he knew better than the mainstream Mormon Church, just like other fundamentalist leaders before him. He would become the one true living prophet, the one mighty and strong, and he would lead people to Zion at the second coming of Christ.

Chad showed up at a woman's house one morning before any of the murders. Her husband was not at home. I cannot reveal her name to keep her privacy. She knew of Chad and actually believed in him and a lot of his beliefs. I met this woman and she told me about her experience. She was impressed by him coming to her house. It made her feel special, but she didn't invite him inside. She said that would not have been proper since she was home alone.

She still has the belief system, but knowing what she now knows about Chad, she is extremely freaked out about the episode. She says it got awkward when he just wouldn't leave, and she finally had to shut the door on him. What impressed me most about her telling me about this was the fact that she still holds the beliefs. In fact, she still believes that Chad had visions and holds a higher standing. He just went off track somehow. Bizarre, I know, but I really don't think she is the only person in Rexburg who feels this way.

Rexburg, Idaho, while not exactly isolated, is somewhat off the beaten path. You don't drive through Rexburg by mistake or on your way to somewhere else. It's also extremely monochromatic and populated with people of mostly the same beliefs and even the same religion. There are positives and negatives associated with this. The positives can be easily seen. It's clean, there is little poverty, little crime, and the people are outwardly friendly.

The negatives that come with any city like this are harder to see. Because people there all have much the same beliefs, it's easy to take those beliefs to an extreme. There are no opposing factors or arguments. This can lead to what I would call not exactly corruption, at least not intentional corruption, but more of a tendency to do things your own way or to think you know what is best.

I'm struggling to describe it, but we've all experienced someone thinking they know better than you or better than the law or the rules. In the case of Rexburg, I think it was easy for people to think they knew who the good guys were and who the bad guys were. I think someone's standing in the community, which translates to their standing in the church, may influence what someone thinks of them or what they might be capable of. Not that anyone intentionally tried to cover up Chad's crimes, but they might not have been able to see his crimes because of their preconceived notion of him.

Even knowing that Chad murdered his wife and his new wife's children, I don't think people in Rexburg wanted to see that he may have been capable of even more right under their eyes.

Chad had a neighbor named Eldon Clawson. Eldon was very involved with Chad's church and kind of a busybody. He would walk the neighborhood regularly. His normal path would take him around Chad's property, and he always knew what everyone in the neighborhood was up to. In fact, if something in the neighborhood wasn't to Eldon's liking, you would probably hear from him.

Chad's property of 3.75 flat acres contained a 1,900-square-foot house and a storage shed. Attached to the house was a structure the family called the "cozy cone," which could be accessed from the house via a staircase. The house was set toward the front of the property, and the back of the property was pasture or had been used as pasturage in the past. There was a small usually dry pond with a tree next to it. This is where JJ's body was found. There was a pet cemetery behind the house where Tylee's remains were found.

The neighborhood was rural. Houses were separated by the land surrounding them. There were no sidewalks or street-lights like you see in more modern neighborhoods. The houses in Chad's neighborhood appear to be mostly built in the 1950s or 1960s. I think they were originally built as small farms. An irrigation ditch runs along the north side of the property and would have provided water for crops and livestock.

Eldon's death is another suspicious death to me. He was in his sixties, healthy, and died of a pulmonary embolism just six days after we now know that JJ died. I always wondered how two bodies could have been buried, one of them burned first, and no one noticed. Maybe Eldon did see something. It's a little coincidental that Chad's neighbor Eldon, Lori's brother Alex, and her ex-husband Joe Ryan all conveniently died of the same cause. According to forensic pathologist Dr. Erik Christensen, a pulmonary embolism can have many causes, not all of which would be obvious.

I have also heard that the reason Chad and Lori were so comfortable moving on with their lives after committing the murders is that they thought people in Rexburg would cover for them. I don't believe anyone in Rexburg would cover for their crimes, but I think Chad and Lori may have thought they were above suspicion.

This is a little off topic and maybe a little "out there," but my mind keeps going back to the Salem witch trials in Massachusetts. Between February 1692 and May 1693, fourteen women and five men were hanged after being accused and convicted of being witches. When you think about it, there are undoubtedly parallels between those events and the events in Rexburg in 2019. I will point out right away that one big difference is that the witch trials were conducted by the government (not our government; we were still English colonies at the time).

My point is that what led to the witch trials was people's belief in the idea that someone could be taken over by an evil force. They had to be hanged to kill the witch and free the soul. And the accusers were always someone who had something to gain by the demise of the "witch."

I think the reason I keep thinking about it is that the question is the same. How did we get to that point? In Salem, Massachusetts, in 1692, people somehow got to a place where they hanged women and men and jailed many children in unimaginably filthy and unhealthy jails. What could possibly have led them to a place where they thought that was the thing to do? Same with Chad and Lori. How could they possibly have gotten to a place in their minds where they thought murdering Lori's children was the thing to do? I'm going to leave it at that and move on. Too big of a rabbit hole, but hopefully the comparisons will at least encourage some thought.

Chad used these early influences in his life to make choices. I think this is where we really learn about who Chad is. Millions of people have had the same upbringing, the same religious teachings, and the same background really. What made Chad different was that he chose to see things his own way. He chose to believe the voices in his head that we all have are the voices of spirits, angels, Jesus, or God. He chose to believe he had NDEs and because of them he could see through the veil. He chose to believe he could predict the second coming of Christ. He chose to believe he would lead the 144,000.

In total, he chose to believe he was a prophet, the one mighty and strong. He chose to believe that he had the right to not only control people's lives, but that he had control over who lived and died.

Sometime around 2014 Chad met Julie Rowe who claimed to have had a near death experience in 2004, which gave her insight into the second coming of Christ. She was excommunicated from the Mormon Church in 2019. Why she was excommunicated and Chad was not until the children's bodies were found is a question I have that I would love to ask. Chad's company published the book that got Julie Rowe excommunicated. Both Chad and Julie Rowe wrote about visions and revelations and being able to see into the future. Maybe it was because she had such a huge following. Anyway, I think Chad was envious of her success and wanted to follow in her footsteps—at least until he could pass her up. He started writing about his own NDEs and his visions of the future.

This is also about the time he became involved with Preparing a People, a group that took church doctrine and beliefs and added their own ideas—the idea that the second coming of Christ was about to happen and people needed to prepare for it. They believed that good Mormons would survive the coming apocalypse in the area of Rexburg. Being a good Mormon meant being a prepared Mormon.

9

CHAD MEETS LORI

What did Chad need to help him along his path to glory? He needed a woman by his side. And not just any woman. In Chad's mind, his wife Tammy fell way short of what he needed. We know he was wrong about that, of course. Tammy was one of the two solid things in his life. The other being the church. Tammy supported him financially and every other way that can be expected of a wife. What she didn't do, however, was follow him down the path he was choosing. She didn't believe a man needed multiple wives to make it to the celestial kingdom. She didn't believe Chad could see through the veil. She didn't believe in past lives, multiple probations, zombies, and the second coming happening on any certain date.

So, for Chad, Tammy just wasn't cutting it. And just when he is beginning to come to terms with that, who shows up at his table at a Preparing a People conference in St. George, Utah, on October 26, 2018, and helps him sell books? Lori Vallow of course.

This was the first time Chad had seen Lori. She was a beautiful, outgoing woman with long blond hair and a lilting voice, and she was all over Chad.

I can almost see why he thought it was meant to be, like God must have had a hand in their meeting. The timing was too good to be true. That must be what gave him the inspiration to tell her they had been married in previous lives and had walked the earth together many times. Whatever his thoughts were, he now had a strong woman by his side who shared his beliefs, and he wasn't letting go.

As a bonus, Lori brought her inner circle with her, a group of people with similar beliefs. Her brother Alex Cox, Melanie Gibb, Melani Boudreaux, David Warwick, Zulema Pastenes, and others. We think of Chad and Lori as this perfect union, but really it was more than just those two. It wasn't just Chad and Lori who came together at that conference. It was a group of six or eight like-minded people who came together. Chad and Lori couldn't have done it all by themselves. They needed their hitman Alex and a group of leaders to help gather in their following.

I don't know if Chad used his pendulum necklace on Lori. He had an owl necklace that he would use to tell people what their future held. He would actually hold it in front of someone's face and swing it back and forth. It was just a cheap piece of jewelry on a fake gold chain, but Chad claimed it had mystical powers. It's such a childish idea, it's really hard to believe some people fell for it, but they did. It reminds me of when Chad told Lori he had a "storm in his pants." To me, it's very telling about what kind of people these were. Naive, gullible, ignorant, and looking for something to fill a void in their lives maybe? Thankfully I can't relate.

In November of 2018 while Tammy was still alive, Chad and Lori were sealed in the Mormon Temple in Arizona.

Accompanying them were the angel Moroni and Jesus. Being sealed means a couple is sealed for eternity. It's like being married, but in the Mormon world it holds more weight. Once you are sealed, it is for eternity, and you are now ready to start building a family that will follow you into this eternal existence. This was just a formality since they had already been married multiple times in past probations. Of course, this was not a real sealing approved by the Mormon Church. Lori later told her friend Melanie Gibb about the sealing, so the inner circle knew that even though both Chad and Lori were married to other people, according to them, they were now married to each other and free to carry on accordingly.

Did the inner circle also know about Chad and Lori's plan to kill Charles? Did they know Lori was making Charles's life a living hell? He would die at the hands of her brother Alex in July of 2019.

10

KILLING CHARLES

On December 5, 2018, in a Preparing a People podcast, Lori told Melanie Gibb that she had a dream that Charles (Lori Vallow's fourth husband) would die in a car accident. It was more of a vision or prediction apparently because when Charles later showed up alive, Lori claimed Satan interfered and prevented the accident that would have caused Charles's death.

In court in the Lori Vallow Daybell trial, we saw texts from Charles to Brandon Boudreaux. Brandon was the husband of Lori's niece, Melani Boudreaux, at the time. Charles told Brandon that Lori was accusing him of infidelity. We know Charles was not the one having an affair. It was Lori who was having an affair, but Lori was very good at lying and manipulating. Time and time again she would accuse others of doing what she was actually doing. She used this to get people on her side and turn them against people who she wanted to hurt. She had gained a "temple recommend" by saying that the church should either give it to her or she would kill her third husband, Joe Ryan. That sounds far-fetched, but I can imagine her telling the church authorities that Joe Ryan was abusing her and her children and she was on the verge of doing something terrible. She needed to get into the temple to temper herself against her desire to hurt him.

Charles Vallow with his adopted son, JJ, during a family trip. Photo provided by Melanie Vallow.

Church leaders have to give a person a temple recommend for that person to be able to enter a Mormon Temple and not all Mormons have it. She was really good at this type of manipulation. She had used it her whole life. She could turn it on or off. If she needed to gain something from someone or if it were to her benefit to accuse someone of something, she would just turn it on, lying without remorse—apparently pretty convincingly and usually accusing someone else of doing exactly what it was that she was doing.

Lori later claimed that Charles was possessed by a demon named Ned Snider and they needed to perform castings to get Ned out of him. These castings started out as small prayer groups. They would gather around in a circle, hold hands, and pray. This wasn't enough, and Charles kept having new demons or zombies enter his body. The problem was that each time a new zombie entered Charles, it would be a stronger evil spirit than the one before.

We heard a lot of testimony about zombies or how a person can be taken over by evil spirits from several different witnesses. If a person weakens himself by drinking alcohol or watching porn or anything considered sinful, that person opens himself up to being invaded by an evil spirit.

In the book *Visions of Glory*, the protagonist Spencer describes being in a bar and being able to see spirits lining up in a queue waiting for the patrons to become intoxicated. Once a person is intoxicated, an evil spirit could jump into his skull. The evil spirit would actually rip open the skull and jump inside and I guess the skull would close up behind it. The more one drank or the more often one drank or participated in sinful acts, the more susceptible one became of being possessed. Of course, only Spencer could actually see this happening because his veil had been torn.

The point of this section of *Visions of Glory* was that once people realized this was happening to them, every time they drank, watched porn, or participated in any sinful activity, they quickly quit doing that activity. I mean it's a little extreme. Most of us have sat through a sermon listening to a preacher tell us drinking or other sinful activities are bad for us, but to say demons rip open our skulls and invade our bodies is a little much.

In late January 2019, Charles came home from a business trip to find that his truck had been removed from the airport parking lot. When he finally got home, the locks had been changed on his house, and his business bank account had been drained of the $35,000 that had been in it. He called the police, and we watched bodycam footage of Charles pleading with police to do something. He was afraid for his life and for the lives of the children. He was unable to pay his business expenses and employees. He told police that Lori was mentally unstable and needed help.

Police in Arizona looked for Lori, intending to commit her to the Community Bridges mental health facility. Lori somehow caught on to the plan because she admitted herself to Community Bridges. She was evaluated and quickly released. That's how good she was at manipulating people. She not only lied to the police and had them believe her, she lied to the psychologists at Community Bridges, and apparently they believed her.

A few days later Charles filed for divorce, claiming Lori viewed herself as a god preparing for the second coming of Christ. Charles apparently still had hope because he later halted the divorce proceedings. About this time in February 2019 Lori just disappeared, and Charles had no idea where she was. He needed help taking care of six-year-old JJ because he needed to work, so he contacted his sister, JJ's grandmother, Kay Woodcock, for help. Kay and her husband, Larry, loved JJ dearly and were more than happy to do so. They went back and forth between Arizona and their home in Louisiana to help Charles.

Since Lori was doing nothing for JJ, and Kay and Larry were the ones who proved to Charles that they would always be there for him, Charles changed the beneficiary on his life insurance policy from Lori to Kay. I think he knew he was in danger and that something might happen to him, and he wanted to make sure that Kay would be able to take care of JJ. When Lori found out about this after allegedly conspiring to murder Charles, she said, "It is like a spear through my heart."

Charles also moved to Houston to be closer to Kay and JJ. He traveled for work, and it really didn't matter what city he lived in. It turns out that Lori was in Hawaii during this time. She was gone for fifty-eight days. She never reached out to Charles or JJ the whole time she was gone. In March she came back to Arizona and continued her affair with Chad, whom she flew from Idaho to Arizona. She contrived an email claiming to be Charles asking Chad to come help with a book he was struggling to write. This was done to fool Tammy and give Chad an excuse to go stay with Lori while Charles was out of town.

In April, Lori moved to Texas to live with Charles, and Charles halted the divorce proceedings. He still loved Lori, and he wanted to try to make it work. The problem was that Lori was still conniving behind his back, planning her life with Chad. In May 2019 Chad and Lori both searched the internet for malachite wedding rings. We were shown pictures in court of Chad and Lori on the beach in Hawaii, both wearing white linen clothes, getting married and wearing the malachite wedding rings. On May 17, 2019, JJ visited grandparents Kay and Larry in Louisiana, and this would be the last time they would see him alive.

Zulema Pastenes testified in court in Lori's trial that, in June, Chad and Lori told her that Charles was now possessed by a strong demon named Hiplos. It was about the same time that Charles and Lori moved to a new house in Chandler, Arizona, and Lori told Melanie Gibb that Tylee was dark. In fact, according to Chad, Tylee was moving further down the dark scale.

I think some of the people in Chad and Lori's inner circle were extremely dishonest, but some were just fools. Zulema is a fool. I think she truly believed everything Chad and Lori were telling her. Listening to her on the witness stand, I could tell that she still believes that certain people can see through the veil or that certain people have a higher spiritual standing and communicate with spirits. I think she now thinks that Chad and Lori lied to her and took advantage of their higher spiritual standing. The really scary thing to me about people like Zulema is I think she could still be manipulated by them in spite of what she now knows.

This is about the time when things really begin to happen. Melani Boudreaux filed for divorce with her husband, Brandon, claiming that Brandon was abusive. She used this argument in divorce court, trying to get parental rights for their children. The fact was that Melani was using what she had learned from Lori. She was using disinformation against Brandon. Brandon wasn't going along with the whole idea of translated beings and zombies, and he needed to go.

After weeks of trying to get through to Lori, as a last-ditch effort to save his marriage with her, on July 1, Charles told Lori that he was going to Idaho to tell Tammy all about Lori and Chad's affair. He didn't actually talk to Tammy in person, but he did send a letter to Lori's brother Adam, hoping Adam could somehow help. The rest of the family had not believed anything Charles told them about Lori, and he was "blackballed" by them.

Finally giving up- but still feeling responsible for Lori, Charles rented her a house in Arizona where she, JJ, and Tylee could live. It might seem strange that Charles would rent his estranged wife a house of her own. It seems like he would have been angry. She was the one who didn't want to live with him, so why should he provide her with a house? She had stolen from him, lied to him, lied about him, and just generally made his life a living hell. That's who Charles was though.

When they were first married, he built her a dance studio in the basement of their house because he knew she loved to dance. The walls were covered with mirrors and she would dance alone for hours looking at herself in the mirrors. After she met Chad, she would send him videos of her dancing. Charles found those videos. According to fellow inmates, she still dances in jail. Dr. John Matthias says she is celebrating her crimes. Larry Woodcock says it's her escape.

Charles set up a visit with JJ on the morning of July 11. He was to pick up JJ and drive him to school. Charles was excited to see JJ because it had been a while. According to Lori's brother Adam, he and Charles were supposed to meet later that day to talk about what to do about Lori. Charles never made it to that meeting. Lori had a plan and Charles seems to have had no idea of what he was walking into when he walked through the front door of that house.

There are two separate stories about what happened next. The one given by Lori, Tylee, and Alex has been disproven, so I'll give you the true account of what happened. Lori's brother Alex had spent the night with her. She claimed she had asked him to because she felt unsafe around Charles. I have listened to the testimony in court and talked to Charles's family. Charles, although he was a big guy, was a gentle soul and never had used violence or even the threat of violence. It just wasn't his way. Alex told police that he stayed at Lori's house only because they had plans to spend the next day together. He denied staying with Lori because she felt threatened by Charles.

In *Money, Power and Sex* I wrote about what people close to Charles had to say about him. What actually happened in that house was that JJ and sixteen-year-old Tylee had been sent outside. JJ was buckled into his car seat, and Tylee was sent out to sit with him while Alex shot Charles with a .45 caliber handgun. He shot him one time and knocked him down and shot him again while he lay helpless and bleeding on the floor. We know the second shot was taken after Charles was laying on the floor because the police found a bullet lodged in the floor under his body.

Alex had claimed to police that he had to shoot Charles twice to stop him from attacking him with a baseball bat. Alex did have a small cut on the top of his head, and he claimed that Charles hit him there with the bat. I doubt it. I think the wound would have been more than just a small cut. Charles was big, strong, and fit and had been a minor league baseball player.

Alex waited forty-five minutes to call 911. I think he was waiting for Charles to bleed out. The 911 operator tried to walk Alex through CPR, but when police arrived, they could tell that Charles hadn't been touched. They said that if Alex had administered CPR, there would have been more blood that escaped Charles's body. They also found that Alex was now at the house by himself.

After Alex shot Charles, Lori had taken Tylee with her to drop JJ off at school. On the way, they went through the drive-through at Burger King and stopped at a store to buy Tylee flip-flops. When Lori and Tylee returned, they were interviewed by police. The interview was videotaped, and in it we see Lori and Tylee laughing and making jokes about being the new neighbors. They both seem eerily unaffected by the death of Lori's husband and Tylee's stepfather. Tylee and Charles were actually pretty close. Charles was a good stepfather to her. He helped her buy her Jeep and supported her in any way he could.

Lori, Alex, and Tylee were questioned further at the police station before being released. This was videotaped also. We see Lori being manipulative. We see Tylee looking very uncomfortable but going along with what she knew her mom would want her to say. While Tylee is in the interview room by herself waiting to be interviewed, she constantly snaps her finger joints and can be heard humming a song from the movie *Moana*.

I have watched it over and over, trying to get some insight into Tylee, and it really haunts me. I know Tylee had been manipulated by her mother since birth, and I'm pretty sure by this point she was terrified of her mom, seeing firsthand what she was capable of. Lori didn't have to tell Tylee to lie for her. Tylee would automatically say what she knew her mom would want her to say. This is one of the most intriguing aspects of this case to me. In my first book I write about the idea that Tylee had been conditioned by Lori her whole life. So much so that Tylee would automatically know that she needed to lie to protect Lori. She would do so without even thinking about it.

What I didn't really think about when writing *Money, Power and Sex* was that Tylee must have been terrified of Lori. Tylee was smart, so by the time Charles was murdered, she had enough information about Lori to know that Lori would kill her. She knew she was in danger. She knew she had been declared dark by Chad, and people who were dark had to die as she just saw happen with Charles, but she didn't know enough about the world to know she had an opportunity right then and there to save herself. She had witnessed her mom manipulating people her whole life, and she probably didn't trust the police to save her from Lori.

The father side of me is really sad about that. Mostly that she might have been right. I know that any individual police officer would most likely have done whatever it would have taken to save Tylee, but nothing regarding Lori was that simple.

This whole thing had been planned by Chad, Alex, and Lori, and Alex pleaded self-defense. Unfortunately, and in spite of conflicting stories from Alex and Lori and the bullet in the floor, police in Arizona bought the story, and Alex and Lori were free to go. In fact, they held a party at the house later that day. Or at least had some family members over for a swim.

I have gotten conflicting information about that. In the police interviews of Lori, Alex, and Tylee right after the shooting, they all seemed to be bizarrely unaffected by the death of Charles. It seems like the police could have caught on at that point, especially since Charles had called the police earlier and claimed that Lori was threatening his life. And if they had, maybe Chad and Lori would not have committed the crimes that followed. Too bad. What if they had arrested Alex and Lori right then and charged them with the murder of Charles? It certainly looks to me like they would have had cause to do so. Sadly, this story could have ended right there.

As soon as Lori's trial in Idaho was concluded, Arizona extradited her and charged her with the murder of Charles. A little late unfortunately.

11

REXBURG POLICE GET A CALL

On the morning of October 2, 2019, Brandon Boudreaux was driving his black Tesla home in Gilbert, Arizona, after dropping his kids off at school. Just as he was about to pull into his driveway, he noticed something sticking out of the back window of a green Jeep Wrangler that was parked across the street from his house. At the very instant he noticed it, he saw the muzzle blast and his driver side window exploded. In shock, but still able to think, Brandon sped off and quickly dialed 911. As he did so, he saw the Jeep pull in behind him. Brandon was terrified, but relieved to see the Jeep turn away and speed out of the neighborhood. It all happened just that fast.

Who was shooting at him and why? Gilbert police questioned the neighbors and the neighbors reported seeing a dark Jeep Wrangler with Texas license plates idling across the street from Brandon's house. The Jeep later showed up on traffic cameras coming from and going to Idaho. From these cameras, the police were able to get the license plate number from the Jeep and found that the Jeep was registered to Charles Vallow. The Jeep showed up on video surveillance at 4:30 a.m. in Rexburg, Idaho. Gilbert police contacted Rexburg police who were quickly able to track it down.

Rexburg Police Lt. Ray Hermosillo (left) and Captain Ron Ball (right) discussing the case outside the courthouse. Photo provided by Ray Hermosillo.

Rexburg police, now involved in the case, seized the Jeep and started looking for evidence. And there was a lot of it. They found Alex Cox's DNA in the Jeep. They found gunshot residue around the back window. They found video footage of Chad and Lori putting the spare tire from the Jeep in Lori's storage unit before the shooting. They found video footage of Alex and Lori taking the spare tire back out of the storage unit after the shooting. On this model of Jeep, the spare tire had to be removed in order to open the rear window. This is significant because it shows that all three were involved.

Rexburg police interviewed Brandon's ex-wife, Melani Pawlowski, and she denied knowing anything, but she was not able to account for where she was and what she was doing at the time of the shooting. My thought is that she was hanging out with Chad and Lori, waiting to hear that Alex had successfully murdered her ex-husband. Melani would never say or do anything that would put Lori and Chad in jeopardy. In fact, she had said that she would go to prison or die before she would do anything that would hurt them. She had moved into the same apartment complex as Alex and Lori with her new husband, Ian Pawlowski, following them to Rexburg.

Melani and Brandon's divorce was not a happy one. They had been fighting over custody and visitation rights of their children. Brandon had filed a restraining order against Melani hoping to keep her away from them. In fact, Melani and Brandon's story is very similar to Lori and Charles's. Both Melani and Lori were telling lies about their husbands, both were embracing fanatical religious beliefs, both were involved in divisive divorces, and I think both had tried to murder their husbands.

In November 2019 the police were called as Melani tried to break into Brandon's house while the kids and Brandon's father were in the house. When the police showed up, Melani argued with them and was unreasonable. She was playing the part of a mom who was worried about the safety of her children, but police could see right through that. They already had a restraining order against Melani, and she wasn't supposed to be there. Watching police cam footage of the event, I could see the police eventually realize that Alex was there sitting in his pickup truck. Of course, they didn't know the significance of that at the time, but it shows that Melani was involved with Alex, who we all now know was the hit man.

Police in Rexburg knew they were on the right track and just needed to find proof of what had happened. That would take a while, and it would become part of the bigger investigation into the murders of Tylee and JJ. They eventually found that Alex and Chad had been talking on burner phones while Alex was on his way to and from and in Gilbert, and that Alex had called Chad right after he attempted to shoot Brandon.

We see criminals use burner phones in the movies, but criminals in the movies might be smarter than Alex, Chad, and Lori, and the police might be smarter than the police in the movies. At least, the technology is better. Sitting in the jury in the Lori Vallow Daybell case, I listened to FBI specialists explain how they were able to track down the burner phones and access the information stored on them. The evidence was a tangled web, and investigators would have to untangle it in just the right order. They did untangle it strand by strand, and they explained to us how they were able to do it. A lot of it was over my head honestly, but I was able to get the gist of what they were trying to tell us.

Once they had the number of one phone, they could see what other numbers that phone had called. They used these numbers to determine that fifteen burner phones had been used. They gained access to those phones. Once they had a search warrant for the phones, they were able to retrieve the information on those phones. Chad, Lori, and Alex had used the phones to gain access to their email accounts also, so the police had texts and email messages sent between the trio. It also gave them access to the email accounts. This is how they were able to determine that Alex and Chad had been talking. They also found that Alex had searched the internet for Brandon's address. They found that Lori had searched the internet for "man shot in Gilbert Arizona" right after Alex attempted to shoot Brandon. That piece of evidence is pretty damning for Lori.

There was no direct evidence, however, tying Melani to the attempted murder. I have found that following this case requires a lot of patience. We want to see justice served. There is a lot of evidence that Melani was right there with Chad and Lori while Alex was trying to murder Brandon. It's obvious that she was directly involved in a conspiracy to murder Brandon. But police need direct or at least solid circumstantial evidence. The fact that Melani was hanging out with Chad and Lori when Alex was in Gilbert just wasn't enough.

However, new evidence keeps coming to the surface, and I still have hope. When all of Chad and Lori's trials are concluded and they no longer need Melani as a witness in those trials, maybe she will be charged.

It's interesting that things all kind of came together in this investigation at the time of the attempted murder of Brandon. Police started to realize there were things going on and things weren't what they seemed. They had the phone call from Kay Woodcock asking them to investigate the whereabouts of JJ and they had Alex's attempted murder of Brandon, and it all pointed directly at Chad, Lori, and Alex. Time to step up their investigation.

On April 11, 2023, in the Lori Vallow Daybell trial, we listened to Rexburg Detective Ray Hermosillo on the witness stand testifying about his first encounter with Lori, Alex, and Chad. Detective Hermosillo said he knew they were lying to him, not only because of his experience in interviewing suspects, but also because some of what they said he knew to be false.

Lori told him JJ was with his grandmother in Louisiana, and he knew that was a lie because Kay was the one who called police asking for help finding JJ. Also, Chad lied about Lori. Chad and Lori were married by this time, but Lori told Hermosillo that Chad was her brother's friend.

Melanie Gibb (don't confuse her with Melani Boudreaux) initially covered for Lori, telling police she had JJ in Arizona. Lori had called Melanie asking her to do so, and Chad asked her not to talk to the police. He asked her to just not answer if the police called her. Lori told Hermosillo that JJ was with Melanie and she took him to see the movie *Frozen*.

Later, on December 8, 2019, I assume because Melanie got scared, she recorded a call with Lori and handed the recording over to the police. We listened to the call in court while Melanie was on the witness stand testifying. Answering the phone, Chad calls her "sweet Melanie" and Lori calls her "babe." In the call Melanie asks Lori where JJ is, and Lori replies that he is safe. She refused to answer when Melanie kept pushing for more information.

Lori blames Kay, saying she is keeping JJ safe from her. Melanie asks if she is in danger, and Chad says that she would be if she knew where JJ was. The call goes on with Melanie pushing for information about JJ and Chad and Lori blaming Kay, saying that JJ is happy and safe. They go on into some religious fanaticism, and it all kind of boiled down to Chad and Lori using it to manipulate Melanie in a kind of passive aggressive way, which they were very good at.

Thankfully Melanie was seeing through it all by this point and working with police. It's just too bad she didn't do that sooner. I don't know if Melanie knew the children were in danger, but I don't know that she didn't. As I write this, I am hoping to get more information that will lead me to a conclusion.

12

KILLING TAMMY

Much like Chad, Tammy Douglas was born into a typical Mormon family. She was born on May 4, 1970, in Pasadena, California, but moved with her family to Springville, Utah, when she was thirteen. Family members say she had a happy childhood.

She loved going to Disneyland. She was a gifted student. She was outgoing and loved to put on plays for her family and friends. She played in the Springville High School band and was yearbook editor her senior year. She created her own library with library cards, lending books to her siblings. When books weren't turned in on time, she fined them.

After high school she moved on to Brigham Young University where she unfortunately met and married Chad Daybell in 1990. After marrying Chad, she went to work for the Springville parks department where she typed thousands of handwritten burial notices into the computer system. People considered her a computer genius, and she eventually took a job as a computer teacher at Art City Elementary School.

Tammy Daybell. The photo was taken at the last luncheon that Vicki put together for the girls, aunts, and cousins. Photo provided by Vicki Hoban.

The description of her life goes on like this. She was a wonderful mother and juggled that with working with children to help support her family. It would be impossible to ask for a better wife, but as we know, she wasn't enough for Chad Daybell.

As I sat in the jury box during the Lori Vallow Daybell trial, listening to testimony about Tammy, the anger I had toward her husband, Chad, was hard to hide. He so selfishly deprived his five children and two grandchildren of their mother and grandmother. And for what? As I said in my last book, it was money, power, and sex.

One of the reasons I hung out in court every day during the Chad Daybell trial is that it gave me the opportunity to get to know people who were there waiting to see justice served. I got the chance to meet several of Tammy's family members.

I spent hours and hours with Tammy's aunt Vicki. She is such a warm person and we spent so much time together that I got to thinking of her as Aunt Vicki. She's just that kind of person.

I interviewed Tammy's aunt Vicki at the courthouse during the trial. Photo by Lauren Matthias.

We talked a lot about Tammy. It often led to tears and sometimes to laughter, but I always loved hearing Aunt Vicki talk about her, and Aunt Vicki had a lot to say. Listening to Aunt Vicki reinforced everything I heard from the witness stand from family members, friends, and workmates. Tammy was a good-hearted, loving, dedicated mother, wife, and educator. She was a good Mormon and had none of the radical beliefs Chad had. She was loved and valued by everyone.

Chad and Tammy's house was just about five miles north of Rexburg, Idaho. There are a few houses around, but it's not a typical neighborhood like you would see in the suburbs. Their daughter Emma and her husband lived across the street and a little down the road. The house sits on the corner of an intersection, and there is another house across the other street.

It was fall and the days were getting shorter. There are not a lot of streetlights or porch lights, just a blinking yellow light at the intersection. Just as it was turning dark on the evening of October 9, 2019, Tammy pulled into her driveway, got out of the car, and opened the back door to get the bag of groceries she had just bought. She was probably thinking of the dinner she would cook that evening for her family.

As she straightened up with the groceries, she was startled by a man dressed in camo, wearing a black facemask pointing a rifle at her. The man immediately fired twice from very close range, and Tammy dropped the bag of groceries. Tammy stood there in shock as the man quickly ran away. She gathered her wits and her groceries and ran into the house where she told Chad what had just occurred. Chad didn't seem overly upset and didn't even go outside right away to see if the man was still around.

Tammy called 911 to report the incident. On a recording of the call, we hear Chad in the background telling Tammy to tell the police it was a teenager with a paintball gun. Tammy was still in shock and really didn't want to believe someone had just tried to kill her. Things like that didn't happen to people like Tammy, especially in the Rexburg area, so in spite of what she had just witnessed, she went along with the paintball gun idea. I'm not really sure if she was convinced though.

Emma's husband, Joseph, had witnessed the attempted shooting from across the street and also called the police. Having listened to Joseph testify in court, I'm surprised he called the police. He was called on by John Prior as a witness for the defense. He was a terrible witness and, in fact, did more to prove the prosecution's case. During cross-examination it became very apparent that he did not like the police. He said he would rather do any other job than be a cop. He showed disdain for the police and prosecution, and it felt to me like he was willing to lie to protect Chad.

Anyway, it was eventually decided that it must not have been a man with a rifle trying to shoot Tammy. It must have been one of the neighborhood teenagers pulling a prank, and it was left at that.

We know it was Alex, and it was a real rifle shooting real bullets. It was fitted with a suppressor so it probably didn't sound like a real gun to Tammy. The prosecution brought the rifle into court to show the jury during the Lori Vallow Daybell trial. I can see how someone could mistake it for a paintball gun. It had a scope that would have looked similar to a hopper on a paintball gun. It was most likely the same rifle Alex had used when he attempted to shoot Brandon. One thing I can say about Alex is that he was a terrible shot.

This episode raises an interesting idea for me. Was Alex incapable of murdering anyone on his own? The two times we know of him attempting murder by himself were both failures. And if he couldn't do it on his own, who was with him at the time of the successful murders?

Somehow, even at that close range, Alex managed to miss. Lori later said to Chad in a phone call that Alex was a screw-up and couldn't do anything right. I wonder if Alex panicked at the last minute and was unable to murder in cold blood, the defenseless Tammy.

There should have been shell casings left at the scene and possibly bullets embedded in a house or trees or something across the street, but it doesn't seem like police thought to look. It seems like they made the assumption that it was a prank and left it at that. Unfortunately, like a lot of things that happened early on in this case, police didn't believe what had really happened, and it's hard to blame them, considering Tammy wasn't sure herself.

The prosecution tried to convince the jury that it was indeed an attempted murder by Alex, but they really didn't have any direct proof. They did, however, have a lot of circumstantial evidence including the actual murder of Tammy ten days later.

On the morning of October 19, 2019, police again received a 911 call from Chad's house. It was Chad and Tammy's son Garth who placed the call, but Chad quickly took over saying his wife had died in her sleep. On the 911 call, we could hear Chad crying as he talked to the operator.

"Hello, I'm Chad, the husband, she's clearly dead," Chad sobbed. "Oh no . . . yeah she's not even . . . she's frozen," he went on.

It sounded very contrived to me. I don't believe Chad is capable of that kind of emotion. Certainly not over the misfortune of someone else. Even his own wife. When the police and coroner showed up, Tammy was lying on her and Chad's bed with pink foam coming out of her mouth. Chad explained that when he woke up, Tammy was lying half out of the bed and that he had awakened Garth to come help him put her back onto the bed. Chad said she had been sick the night before, throwing up, but she wouldn't let him take her to the doctor. He said she preferred to treat herself with home remedies.

When police showed up, her body was cold and she had that pink foam coming out of her mouth. They again believed that nothing nefarious had happened to her. The coroner said she died of natural causes, and it was left at that. No autopsy was performed.

On October 22, just three days after she died, Tammy was buried at the Evergreen Cemetery in Springville, Utah. People in Rexburg who were close to Tammy thought it was odd that Chad would have her buried there. My thought is that Chad thought that if he buried her in a different state, the police wouldn't bother to exhume her if they thought they needed to. Of course, police had no problem going to Utah to exhume Tammy's body, but that's how simplistic Chad's thinking is.

In spite of the coroner's determination that Tammy died of natural causes, some people were becoming suspicious of Chad. Steve Schultz, the director of Springville Mortuary, knew Chad and Tammy well. Before Chad and Tammy moved the family to Rexburg, Schultz had been their neighbor. After the coroner and police left, Chad called Schultz to come pick up Tammy's body and prepare her for her funeral in Springville. This was Saturday morning and Chad told Schultz he wanted the funeral to be the following Monday.

When Schultz asked Chad if there was to be an autopsy, Chad said no. Schultz explained to Chad that an autopsy was important for two reasons. One of course being that it would explain how Tammy died and the other being that she may have died of something that could be hereditary. It would be important to Chad's kids to know if there was something they should be aware of. Still, Chad refused the autopsy.

Schultz explained that they couldn't possibly do the funeral on Monday, and he and Chad agreed on Tuesday. Even though Schultz had always thought a lot of Chad, he became suspicious of him. Schultz took the liberty of examining Tammy's body when he prepared her for her viewing, but didn't find anything too suspicious. He did note the bruising on Tammy's arms, but it wasn't enough for him to have anything more than a little awareness that things might not be what Chad was claiming.

And other people who knew Tammy well were also questioning how she could die and why the funeral had to happen so fast and so far away. Springville is a four-hour drive from

Rexburg, and people who worked with Tammy and loved her wouldn't be able to attend. They decided to have a memorial for Tammy in Rexburg.

Hearing all of this in court made me feel extremely sorry for what was done to Tammy. She was a great mom, wife, grandmother, and teacher. She was valued by so many people. People close to her were not convinced that she had died of natural causes. I have a feeling that those people may have known something was not right in Tammy's world because they contacted police and said they didn't believe she died of natural causes.

Samantha Gwilliam, Tammy's sister, testified that she knew Tammy was in very good physical condition, and in fact she was preparing to run a 5k. All of the people who died around Chad and Lori were in good health, and they expected us to believe that they died of natural causes. How stupid do Chad and Lori think people are? One thing I have learned about people is they are incapable of understanding that others might be smarter than they are.

We heard in court that police discovered that Lori had been searching the internet for wedding dresses at the time Tammy was murdered. We also heard Zulema Pastenes testify that Lori had told her that Chad would be moving in with her. Zulema said she told Lori that it was too fast and there should be a grieving period.

Just one week after Tammy's death, Chad told his friends from church that he had met the woman he was going to marry, and a few days after that he introduced Lori to them. They said Chad and Lori were very affectionate to each other, and it bothered them. "They looked like teenagers," they said, and they were very embarrassed. Lori also told them that her husband died of a heart attack and they had recently lost a daughter. She also said she was an empty nester. All lies of course.

Not long after Tammy's death, police started to realize things in Chad and Lori's world were not what they appeared to be. They started putting the pieces together. Charles had been shot to death by Alex, there had been an attempted shooting of Brandon, there may have been an attempted shooting of Tammy, Tylee and JJ were missing, and they knew Chad and Lori had been lying to them.

In the early morning of December 11, 2019, they quietly exhumed Tammy's body and had an autopsy performed by Utah medical examiner Dr. Erik Christensen, who determined that she had died of asphyxiation. We were shown pictures of her exhumed body in court, and the medical examiner pointed out some bruising on her arm, which he said would have been consistent with someone holding her down.

Dr. Christensen checked the contents of her stomach and found everything she ate the night before. This was inconsistent with what Chad said about her vomiting the night before. Dr. Christensen explained that the pink foam coming out of her mouth would have been consistent with asphyxiation. As the flow of blood slows, fluid builds up in the lungs causing a foam that can come out of the mouth and nose. He declared her cause of death to be asphyxiation and the means to be homicide.

Using cell phone location, the police determined that Alex's phone was just a few blocks away on the night of Tammy's death. Why would Alex have been so close by in the middle of the night? Might he have parked his car away from the house and left his cell phone in it in order to not disturb Chad and Tammy's adult son Garth who was living in the house?

I have seen Chad and Tammy's house. It's very small for that many people, and it must have been hard to murder Tammy with Garth sleeping in another room just a few feet away. This, I believe, bolsters my idea that more than one person helped Chad murder Tammy. The fact that Tammy had very little bruising, in my opinion, points to the idea that at least two people held her down while another person somehow asphyxiated her, either with a pillow or by holding his hand over her mouth and nose.

Another possibility is that the murder occurred while Garth was at work at the haunted mansion. According to Garth's testimony he worked until 1:00 a.m. the night Tammy was murdered. This idea lines up with the information police got from Alex's phone. Alex was known to be traveling toward Chad's house at 10:45 p.m. on October 19. According to Rexburg police Tammy's time of death was between 12:30 a.m. and 2:00 a.m. Alex's phone was apparently turned off between 10:45 and 11:53 p.m. on October 19.

Okay, so we know Chad for sure and Alex almost for sure, but who would the third person have been? Even though Garth was there that morning and backed up Chad's lies, I don't believe he would have been involved. Garth and all of Chad and Tammy's kids are victims of their father. They may not know that yet or they may not be willing to admit that to themselves yet, but they are. They have all defended him so far, saying they don't believe their father would do what he is accused of, and even if he had, he would not have buried Tylee and JJ in his backyard. They say they think he was set up by Lori and Alex. I think that will be the defense's argument in court also. The witness list is sealed, but I think Chad's defense lawyer, John Prior, will call them in to testify. That would be hard to see. I hope they are able to move on with their lives.

Among Tammy's friends and coworkers, there is a lot of doubt about her death. They have all been told conflicting stories from Chad about the night of her death. To one he said he was upstairs when he heard a thump and went to check on her and found her half out of the bed dead. To another he said he was in bed with Tammy when he heard the thump and woke up to find her dead. He also contradicted himself about the time of her death.

At her memorial he spoke about his deceased wife to the mourners and called her lazy. They all knew that Tammy was anything but lazy, and they thought it was really strange that he would say such a thing at his wife's memorial.

These are the questions I am left with regarding Tammy's death. I'm sure Alex was there. Why wasn't there more bruising on Tammy's body? Could there have been more than one person holding her down while she was fighting to breathe? I think there must have been or there would have been more bruising. How could they have done this to Tammy without waking Garth sleeping in that small house, or was she murdered when Garth was at work? What did Chad do between the time he murdered Tammy and the time he called 911? There were several hours between. Did he just lie down next to her dead body and go to sleep? Why did Chad and Lori feel they had to murder Tammy?

I think I know the answer to that last question. She was in the way. Chad and Lori wanted to be free to carry on their relationship without Tammy being in the way all the time. Chad had already said he thought Tammy would die young even before Lori came along. I think Chad tried to get Tammy to go along with some of his fundamentalist beliefs, and with what I know about her, I don't think she wanted any part of it.

The main belief Chad had that I think would have caused a problem for Tammy was the idea of plural wives. Chad was meeting a lot of women through the writing of his books, his speeches, and his participation in Preparing a People, and they all had similar beliefs. Some of the main people involved in Preparing a People were fundamentalist Mormons who believe in polygamy.

Chad was getting attention that he had not gotten before. Julie Rowe claimed Chad had molested her. I wish some of these women would talk. I also think that Tammy must have been suspicious of Chad and Lori. If she hadn't caught on by the time she was murdered, I think she would have been about to. We know Charles was on to them and had sent Tammy an email detailing the affair.

Now that the Chad Daybell trial is over, I have more answers and more questions. Garth did testify for the defense. He stated that he worked until around 1:00 a.m. that night. When he came home, he walked by his parent's room and saw two forms in the bed and heard his father snoring. All was well and he went to bed.

The problem with Garth's testimony is that it was contradicted by a coworker of his. The coworker said that Garth told him a different story. Garth told him that Chad wasn't home when he got home from work and his mom was dead. Two totally different stories, but Garth came off in court as dishonest and the coworker came off as honest. Also, the coworker would have nothing to gain by perjuring himself and had no one to protect. When he was done testifying, he sat right next to me in the gallery. I had so many questions, but couldn't ask them until there was a break. When the break finally came, he was gone. I did get to verify his story later though.

It made me sad listening to Garth lie for his father—the father who was on trial for murdering his mother. I asked myself why he would do that. Why he would defend his father in spite of all the evidence against him. I watched Garth on the witness stand try to make eye contact with Chad. It appeared to me that he was trying to get Chad's approval. It seemed to me that Chad didn't think Garth was doing a good enough job. He would look down when Garth tried to make eye contact, kind of like disregarding him.

I think Chad conditioned his children from birth in much the same way that Lori conditioned Tylee. Garth would do or say whatever it was that he thought Chad would want him to do or say, and even though Chad wouldn't have to tell him to lie, Garth would know that was what was expected.

I also know that Garth believed Chad was a prophet. He believed Chad could see into the future, and he believed Chad spoke to God. Garth said so when Chad told him that his books were not fiction, but truth. He said he found out the books were true when he heard Chad talking to Julie Rowe about it.

Chad and Tammy's daughter Emma also testified for the defense, and her testimony also worked better for the prosecution. She was obviously coached on what to say even though she claimed she had not been talking to John Prior. She had been talking to Chad though. I'm guessing Chad even told her what other witnesses had said on the stand. She tried to contradict what those witnesses stated, but it didn't go over well. She came off as not credible. She came off as downright dishonest.

I thought they would both come back and testify in the penalty phase and plead for their father's life. They did not. In fact, no one did. That really surprised me, but I guess at that point no one was willing to do that. That silence spoke loudly to me.

Tylee and JJ. Photo provided by Kay Woodcock.

13

KILLING TYLEE AND JJ

This is the hardest part of the story for me to write about. Not only because it is emotionally difficult to write about the brutal murders of such innocent children, but also because it is hard to ask anyone close to them about what happened. It's just too hurtful and I don't want to put them through that.

I hope that in reading this section, people understand that the story of how they were murdered needs to be told. People need to know. Not to sensationalize or because of curiosity or because people like to read about other people's misery, but because we need to talk about what going down the wrong path can lead to. I have become friends with some of the people who loved Tylee and JJ while they were alive. I love my friends, and they know, or I at least hope they know, that I write about this in order to be a voice for those who are still living and in danger.

I just listened to an interview Dr. John and Lauren Matthias did on their *Hidden True Crime* podcast. They were interviewing JJ's grandfather Larry Woodcock. Dr. John told Larry: "It could have been avoided, it should have been avoided." That's exactly why I am writing about this. It should never have gotten to the point it got to, and I want to do whatever my small part is in making sure it doesn't happen again.

I'm nobody. I just happened to be on the jury for the Lori Vallow Daybell trial, and reluctantly I might add. I have never been a writer or author, I have no idea if people who read this are going to think it's any good, but I am going to do what I can whether it's sufficient or not. I am a person who cares and I am going to tell this story. The problem is that it will happen again. It is happening somewhere right now, or at least leading up to it.

Larry went on to say in the interview: "We have not come to grips with this, not totally." What he meant is that the people who have the same extreme beliefs as Chad and Lori, the people who helped lead them down the path that led to murdering the children, are still out there. Some of them are still espousing their extreme beliefs, living on the backs of their victims.

It led to unbelievable extremes in Chad and Lori's case, and while I won't say that everyone who is involved in the prepper movement or has fundamentalist beliefs would go to these extremes, I will say that there is the danger that someone will, and we need to deal with it.

After spending seven weeks as a juror in the Lori Vallow Daybell trial and after doing all of my research for these books after the trial ended, I believe that things are going on that we are unaware of and are being swept under the rug, or we are just not admitting to ourselves that they're happening.

Listening to Zulema Pastenes testify in the Lori Vallow Daybell trial gave me my first real insight into how deep it goes. Her testimony was most interesting to me because I think that she truly believed all of what Chad and Lori were telling her. She believed in past probations, near-death experiences, seeing through the veil, zombies, Chad being a prophet, and all the rest of it. She said she thought Chad and Lori had a higher religious standing and she wanted to follow them and would follow them no matter where they led her. It's terrifying to know there are such gullible people out there, but there are, and they are being taken advantage of by people like Chad.

Just recently a man named Moroni Johnson acknowledged that he was part of a conspiracy with self-proclaimed prophet Samuel Bateman to traffic underage girls across state lines for the purpose of raping them. Their network covered four states. Bateman is the leader of an FLDS offshoot that believes a man needs multiple wives in order to reach the celestial kingdom. Bateman has over twenty wives, ten of whom were under the age of eighteen when he "married" them. He also "gifts" wives to his friends. Thankfully Bateman and Johnson have been arrested, but the core of the problem is still there on the border of Arizona and Utah, and crimes against underage girls will continue until we do something more about it.

Extreme fundamentalism of any kind is dangerous. The Kingston family is still thriving in the Salt Lake City area. The LeBarons are still out there. The Crick and the FLDS within it still exist. We know of their crimes. We know there has been murder, child abuse, spouse abuse, tax evasion, human trafficking, and more. We know these are powerful groups with a lot of influence in government. What is it going to take for us to finally hold to account the people leading these groups? We hold religious freedom to our hearts in this country as we should, but our laws are our laws, and when they are broken, we need to hold people to account.

I know it's complicated, and I know that for a politician who has to get reelected, it's even more complicated, but if our elected officials aren't willing to deal with these groups, what hope do we have of keeping them from committing these crimes?

When the FBI finally raided the FLDS's Yearning for Zion ranch in Eldorado, Texas, on April 3, 2008, they found hundreds of underage girls there who they were sure were either being abused or about to be. Child Protective Services ended up caving under the pressure of being accused of stepping on the right to religious freedom, and the children were given back to the parents who were abusing them. This after saying they found proof that underage girls were being groomed to be married to older men as soon as the girls reached puberty. If the very people we pay to protect these children can't protect them, who can?

We're seeing right now as I write this what is happening in our cities. If we ignore the law, chaos erupts. If there is any law that people think they can get away with breaking, we can be sure there will be somebody out there who will break that law. I have seen firsthand that the police officers and FBI agents who do the footwork in cases like this case are first-rate. They take what they do with the appropriate amount of seriousness. I wouldn't want any of them to think I am being critical of them. The problem is not with them, and in fact I would say that if there is any hope of dealing with these criminals, that hope resides with them.

The real problem is higher up at the upper levels of government. Politicians just don't seem to have the stomach to deal with them. The only way we're going to make change is if we take it seriously like we did with organized crime in the 1980s and terrorism after 9/11.

Larry Woodcock goes on to talk about Chad and Lori's inner circle. They were witnesses in the Lori Vallow Daybell trial and will be witnesses in Chad's trial. None of them have been charged with crimes, but to differing degrees, they were all aware of what Chad and Lori were doing. They could have said something to stop Chad and Lori, and they did not. They could have at least said something once they knew or at least suspected that Tylee and JJ had been murdered, but they did not. They may have been afraid for their own lives, thinking Chad and Lori could just as easily add them to the dark list and murder them. They may have been afraid that the police would come after them. So what? These are not honorable people.

Larry wonders how they can look at themselves in the mirror. So do I! These are all our children. They are not your children or my children; they are all our children. They are helpless, small, and weak, and we are all their protectors. A crime against any child is a crime against us all.

At the very least, I hope that people who were in Chad and Lori's inner circle know that we see them. I want them to know that. I wanted them to know that as I sat on the jury, and I would have loved an opportunity to tell them that I see them for what they are. Of course, I didn't get that opportunity as a juror, but I get it now.

This is why I am writing about the murders of Tylee and JJ—the fact that if these extreme groups are allowed to proceed unchecked, if we turn our heads away from it, if we don't allow ourselves to believe that human beings can be so cruel, if we think that places like Rexburg, Idaho, are above this kind of crime, we are responsible for their deaths.

As I said earlier, when Judge Boyce was reading Lori Vallow Daybell's sentence to her in the Fremont County Courthouse, he said to her: "I don't believe a God in any religion would want what happened here to happen." He's right, of course, but Tylee and JJ's mom did. She had gone down so far into her rabbit hole that she actually believed and I think still believes that murdering her children was the right thing to do.

How do you convince a mother that brutally murdering her children is good for them? How do you do that, Chad? I really want to know. (I apologize to my readers. I'm not a cop who makes a living hiding my emotions. I'm not a doctor or scientist. What I am is a father, and a member of the human race.) People like me sit on juries. We are your peers. And we don't approve of what you did. The law puts us in a position to do something about that. Sadly, our judgments come after horrible events happen.

Anyway, these extreme religious beliefs and the people who use them to gain power and influence are dangerous. Don't misunderstand me. Lori Vallow Daybell is responsible for her children's murders. She was their mother and their protector. She deserves every bit of the sentence she got and I believe that if there is a God, there will be a reckoning for her with him. But this book is about Chad, or at least is focused on Chad's part in the lives and deaths of the people whom this story is really about. Chad is the one who used extreme religious beliefs to promote himself. He used people like Lori and Zulema and Melanie and Alex and many more. He destroyed them just as brutally as he destroyed Tylee and JJ, and he did it with no remorse in spite of the cost to those people.

I think Chad still believes that he is the one mighty and strong and he's justified in ruining so many lives. He is so narcissistic and so wrapped up in his own mind that he is incapable of having any remorse or sympathy for any of his victims. He has chosen so many wrong paths to get to where he is presently.

My hope is that after reading the first few pages of this chapter, you understand why I think it matters how Tylee and JJ were murdered and will excuse me for what comes next.

14

TYLEE ASHLYN RYAN

(SEPTEMBER 24, 2002–SEPTEMBER 9, 2019)

When I was writing *Money, Power and Sex*, I hadn't yet realized that my mind was playing tricks on me. That's what happens to you when you are subjected to the things I was subjected to as a juror in the Lori Vallow Daybell murder trial.

I have done a lot of research and a lot of contemplating since the trial ended, and my thinking has evolved. I believe I have come back to rational thought and reality. My brain is able to admit to itself the truth of what I saw and heard in that courtroom. I don't think I could have withstood the truth until some time had passed. Now I am sure of what happened to little JJ and Tylee, and now I have to grieve again for these two kids whom I know so well even though I never met them.

Tylee Ashlyn Ryan. Photo provided by Kay Woodcock.

While writing my first book, I thought a lot about Tylee's trip to Old Faithful with her brother JJ, Uncle Alex, and mom Lori—mostly about the trip back to Rexburg. My inability to comprehend that Lori, Chad, and Alex could do what they did to JJ and Tylee made me want to believe that Tylee had been drugged on that trip home. I wanted to believe that there was at least a chance that something had been slipped into her drink when they stopped for dinner. That would have not only saved her from the pain, but also saved her from knowing that her mother and uncle were murdering her.

There is nothing to suggest that, however, and in fact the truth that I have learned suggests otherwise. The murders of Tylee and JJ were ritualistic in the extreme. They had to be done in a particular way in order to save their souls. At least this is the belief that Lori had, which was put into her head by Chad and others who had the same extreme beliefs. It was handed down through Chad to Lori and through Lori to Alex. The kids were dark. Their bodies had been invaded by zombies, and their only hope for salvation was to kill the bodies and save the souls.

Further, it would save the kids from having to live through the apocalypse, which was going to be a horrendous time, and send them directly to heaven, where they would be busy doing good works in the arms of Jesus. And the apocalypse was only a few months away.

As we know sixteen-year-old Tylee died on September 8 or 9, 2019, and the great earthquake on the Wasatch Front (the mountain range just east of the Salt Lake Valley) was to happen on July 22, 2020. Very few would survive the earthquakes, floods, and plagues, and those who did survive would be put through hell before the Mormons led by Chad were able to make things better. In fact, Chad and his followers would eventually make things on earth ideal for the survivors. The survivors would only be those who were extremely worthy, and Chad did not think Tylee and JJ were worthy. They were dark. At least that was his excuse for getting them out of his way.

The last proof of life we have of Tylee was a picture taken in front of Old Faithful in Yellowstone National Park on September 8, 2019. The picture was taken by Lori and shows Tylee, Uncle Alex, and JJ, all with smiles on their faces. It looks like a happy moment, and I think that is the point of the picture. Lori and Alex had plans for Tylee, and this picture would throw the world off track. I've looked at that picture for hours, and when I look at Tylee, I see what looks like a knowing smirk on her face.

Shortly after that picture was taken, they made the two-hour trip back to Chad's house at 202N 1900E, Rexburg, Idaho. The contrast between the beauty of the drive between Yellowstone and Rexburg, which I have made myself more than once, and the bleakness of Chad's house and property is striking. Along the way they stopped for dinner, possibly to let some time pass before arriving in Rexburg. What happened next is still somewhat unclear, but we do know some facts.

I should probably go back at this point and tell you about some of the things leading up to Tylee's murder and some of the testimony I heard in court.

The testimony against Lori Vallow Daybell given by people like Zulema Pastenes, April Raymond, and Melanie Gibb, among others, was pretty damning, as was the testimony given by the police and FBI. Zulema talked about how Lori and Chad described casting out zombies in order to save souls. According to Chad and Lori's extreme beliefs, burning and binding was what it would take. If it wasn't done in a particular way, their souls could not be released to heaven.

They also had the belief that an autistic person like JJ was held in special regard in the spirit world. His body would have to be left intact. He had a higher spiritual standing, and it was not necessary to burn him and hack him to pieces. It wasn't necessary to make him suffer that much. He would make it to heaven without that.

Rexburg Detective Ray Hermosillo testified about what they found when they served a search warrant on Chad's property on June 9, 2020. I describe the exhumation of both Tylee and JJ in *Money, Power and Sex,* so I won't rehash that part any more than necessary here.

What happened between the time the picture was taken in Yellowstone and the next day? In the picture we see a beautiful teenage girl. The next pictures we see of Tylee were after the police and FBI exhumed what was left of her in the "pet cemetery" in Chad's backyard nine months later.

I think about the time between that picture and when they found the remains. I think about what people had to go through and how hard it must have been for them. The family, their friends, the community, the police, the whole country. All hoping to find them alive. Doing everything they could to find them. The family, grandparents Kay and Larry in particular, pushing for answers and never giving up. The police were searching and asking questions, investigating every possible lead. People in the media like Nate Eaton of EastIdahoNews.com following every step of the investigation. The community, people like Jeanine and Clint Hansen, doing whatever they could. They built a wall along the fence of Chad's property where people could come to contemplate and pray and place cards, flowers, and candles. They held vigils. When they found Tylee and JJ buried just feet from that wall, it turned into a memorial.

We know Alex, Lori, Tylee, and JJ stopped for dinner on the way home. Surveillance video shows Alex's pickup leaving Yellowstone at 6:40 p.m. It's a little more than a two-hour drive back to the Rexburg area, and we know they stopped for dinner, so we can surmise that they got back around 9:30

or 10:00 p.m. According to police testimony, Alex's phone was at Lori's apartment at 11:15 p.m. and again between 2:42 a.m. and 3:47 a.m. At 9:21 a.m. he is in Chad's backyard and leaves fourteen minutes later.

At 11:53 a.m. Chad sends a text to Tammy saying he shot a raccoon in the backyard and buried it in the pet cemetery. When police were scraping away at the pet cemetery, they found the remains of a cat and a dog, but no raccoon.

We can assume that Tylee was not murdered at Lori's apartment. Dr. Christensen, the medical examiner, couldn't determine what Tylee's cause of death was, but the way she was murdered would have left evidence at the scene. So I think we can assume that she was murdered in Chad's backyard while Lori was at home in her apartment. She must have been murdered between 11:15 p.m. and 2:42 a.m.

Another possibility is that she was murdered between 3:47 a.m. and 9:21 a.m., but it would have been getting light by about 6:00 a.m. I think she was murdered by Chad and Alex between 11:15 p.m. and 2:42 a.m. and she was buried by Chad after Alex left and Alex came back later that morning to check on things. Either that or Alex murdered Tylee while Chad hid in his house.

I'm actually leaning that way because Chad lived in a fantasy world, and he is a coward. He was fully capable of ordering the murders, but I'm not sure he was capable of actually participating in the murders. That was Alex. Alex was a cold-blooded killer. Chad was capable of burying what was left of Tylee when Alex was done because he needed to hide the evidence of what he knew was a horrific crime that he would pay dearly for at the hands of his fellow mortal human beings.

The FBI Evidence Response Team found tools in Chad's shed and sent them off to Quantico for examination. Tylee's

DNA was found on a pick and a shovel. The only way I can see that it could have been there is if they used those tools to hack her body and to bury what was left of it when they were done hacking and burning. That furthers the idea that Tylee was murdered in Chad's backyard. We have the pick and shovel, the fact that she was buried there, and cell phone location on Alex's phone all pointing to the idea that she was murdered there.

In court during the Lori Vallow Daybell trial, the prosecution showed us pictures of Tylee's bones that police had exhumed in Chad's pet cemetery. There were her left and right partial femurs and left and right hip bones. The femurs were burned and what was left was about the upper third.

Dr. Angi Christensen, an FBI forensic anthropologist, explained what we were looking at. The hip bones were two of the few bones left intact enough to recognize. We could see that they had five creases, and Dr. Christensen said they would have been caused by something like a pick or ax striking it.

The question I had at the time and still have is: Was it done after Tylee was dead and they were dismembering her body or was it how they murdered her? Dr. Christensen, who examined Tylee's remains, testified that there was no way to know if they were postmortem or perimortem (after death or while killing her). What we do know is that Tylee's body was dismembered and burned. The only person alive who knows for sure is Chad Daybell, and I hope we find out during his trial, but I doubt we will. At the very least, I hope that new information comes to light so we can make some kind of conclusion. (New information did come to light in the Chad Daybell trial. I explain it in Part II of this book.)

Listening to the testimony in court, I honestly have to say that I did my best not to think about how she died. I was convinced that she was murdered and that was enough for me for the purpose of coming to a verdict. I put the rest out of my head because it was just too horrible to contemplate.

Other evidence that the Evidence Response Team found close to the burn pit was a bracelet and a charm that were known to be Tylee's. They showed them to the jury in court and a picture of Tylee alive wearing the charm on a necklace.

What I am sure of now is that her murder was brutal and unmerciful. The reason I think that is because of the way they said it had to happen in order to cast out the zombies. They also had a strong belief that in order to get to heaven, you had to suffer terribly.

Chad talks a lot about suffering in his books. They are full of violence, suffering, and death. In order for a person to get to the new Jerusalem, that person would have to survive what was happening on earth. Not just the floods, earthquakes, and plagues I mentioned earlier, but also wandering bands of murderers and thieves. If someone finally made it to the new Jerusalem, they would show up starving and in rags. They would have suffered sufficiently for Jesus Christ to accept them. They would have proven themselves to be worthy.

Was Tylee taken straight to Chad's after getting back from Yellowstone? Considering the timeline, I think Alex dropped Lori and JJ off at her apartment and took Tylee to Chad's backyard. They would have had to time it just right since Chad still had Garth living at home and he would have to be asleep or at work.

Tammy was also still alive, and she would have been home, presumably sleeping in her bed. Did Tylee know on the trip from Lori's apartment that Alex was about to murder her, or did they trick her some way? Tylee was a fighter, and I think she would have had to be either bound or drugged while in Alex's truck, or she would have left evidence of a struggle. She would have kicked out a window or something the police would have found later. Or maybe she just thought she was going on an errand or something with Uncle Alex.

From conversations I've had with family members, I get the idea that Tylee and Lori had a mercurial relationship. A lot of fighting and yelling. I think Tylee was pushing back against her mother's control over her. So maybe Tylee left with Alex because she couldn't stand being with Lori. I can imagine a big fight. I can imagine Lori telling Alex she's had enough, that Tylee has gone too far down the dark scale, she's obviously been taken over by zombies, and it's time to do away with her. She's just causing problems and in the way. She also was a witness to the alleged murder of Charles and might have been threatening to tell someone what she knew. That would certainly be a motive to kill her.

She was a smart girl, and I think it would have been hard to trick her. This is where it gets even sadder for me. I think Tylee knew that she had been declared a zombie, and I further think she knew that put her life at risk. Melanie Gibb testified on the witness stand that she listened on the phone to Lori calling Tylee a zombie and Tylee saying: "Not me, Mom."

She would have been defenseless and helpless at the hands of 6 foot 1, 227-pound Uncle Alex. She also probably thought that her best hope was to reason with Alex and plead for her life.

The way Alex later died himself I think indicates he couldn't live with what he had done. I think Alex thought he had to die to protect his sister, and he was willing to do that. I don't know what drugs he might have been given or have taken himself to cause his death, but I do know that he died of a pulmonary embolism.

Who else died of a pulmonary embolism? Lori's ex-husband Joe Ryan and Chad's nosey neighbor Eldon Clawson. Three healthy people who conveniently died the same way. Also,

Alex took a quick trip to Mexico right before he died. Was the trip a way for him to buy drugs he could kill himself with? Or was he duped into buying the drugs Lori and Chad would use to murder him?

So Tylee was taken at night to Chad's backyard. From what I know about Chad, I'm thinking he probably didn't participate in her actual murder. I think he probably hid in his house while the actual murder was taking place. I think Chad gave Alex explicit instructions on how to carry out the murder. He would have done this as the prophet, the one speaking directly to God, and he probably gave Alex his instructions on how to murder Tylee in the form of a blessing.

I think Alex dragged Tylee into Chad's backyard and went to work on her, probably knocking her unconscious and not stopping until the biggest part of her body left was the hip bones we were shown pictures of in court. Alex would have had to have done it in a frenzy, not stopping until she was reduced to bits of flesh and bone. I'm guessing the hole her remains were buried in had been dug previously in preparation for this, indicating that it was all planned out ahead of time.

I think Chad may have dug the hole while Alex, Lori, Tylee, and JJ were at Old Faithful. I don't think Alex would have had time to dig the hole, hack up her body, and burn her in the three hours and twenty-seven minutes between the times he was known to be at Lori's apartment. He would only have had time to hack her up and burn her. I also think the burning of her body, or what was left of it, was done in a hurry.

When police dug up the pet cemetery in June 2020 and found her remains, they found partially burned pieces of human tissue and bone fragments. There was a mostly melted green plastic bucket with tissue and bone, and underneath that they found a partial human skull. They couldn't tell for absolute sure at the time, but they assumed it was Tylee. DNA testing and dental records quickly confirmed what they suspected. They also found the pieces of jewelry I mentioned earlier that belonged to Tylee around the pet cemetery and some of Tylee's teeth when they sifted the soil.

We know that Chad was in his backyard when he texted Tammy the next morning, and I think he was doing what he could to clean up after Alex. Probably raking the ground and doing what he could to hide the fact that Tylee was so disrespectfully buried there in the family pet cemetery. At 11:53 a.m. Chad sent Tammy a text saying he had shot a raccoon in the backyard while he was burning brush. The now infamous raccoon text was meant to give Chad a reason to be burning and raking around the burn pit and pet cemetery.

So obviously some of what I wrote above is conjecture. I had to piece it together. The facts that I have were given to me in reverse order by the police officers and FBI agents as they described how they painstakingly exhumed Tylee. It brought tears to my eyes and the eyes of several of my fellow jurors, listening to their testimony. Not only for Tylee and what she went through at the hands of Uncle Alex, but also for the people who had to deal with it all firsthand. We had to look at pictures of what they found. The pictures were so horrible that the computer monitors in court were turned to face the jury so the people sitting in the gallery would not be subjected to the horror.

The other thing I want to tell you about Tylee is that she had been manipulated by her mother her whole life. I describe that in *Money, Power and Sex,* but I need to reiterate that fact here. Go back and read that section if you haven't already or don't remember it. It's an important thing to know about Tylee and Lori's relationship, and it adds to the sadness about Tylee's short life.

Joshua Jaxon Vallow. Photo provided by Kay Woodcock.

15

JOSHUA JAXON VALLOW

(MAY 25, 2012–SEPTEMBER 23, 2019)

J came into this world under tough circumstances. His mother and father were drug addicts and unable to care for him. He had autism. In spite of his circumstances, JJ was blessed.

One of the reasons families are so important is that not everyone's lives are what we would like them to be. There needs to be a safety net for the children. JJ's family was that safety net. Grandparents Kay and Larry did not hesitate to take JJ and provide a loving home for him. In spite of their age, they would have made any sacrifice and they wouldn't have even considered it a sacrifice. To them, having JJ was nothing but a blessing. Kay and Larry believe JJ would have gone on to do great things with his life. It's not uncommon for people with autism to do just that. JJ was brilliant and energetic so I think he might have. Larry says JJ knew his ABCs forward and backward and had the ability to disassemble and reassemble things in order to understand how they worked at an early age.

It makes me sad to think of a lot of the families today. Single parents doing their best, broken families. Where is their safety net? The government? Does the government feel blessed when a helpless child is left to their care? I'm sure there are good individuals within the government who would say yes, but do we really want to leave helpless children in the hands of what at best is a crapshoot? Wouldn't it be better if we embraced and promoted the family instead of tearing it apart and dividing it?

Lori and Charles had a solid marriage and family when JJ was an infant and the family decided that JJ would be better off with them. It was hard for JJ's grandparents, Larry and Kay, but they only wanted what was best for JJ. Kay's brother, Charles and his wife Lori, legally adopted JJ and did provide a loving home and family until about the time Lori met Chad Daybell. That family was Charles, Lori, Lori's daughter Tylee, her teenage son Colby, and JJ. Kay and Larry stayed very involved in JJ's life. They visited as much as possible and FaceTimed with him daily. That's why Kay and Larry became very worried when they quit hearing from him or Lori. Lori would talk to them only reluctantly, and she always had excuses for why JJ couldn't talk to them.

The last picture we have of JJ is one that was taken in Lori's apartment in Rexburg, Idaho, on September 22, 2019. JJ is sitting on the couch in his red pajamas. The same red pajamas police found him in when they exhumed his body in Chad's backyard on June 9, 2020.

Just like with Tylee we on the jury were shown pictures of JJ's exhumed body, and again, the monitors were turned so only the jury could see what was on them.

On the night of JJ's murder, Lori had guests staying with her in her two-story apartment on Pioneer Road in Rexburg. Melanie Gibb and her boyfriend David Warwick were at Lori's to record a Preparing a People podcast. Warwick testified under oath on the witness stand in the Lori Vallow Daybell trial. He said that he slept in JJ's room, Melanie slept in Tylee's room, and JJ slept in Lori's room. Tylee's room would have been available since we know she had already been murdered. Lori had an unbelievable story about Tylee being a student at Brigham Young University even though she hadn't graduated from high school yet.

At about 10:30 p.m. while recording the podcast, Warwick saw Alex come in with JJ asleep on his shoulder. Alex took JJ upstairs presumably to put him to bed in Lori's room.

Warwick says he had a terrible dream in the middle of the night, was screaming in his sleep, and Melanie came to his room and woke him. After waking Warwick, Melanie thought it would be a good idea to have Chad come and give him a blessing. She must have thought that would calm Warwick. She went to Lori's room to wake her and have her call Chad. The door was locked, and Lori didn't respond to her pounding on the door. I have to say that the whole nightmare story is unbelievable to me. The whole story is just so strange. I wonder if Gibb and Warwick made the whole thing up to cover for themselves. Why would Lori have to call Chad? Didn't Melanie have his number? In my opinion, Warwick and Gibb are insincere and downright lying to protect themselves.

The next morning when Melanie questioned Lori, Lori said that JJ had an episode that night and was crawling all over the cabinets and had even knocked over a picture of Jesus Christ, breaking it. Lori did have religious pictures all over her apartment. I could see them in the police bodycam footage, but it still struck me as unlikely the way she described JJ getting on top of cabinets and the refrigerator. Warwick asked Lori if he could see JJ and give him a blessing, but Lori told him Alex had come and taken him. Warwick stated that at the time he didn't have any reason to suspect foul play.

So, horrible nightmares, a kid climbing onto the top of the cabinets, and people wanting to give and get blessings. It all just sounds too crazy.

But foul play there was. On June 9, 2020, police felt like they had enough evidence, and early in the morning they served a search warrant to search Chad Daybell's property. Rexburg police, Fremont County Police, the Fremont County prosecutor, and the FBI Evidence Response Team showed up at the Mormon Church just a short distance from the Daybell property. They briefly discussed their plan and went to 202N 1900E. Around fifty officers in all and several police and FBI cars, trucks, and vans. The two roads that go by the house were shut down.

FBI Agent Steven Daniels testified in court about how they began the search for Tylee and JJ. They knew that Alex had spent time around the dry pond in Chad's backyard, and they knew that Chad had spent time around the burn pit the day Tylee went missing. The team split into two groups and started their searches. Daniels immediately noticed a berm and an area where the grass was shorter than the surrounding grass next to the dry pond right where Alex's phone had been when JJ went missing.

The team immediately, but very methodically, started removing the grass and dirt in that area. They quickly uncovered four large stones placed in an unnatural way. They removed the stones and found plywood underneath. As soon as they removed the plywood and a thin layer of dirt, they could see what appeared to be a black plastic garbage bag and they could smell the smell they all knew to be the smell of human remains.

The configuration of the stones over JJ's body.
Author's drawing.

I could feel the emotion in the courtroom as Agent Daniels described the moment they knew they had found what they were looking for—but were hoping so hard not to find. Agent Daniels very professionally described the process of exhuming JJ to the jury.

JJ was buried in the same red pajamas, but now his body was wrapped in garbage bags. A white plastic garbage bag over his head and a larger black plastic garbage bag over his whole body. His wrists, arms, legs, and head were wrapped in duct tape. The duct tape had been wrapped around him in many layers, way more than would have been necessary to contain him and keep him from fighting back. That's how I know the murder of JJ was ritualistic. That and the fact that Lori and Chad espoused one of the ways to save a soul was that bodies had to be bound in order to release the zombie that had entered it.

JJ had been stuffed into garbage bags and bound, struggling to breathe until he died of suffocation. Since we know Lori was not in her apartment that night, I think we can assume she was with Alex when he murdered JJ. Also, FBI agents testified in court that they found a hair that DNA testing concluded was Lori's between the plastic bag and duct tape.

We can't say for sure if Chad was there or if he was again hiding in his house when the murder actually happened, but we can say for sure that he was the one who called for JJ's murder and laid out how it was to happen. He's the one who said JJ was dark and his body had been taken over by a zombie.

I remember wondering while listening to testimony if JJ might have already been dead when Alex carried him up Lori's stairs. I thought that could be the case at the time, but again, I was fooling myself. My mind was playing tricks on me, not wanting to believe how the murders of Tylee and JJ actually happened.

Forensic pathologist Dr. Garth Warren testified that they found a small amount of HGH in JJ's blood. At the time I wanted to believe that JJ had been drugged, but Dr. Warren went on to say that it could have been there because it was a component of his autism medication, and anyway it wasn't enough to hurt him or have any kind of effect on him. Also, JJ had scratches on his neck and enough bruising around his body to indicate that he put up a fight.

According to Chad and Lori's extreme beliefs, we know they thought a person had to die from being bound or being burned. Since we know Tylee was burned and we know that JJ's body was bound when police found it, I think it's safe to say that he died of asphyxiation, not being able to breathe through the two layers of plastic and multiple layers of duct tape. Also, why would someone use so much duct tape on an inert body? Dr. Warren's conclusion was that JJ died of asphyxiation due to the plastic bag over his head and duct tape over his mouth.

Lori's cruelty toward JJ didn't just happen on the night that he was murdered. She had quit giving him his autism medication that he needed to keep himself calm, she had taken away his sister who was his primary caregiver and whom he loved, and she had taken away his dog. He loved his dog, and like a lot of people with autism, he depended on his dog for comfort.

I thought a lot about Lori getting rid of the dog and why it was done. I think that she just figured JJ's days were numbered anyway so why deal with a dog. The dog was a specially trained service dog, and Lori had signed an agreement that she would not just give the dog away. If for any reason the dog wasn't working out for JJ, she was supposed to return the dog to the agency that provided it. She did just give the dog away though.

I have heard a theory that Lori killed JJ in a fit of rage, unable to control her anger. The idea is that JJ was out of control, and Lori lost herself and strangled or somehow suffocated him. I don't think this idea is accurate for all the reasons listed above. It was planned and coordinated.

I also wonder about Warwick and Gibb. Gibb for sure was in Chad and Lori's inner circle, and I have a hard time believing she didn't know something was up. She did cooperate with police when they became suspicious, but could she have said something in time to save Tylee and JJ? She must have been wondering on the night of JJ's murder where Tylee was. Did she believe Lori's story that Tylee was a student at BYU? It seems unlikely to me. She was very close to Lori and definitely part of Chad and Lori's inner circle. I've listened to her talk a lot, and she doesn't come off to me as stupid.

I think one would have to be extremely stupid to be that close to Chad and Lori and not know. Some people think that because she cooperated with police, Gibb is one of the least guilty of the inner circle, but I think it's the opposite. I think that she is the most self-serving, arrogant one besides Chad and Lori. She expects the police and all of us to believe her, but I don't. I see right through her.

16

WHO WERE JJ AND TYLEE?

Okay, enough of all of that. I have learned so much about JJ and Tylee's lives. Who they were, who loved them, and what they might have been.

Tylee was sixteen years old when she died and looking forward to her upcoming seventeenth birthday. She had been moved around a lot, but she was able to make some lasting friendships. She did not want to move to Idaho with Lori and probably could have stayed with Charles in Arizona where her friends were, but she didn't want to leave JJ. She loved JJ more than anything and would do anything for him. In fact, she did do everything for him, especially after Lori met Chad and wasn't as present as she had been.

JJ required a lot of care. According to Kay and Larry, you couldn't leave him alone for a minute, and Tylee was the one who was there for him. I think that caring for JJ gave her her only sense of purpose in life. She was so manipulated by her mom that she had no freedom of her own. She had been moved away from whatever friends she had. JJ was the one constant person she could count on.

We know that a lot of people loved JJ, starting with Kay and Larry, who took him in right after he was born and gave him love and a home. Kay and Larry would have been more than happy to keep and raise JJ, but at the time they thought Charles and Lori could provide a better home for him. JJ would have a family with siblings. The love shines through on Larry's face when he talks about his time with JJ. He says JJ was so full of energy, and you couldn't leave him unattended for a minute or something was sure to be destroyed. Not maliciously, but just because JJ couldn't control himself. And Kay and Larry loved that about him.

Larry thinks JJ would have grown up to be something really special. Kay and Larry were certainly special to JJ in the way only grandparents can be. Kay tells of how when they brought JJ home from the hospital as an infant, the only thing that would calm him down is to have him lie on Larry's chest. She says that was magical.

Charles also loved JJ and would have done anything for him. In fact, Charles was coming to pick up JJ and take him to school just to be able to see him when he was so callously murdered. I think Charles may have known that something was up, but he was willing to take the chance for JJ's sake.

We know that Charles helped Tylee buy the Jeep she loved so much. The same green Jeep Alex used in his attempted murder of Brandon Boudreaux. Tylee was already dead by that time, so I guess the Jeep was available.

The last thing that Chad and Lori needed to do was murder JJ and Tylee if their motive was just to get them out of the way. They could have handed them off to people in their own family or any number of good families in Rexburg, further bolstering the argument that the murders were ritualistic and that religious zealots can be dangerous.

As I write this, JJ would be just turning twelve and Tylee would be twenty-one. Lori said in her allocution statement at her sentencing that they were busy in the spirit world doing good things. She put them where they are today. She took it upon herself to play God and make the decision to murder her children. It's what makes her think she had that right that terrifies me and is the point of this book. She was and I think still is so sure of her beliefs that she convinced herself that ritualistically murdering her innocent children was the best option for them.

My biggest hope is that we get more information about the inner circle in the Chad Daybell trial. I also hope that those people are held to account. Once they are no longer needed as witnesses for the prosecution, maybe that same prosecution will go after them. I further hope that we can expose the bigger circle of fundamentalist religious zealots. They are dangerous, they are real, and they are committing crimes against innocent children.

I listened to Lauren and Dr. John Matthias interview Larry Woodcock. Lauren said, "Forgiveness is part of healing" and she asked him if he would ever be able to forgive people in Chad and Lori's inner circle. I don't think Larry quite knew how to answer that. I don't think he has gotten to that stage yet. He is still and always will be grieving. I think what was missed in that conversation, though, is that people have to ask you for forgiveness. If they would admit what they had done and pay for their role, then we might be able to forgive them, but so far, that hasn't happened. Not one of them has stepped up, and I don't think they ever will. They didn't step up when lives were at stake, so why would they now? They are just extremely selfish, self-serving individuals who can somehow sleep at night and look at themselves in the mirror in the morning.

I hope you can forgive me for putting you through this last chapter, especially if you were close to Tylee and JJ, but even if you weren't, it's the stuff of nightmares. Believe me, I know. We have to take our strength from people like Kay and Larry. We have to be willing to accept what happened, and we have to be willing to do the hard work of doing whatever it is that each of us can do, to stop it from happening again.

There is something that each one of us can do. Maybe it's as simple as valuing our own family and raising our kids right, being good mothers and fathers. Maybe it matters how we vote and what kind of people we vote for. Maybe it's supporting what is good in our communities and pointing out what is bad. There are all kinds of ways of showing the kids in our communities that we value them and ways of having a good influence on them. I could literally go on for a hundred pages about this, but you get the point.

17

OTHER VICTIMS

Did Chad and Lori have other victims, and, if so, who were they? Let's separate them into two categories, living and dead. Let's look at possible dead victims first.

We know Lori's brother Alex is their victim. We don't know if they murdered him, if he killed himself, or if he died of natural causes like the police report says. Actually, I do know he did not die of natural causes. At least I am thoroughly convinced of it. It's just too convenient for Chad and Lori, and he was a healthy man when he allegedly died of a pulmonary embolism.

Pulmonary embolism is kind of a broad term. It boils down to blood clots in the lungs, but the blood clots can be caused by many things. So, while it is possible, it's extremely unlikely in this case. And Alex was a victim in so many ways.

His family says that he had a head injury that occurred in a car accident when he was sixteen. Some in the family say that he was never really right after that, and others say they don't think the accident or Alex's injuries were that big a deal.

Could Chad and Lori have taken advantage of him knowing he wasn't capable of thinking clearly? Whether he was capable of clear thought or not, they certainly took advantage of him. Especially Lori. The family also says that Alex would do anything for Lori. Chad used his influence on Lori, and Lori used it on Alex. He became their hitman. He did the dirty work for them. He murdered several people, two of whom were his own niece and nephew. He did it for Lori, believing she and Chad were translated beings and that God spoke through them. So, yes, Alex is certainly their victim. I'm not saying that excuses him for his crimes. He was a killer, a child killer, and a victim.

What about Joe Ryan, Lori's third husband? He died similarly to Alex in 2018. He was fifty-nine years old. Lori had said she wished he would die. She even said she would kill him if she could. According to *The Post Register*, an Idaho Falls newspaper, Lori talked about her relationship with Joe Ryan at a Preparing a People conference in 2018.

In a recording obtained by police she says: "I was going to murder him. I was going to kill him like the scriptures say. Like Nephi killed. Just to stop the pain and to stop him coming after me and to stop him coming after my children. I just thought I couldn't take it anymore."

Joe Ryan's sister, Annie Cushing, says Lori wanted to murder him. She has a recording she says of Lori saying she wished he were dead. A friend of Lori's said Lori listened to his last breath. Lori wasn't supposed to have been there when he died. She was accusing him of abusing her children. Lori's son Colby even says he was sexually abused by Joe Ryan. Tylee said she had been abused by him.

Whether we believe any of them or not, it would give reason for Lori to want him dead. It would be a motive for his murder. I talked to a close friend of Joe Ryan's, and, according to her, Joe was a successful, happy, and kind man, and she doesn't believe any of the things Lori says about him are true. According to the friend, Lori took everything he had, ruined his life, and probably murdered him. It rings true to me just because of how we know she treated Charles and that she is accused of his murder.

There are other unanswered questions relating to Joe Ryan. In an article by Annie Cushing, she says Lori had taken photo albums and file folders that reeked of decomposing flesh from his apartment. Joe Ryan had lain dead in his apartment for several days before a neighbor's dog apparently noticed the smell and his owner called police.

April Raymond claims Lori said she paid Alex to kill Joe. Of course, Lori doesn't say in the recording that she does murder him. So a lot of things seem incriminating and are confusing surrounding Joe Ryan's death. One thing I do know is that he died in an apartment. He had been living in a really upscale home that he owned before Lori left him.

The police have looked into the case of his death twice. They concluded their second investigation in 2021 and both times have not been able to come up with anything that would directly point to murder. But that doesn't mean it wasn't murder. It just means they can't prove it was murder.

We know Alex tased Joe and served six months in jail for it. Alex was never sorry for it and said he did it because Joe was abusive to the kids and Lori. Makes sense, but it also points to the idea that Alex would do something like that for Lori.

What if Lori was lying and manipulating Alex? What if Lori was the one who was abusive to her children and turned the tables on Joe Ryan? We know she was capable of that and in fact that was her MO. After learning everything I can about Joe Ryan and talking to Annie Cushing and others, I have concluded that Lori intentionally ruined his life. She was probably bored of him or at least she for some reason wanted to end her relationship with him.

More than that, she wanted what was his to be hers in the process. By the time Joe Ryan died, he had lost his livelihood and his home, which was a very expensive house on beautiful property. He had been reduced to nothing, been ousted by his friends and family, and turned to alcohol by the things Lori did to him and accused him of. I think Melani Boudreaux was following Lori's example and doing the same things to her then husband Brandon.

Lori has two sisters who have died. One died as a baby and the other, Stacey Cope Cox, died at the age of thirty-one in 1998. Stacey was Melani's mom. There is a lot of confusion about her death. Alex was the only one home. The rest of the family was in Hawaii or living in other parts of the country. Alex contacted the family in Hawaii and told them Stacey was dying and being cared for by hospice, and they didn't come home. They didn't even come home for her funeral. That is not normal. Melani Boudreaux, ex-wife of Brandon Boudreaux whom Alex tried to shoot, was Stacey's daughter and in Lori and Chad's inner circle.

I already wrote about Chad's neighbor, Eldon Clawson. Just another suspicious death by pulmonary embolism. He was relatively young at sixty-three and healthy. He walked the neighborhood every day. There is definitely a possible motive in his death since he may have seen something he wasn't supposed to see in Chad's backyard. Chad may have been afraid that as the police started looking for the children, Eldon would become suspicious of what he saw.

But what about the living victims? There are so many. So many people have been hurt to differing degrees. Start with Kay and Larry. JJ, the love of their life, was brutally murdered. Kay's brother was murdered. They weren't as close to Tylee as they were with JJ, but they loved her, too, and she is gone from their lives forever. They have to live with the knowledge of how the kids were murdered. So many other family members. JJ's natural mom died after JJ was found dead, and according to her doctor it was of a broken heart. She struggled for years, trying to get over her drug addiction, hoping to be a mom to her son.

Tammy's mom died in 2023. Her sister Vicki said she died at least knowing Lori had been convicted of her crimes. I had the opportunity to meet and talk to family members who were close to Tammy. Jason and Samantha Gwilliam, Tammy's brother-in-law and sister, testified in court in Chad's trial. They were very close to Tammy, and I could see the anger and anguish in their faces. And what they had to say on the witness stand was that Tammy truly was beloved by her family, her friends, and her coworkers.

Just like Charles, Tylee, and JJ, Tammy was a totally innocent victim. Even when Lori's trial ended, I still didn't know if Charles and Tammy might have been in some way involved in any of the crazy beliefs held by Chad and Lori. It would make sense that they might have at least had some involvement. Charles had joined the Mormon Church after he met Lori.

But it turns out that Tammy and Charles were totally innocent. If they had any knowledge of what Chad and Lori's weird beliefs were, they did what any of us would have done if we were in their position. Both Tammy and Charles were finding out about Chad and Lori's beliefs, but they were trying to cope and hope for the best. They certainly were not taking any part.

I feel very sad for the law enforcement officers who searched for so long for Tylee and JJ only to have to exhume their bodies from Chad's backyard. They were so hopeful of finding the kids alive. It turned out to be their worst nightmare, and don't think they don't take any of this personally. Yes, they are professionals. They all somehow held their composure while testifying in court, but they are also fathers, mothers, and good people. They were shocked and horrified when they found Tylee and JJ. I only had to look at pictures as a juror. They had to experience it firsthand. Also, they are the ones tasked with our safety, and they didn't protect those kids. Not that they could have. They couldn't have, but cops being cops, I'm sure they feel regret for that.

I feel for the community of Rexburg and think about all of the people who were hopeful of finding Tylee and JJ alive. And the state of Idaho. The Lori Vallow Daybell trial cost taxpayers $1.8 million, but what is the real cost? I bet nobody knows. The hours the police and FBI spent investigating. The cost for the jurors to serve for seven weeks. We were paid $1,344.75, and we had to pay taxes on that. It comes out to about $35 per day before taxes.

The travel expenses for the family to attend the trial. I know Kay and Larry spent a lot of time in hotels. The media spent a lot covering the trial, but that is their business, so presumably they made money. That's not in any way to say they covered the case for money. Of course, the networks they cover the trial for are in the business of making money, but the individuals who are covering this case closely have their hearts in it for sure.

Larry says he is very angry at what he calls Chad and Lori's inner circle. He should be mad. They are not good people, but some of them on some level are also victims. People like Zulema Pastenes who truly believed in Chad and Lori were taken advantage of and used by Chad and Lori. People in the prepper world, not in the inner circle, who believed them also. They followed the wrong people and believed the wrong things. We can be mad at them for their ignorance and stupidity, but they are weak and are victims. Chad and Lori played on their weakness and took advantage of it.

I think of Tylee's friends. What must they have gone through when Tylee was missing and when her remains were found. Tylee's best friend was a friend of her whole family. She had tried to contact Tylee while Tylee was missing. She got only brief texts in return, which turned out to be from Lori pretending to be Tylee. This shows a level of coldheartedness that is hard to comprehend.

Chad Daybell and Lori Vallow Daybell have *ABSOLUTELY NO REMORSE FOR THEIR VICTIMS*, living or dead. One of the hardest things for me to understand sitting in court every day is how could Chad or Lori sit there in front of all of the good folks who they had hurt so badly. How could they do it and hold their composure? I don't think I will ever answer that question thoroughly, but I will say I think it's because they really do believe what they have been preaching.

Charles Vallow had adult sons who found out about his death through text messages from Lori. In her text message to them she says, "working on making arrangements," and that she will "keep them informed. I'm still not sure how to handle things. Just want you to know that I love you and so did your dad!"

She didn't even have the decency to call them. She actually texted them to tell them their father was dead!

When Charles's sons pleaded with Lori for more information, she just quit responding to them, not answering their calls or texts. Charles was really into nice watches and had a collection of expensive watches. These watches were important to Charles's sons, not only because they were valuable, but because the watches would have given them something to remember their father by, but when his sons asked Lori repeatedly for the watches, she eventually sent them a cheap Timex. That's pretty cold.

Charles's sister-in-law claims Lori cleaned out Charles's house of anything of value right after she and Alex murdered him. The sister-in-law had gone to Charles's house right after finding out he died and found everything of value missing. Alex was known to be driving Charles's pickup truck shortly after the murder also. Lori just showed absolutely no consideration for Charles's sons, not even offering to share any of his belongings or wealth with them. She selfishly took it all for herself. I think to her own demise. If she had been less selfish and greedy, maybe people would have been less likely to point the finger at her.

She was expecting a big payday from the insurance company after Charles died. His life insurance policy was for $1 million. She could have kept her mouth shut about that instead of saying it was a spear through her heart when she found out he changed the beneficiary to his sister Kay and had an agreement with Kay that she would give each of his two sons $250,000 of it. Also, if she hadn't collected the social security death benefit meant for Tylee and JJ, maybe it would have been harder to convict her of murdering them.

Tammy had so many friends and family who cared for her. Her coworkers and students loved her and depended on her. She was truly irreplaceable, and Chad and Lori took her away from them forever.

The most striking thing to me is that Chad and Lori couldn't care less. They have yet to show the slightest bit of remorse or sympathy for anyone. In fact, they are continuing to victimize people, even as they both sit in prison. A whole new set of jurors is sitting through several weeks of testimony. They are having to listen to Chad's defense attorney, John Prior, drone on about nothing for hours. They will be taken away from their families and their jobs, and for what? This jury will very likely end up being sequestered, which will make it even worse for them. They have to look at the same horrific pictures I had to look at and hear the same sad testimony.

But that's what we do in this country. Even Chad is entitled to his day in court. It's not fair, it's costly, and it's offensive, but he will get the opportunity to prove he is innocent if he can.

How will he try to do that? I think he will blame it all on Lori, even though she did not do that to him. She could have. In fact, it was her only hope, but she wouldn't let her attorneys, John Thomas and Jim Archibald, do that. Chad's attorney, John Prior, will say that the prosecution already proved that Lori was the one behind the murders. The prosecution will counter that although Lori is guilty of the murders, it was Chad who held the power and called the shots. In the end, Chad will have no chance. He is the priest holder, and he is the one who had the light and dark scale. Lori is more guilty of going along with him than anything else.

Anyway, that's my prediction and you, the reader, will know how it all turns out by the time you finish the next section of this book if you don't already know. As I write this, I don't know how it turns out for sure because it hasn't happened yet.

I wonder if Lori will be called on as a witness. She can be. If she is, I wonder what she'll say. Whatever it is, I wouldn't miss it for anything, even though I know it will be a bunch of preposterous religious rhetoric.

Chad will continue to victimize Lori, and he'll do it with a blank face, sitting in court with his hands folded in front of him, staring straight ahead for hour after hour. And he cares about as much as he appears to care, which is not at all.

18

DIVING INTO CHAD'S MIND

Dr. John Matthias has made his living diving into the minds of some of the most inhumane killers. His job was to go into the prisons where they lived and evaluate them and make recommendations to parole boards.

Much to his credit, he said Chad Daybell was the one behind the murders of Tylee and JJ way before I believed it. I thought Lori was their mom, so I guess I just instinctually blamed her. The more I learn about this case and after sitting through both trials, the more I realize Dr. John is right. Lori is their mom and Lori does have to take responsibility for the lives of her children, but Chad is the priest holder, the religious guru, and the one with all the ideas and ambitions. Chad is the one who had the light and dark scale. Chad is the one who wrote books about the second coming of Christ and the turmoil and violence that would come with it. Chad was the visionary and, in his mind, I think, still is.

As I said in chapter 8, Chad needed followers. He believed he was the one Christ intended to lead the Mormons after the second coming. He was frustrated when the elders didn't pick him to be bishop in his ward. He had visions that told him he was to do great things. Why couldn't the powers that were see that? Why didn't the telestial beings on this earth see that he was chosen? He had done everything he could think of to make them take notice. He had written books about what life would be like when Jesus showed back up in human form on earth. In those books, Chad was the one Jesus chose. Chad had lived on this earth and walked with Jesus many times before.

But what got Chad to a place where he was not just capable of murdering children and the mother of his own children, but also where he believed he had the right to decide who lived and who died and how people would have to die?

Let's separate it into two ideas: Chad's ideas about himself and Chad's ideas about others.

I said before that Chad chose different pathways, and those pathways led him to where he is today. Like a highway with on-ramps and off-ramps.

Chad started out pretty normal, with normal ambitions and ideas. As he grew older into puberty, he started to be frustrated. He was stifled by the Mormon Church. In the church there are limitations and expectations. One has to meet those expectations to move up in the church. It wasn't enough for Chad. He studied hard and learned a lot about the history of the church and the beliefs of the church.

This is where Chad takes that first off-ramp heading in the wrong direction. He thought there was more. More than what the church was providing. He started to look for answers outside of the church. Maybe not so much outside of the church, but on the fringes of what the church intended. Chad is not the only one who does this. This is where the prepper groups and the fundamentalist groups come in. They have answers the church won't give or at least they believe they do. This is one of the reasons these groups are so dangerous and why the Mormon Church repeatedly advises its members to stay away from them. There is a reason the church doesn't give answers to these questions. The church doesn't have them. Nobody does.

People who claim to have answers are lying and are dangerous. We all have visions. We envision the future and imagine how we would like the future to be. We plan our futures based on the vision we have. But no one can really see into the future. People who claim to have visions that actually see into the future are liars.

We all pray in one way or another. Some of us pray to God, some of us pray to some other entity we believe exists, and some of us just hope and wish for things. It's all a form of prayer. But no one has an actual conversation with some otherworldly being. No one has the voice of God in their head. Not in any direct way. You can argue that some people are closer to God and that may be true. Some people are more spiritual. They are closer to God because they live a more righteous life. But God does not speak to them. Not directly. He may speak to them in the way they live their lives. There may be rewards for living a more righteous life, but there is no voice telling them the future.

But Chad took that first step in the wrong direction. He started out believing he was special. I think he started out just believing that he had more to offer. That in itself would be a good thing that would lead a person in a good direction. Maybe helping others cope with life and with their questions about religion. It frustrated him when he didn't get the attention he thought he deserved, so he took it a step further, another wrong turn. He started professing to have visions and to be able to see through the veil. Now he had insights and knowledge that the rest of us don't have, and he could use that knowledge however he chose. He chose to use it to manipulate people. It worked and he began to get some of the attention he had craved for so long.

Still, he was limited as to what he was able to accomplish. He had a following, but it wasn't big enough. He had a beautiful, dedicated wife in Tammy, but he was entitled to more. He had his own publishing company, but it was struggling to survive. It all just wasn't enough.

He took things a step further using his standing and his agency within the church to manipulate people who followed him. He took the idea that some people are light and some are dark from scripture. He used ideas that are considered to be scripture and doctrines that we accept as truth and stretched it and added lies where he needed to. And here's the surprising thing: People fell for it. Not everyone, of course, but some people were so malleable that when they listened to his stretched truth and twisted lies, they believed him.

This is what took Chad down the worst possible path. When he found that he could tell what he knew to be lies and people looked up to him, he started using those people for his own gain. That's the biggest sin of all. He used his agency within the church for his own personal gain. Once he became okay with that, he was on a path to destruction, and it was so steep and slippery that he could no longer control himself. Now he actually started to believe his own rhetoric. If people looked up to him so fervently, he must be what he thought he was. He did have the right to manipulate, to lie, and even to decide who lived and who died.

He had the right because he was the one mighty and strong.

God did talk through him. If he had the idea, that idea came directly from God. If God told him he had to accomplish certain things and to do that he had to remove obstacles, he had better do it because the voice in his head was God. And anyway, those obstacles, those people in Chad's way, would be better off in heaven. They could skip the whole seven years of trials and tribulations and be delivered directly to the celestial kingdom. They would be worthy because they would have already made their sacrifice by getting out of Chad's way. Anyway, they were zombies, their bodies having been taken over by Satan. Their souls were in limbo and needed to be released. This has to be true because they are in Chad's way. They are someplace they don't belong, and they are making it hard for Chad to get what he wants or, in Chad's mind, what God wants for Chad.

And Chad had to call them zombies. He had to dehumanize them in order to justify killing them. Alex wasn't going to just randomly kill people because Chad told him to. He had to convince Alex that they were already dead. They were zombies. Their bodies had been taken over by dark spirits.

What about Chad's light and dark scale? This is an interesting concept to me. It actually kind of defines this case and life in general. Whether you say light or dark, good or evil, right or wrong, we all make choices and those choices define whether we live in the light or in the dark, on the good side or the bad side. The bad or dark side is chaos. For instance, if we tell a lie, it doesn't just end there. It may make things simpler in the moment, but soon we find ourselves telling more lies to cover for the original lie. Our lives become complicated and confusing, chaotic. This is where I think members of Chad's inner circle live and their lives must be hell on earth.

If we cowardly turn our heads when we see someone commit an evil act against someone else, we have to live with that. Better to stand up for what is right and live with the consequences of that. Living in the light, doing good deeds, being honest and generous, is much easier, happier, and healthier.

I was contemplating all of this while I sat in court all day for several weeks watching Chad. I couldn't tell if my mind was playing tricks on me or if I was actually watching Chad physically metamorphose in front of my eyes. As I sat there, I felt like I was seeing his body change into something almost not human. I know, it's getting a little weird, but this is what was going through my mind as I watched him. I actually felt like I was seeing a physical change and it really kind of freaked me out at the time.

Looking back, I think Chad's body was changing. I think it shows the power of the mind over our bodies. Outwardly, Chad showed almost no emotion in court, and I wondered about that. How could he sit there in front of everyone he hurt so badly? Now I think he was hurting inside in ways that I can't even imagine. I think he was frustrated to be put into his position by us mere mortals. I think he was humiliated by that. I think he was scared to death to go to prison. I think he knows he hurt people who were sitting there in that room staring at him. I think he probably wondered where his god was. I think he hid all of those emotions from us and held them inside. I could almost feel sorry for him for that. Not in any kind of forgiving way, but in the way that, as human beings, we are aware of our mortality.

Chad was beginning to feel mortal. He was questioning his faith. Some will disagree, but I am sure of it. That is what explains the metamorphosis I was seeing in his body. He was trying so hard to hold it together emotionally, that it was tearing his body down.

If I am right about this, Chad will never make it to his execution. He will rot away in his cell until his body finally gives up and his own demons rip him apart from the inside out. Pretty dark stuff.

THE TRIAL OF CHAD DAYBELL

19

WHAT THE HECK JUST HAPPENED?

As I sit here writing on February 29, 2024, something just occurred that blows my mind. The timing is uncanny, and while it is in no way related to the case I am writing about, it might have a profound effect on it.

In 1973 Thomas Eugene Creech married seventeen-year-old Thomasine Loren White of Boise, Idaho, who later allegedly participated in one of his murders. The marriage was not a happy one. Living with a man like Creech was chaotic and horrific. He was brutal and unable to provide any kind of stability. In fact, life with Creech was the opposite of stable. After living on the road with him for just a short time, White committed suicide in a mental hospital.

After this, Creech moved to Idaho with seventeen-year-old girlfriend Carol Spaulding. While Creech and Spaulding were hitchhiking between Lewiston and Donelly, Idaho, they were picked up in a 1956 Buick driven by two house painters. Highway 95 runs through the mountains and valleys of central to northern Idaho. It's a rural area, and the road is lightly traveled, especially in 1973. People in this part of the country were not used to crime or criminals.

It would have been natural for the house painters to stop and pick up a man and woman hitchhiking. In fact, it would have been rude not to. They would have been totally unsuspecting when Creech shot them both in the back of the head and buried them alongside the road near Donelly.

In 1974 Creech was sentenced to hang until dead in Idaho for those two murders. At the time it was known that he was involved in many other murders in other states. In fact, on the stand in court in Idaho, he confessed to a total of forty-two murders—some of which were ritualistic and, as he said, satanic. He was allegedly a member of the Hell's Angels and the Church of Satan.

Creech seems to have had the same effect on his new girlfriend as he had on his wife. Spaulding also attempted to kill herself by slashing her wrists while in a mental hospital. She survived and was later charged as an adult for her part in the murders.

Idaho's last execution by hanging occurred in 1957. The Old Idaho State Penitentiary has been replaced by a modern facility, but the Old Pen is still there just east of downtown Boise, and the gallows can be viewed by visitors. In 1976 Creech's sentence was reduced on appeal to life in prison. In 1981 he was again sentenced to hang for beating his cellmate to death with a sock full of batteries.

Because of a long, arduous appeals process in death penalty cases, this guy was allowed to sit on death row until February 28, 2024, at which time he was taken to a chamber where he was to be put to death by lethal injection. Leading up to his execution date, we have seen on the news that Creech had been a model inmate for several years. Even the judge who oversaw the trial so many years ago said he thought Creech should be allowed to live.

The lethal injection was unbelievably somehow botched, and Creech is still alive as of this writing. To the horror of the witnesses, his executioners tried eight times to place a needle into his veins and failed each time. It took several months for me to get a straight answer as to whether he had served his sentence and would now get to live out his natural life, hopefully not as a free man, or if he would again be taken to the death chamber for a second attempt. My thought was that he served his sentence and that he would live out his days in jail.

As it turns out, Idaho passed a law in October 2024 that allows the executioners to insert an alternative central line in an artery closer to the heart if the standard lethal injection method fails, and Thomas Creech was rescheduled to be executed on November 13, 2024. This is controversial, of course, and would be the first time Idaho has carried out two death sentences on one inmate. The argument against it states that Creech's sentence has already been carried out and doing it a second time violates the Fifth Amendment's double jeopardy clause and the Eighth Amendment's cruel and unusual punishment clause. Because of that argument, Creech's execution has again been delayed.

What does this have to do with the Chad Daybell case? Absolutely nothing and absolutely everything.

Even though the two cases are in no way connected, the fact that one month before Chad Daybell is faced with the death penalty in Idaho, Idaho has shown that it is too inept to put someone to death, even someone who has committed the most heinously evil crimes imaginable and admitted to doing them. Not only is Idaho incapable of putting someone to death, but they let the convicted serial killer linger on death row for forty-eight years before their botched attempt. If an argument can be made that death by lethal injection is cruel and unusual punishment, something citizens of our country are guaranteed not to have to suffer, by the Eighth Amendment to our Constitution, the Creech situation certainly bolsters it.

Go back and read chapter 4 of *Money, Power and Sex* if you want to hear my thoughts on the death penalty.

Unbelievably, this has happened one month before the Chad Daybell trial is scheduled to begin. The timing is almost as unbelievable as the botched execution.

I thought the botched execution of Creech might have an effect on the Chad Daybell trial. I thought the prosecution might decide to drop their pursuit of the death penalty, possibly thinking a jury would be tentative about committing someone to death in a state that just proved it was incapable of following through with it. I was also worried that all of this might cause a delay in the trial.

Judge Boyce had already denied the defense's attempt to get the death penalty dropped in a pretrial hearing. I wondered if they might make another attempt given the new circumstances. But none of those events happened. Jury selection started on schedule on April 1, 2024, and the prosecution is still seeking the death penalty.

I wondered at the time if that might turn out to be a mistake. I thought it might be hard to find a jury that would be willing to sentence anyone to death in Idaho. Even if the jury could not support the death penalty, they would have the option of life in prison, so I guess the prosecution figured they didn't really have anything to lose.

20

COURTROOM #400,

ADA COUNTY COURTHOUSE, BOISE, IDAHO

Monday, April 1, 2024

da County courthouse sits just east of downtown Boise proper. It's a modern building compared to most courthouses in Idaho. Even so, I am told that we have outgrown it. That's not surprising to me given the growth Boise has experienced in the last five years or so.

The four-story courthouse faces Front Street, which is a busy street through downtown Boise. A big courtyard and steps lead up to the entrance where reporters were stationed throughout both trials.

It felt a little strange to me walking up the steps, past all of the media, and into the courthouse. When I had been a juror in the Lori Vallow Daybell trial exactly one year ago, I was brought to the courthouse in a van and whisked into the basement. Our guards went to great lengths to keep us isolated from the media. This time at the Chad Daybell trial, I can talk to whomever I want to talk to and I plan to.

One thing I thought was an oversight as a juror is that jurors were not subjected to any kind of security check. For Chad's trial, I had to wait in a long line of impatient people to get through security. I had a reserved seat so it was okay. Everyone else was racing to get in line outside of the courtroom. On some days not everyone made it in.

Ada County Courthouse. Personal photo.

Courtroom #400 is the biggest courtroom in the Ada County Courthouse, but it felt small with all the seats filled. The gallery was pretty small and about a third of it was reserved for family, law enforcement, and me. I spent every day there sitting about ten or fifteen feet away from Chad Daybell and John Prior. The prosecution team was directly in front of my front-row seat just on the other side of the rail you always see in courtrooms. I liked that because every now and then during a break in the action, Rob Wood or Lindsey Blake would turn to me and give some tidbit or ask my opinion about something. I also got to sit with some of the detectives, agents, family, and witnesses. There were very few opportunities to talk inside the courtroom, however. Most of the conversations happened in the hall outside of the courtroom during breaks.

The courtroom had the wood typical of a courtroom. I think it was mahogany, but I couldn't say for sure. To my left was a huge window overlooking downtown Boise. I could even see the Boise State football stadium. Somehow looking out that window gave me comfort at times, seeing how civilized our city is compared to what was unfolding in the courtroom.

Today is the first day of jury selection. Potential jurors will be asked questions by the judge, the prosecution, and the defense. They call it voir dire. I wonder what they're looking for in jurors. I wonder what the potential jurors are thinking. Probably the same thing I was when I was sitting in their seat. That, surely, I would not be selected. That my world would be okay. For eighteen of those jurors, though, their lives are about to change in ways they can't yet conceive of.

I'm sure it's different for everyone, but they will all be exposed to the horror of this case, and it will have an effect on them. They will also have the honor of being part of an intact legal system that, for me at least, made me proud and hopeful in a time when I wasn't expecting that, considering all that I had been seeing on the news over the past few years.

As a prospective juror in the Lori Vallow Daybell trial, I was totally unaware of how the prosecution, the defense, Judge Boyce's court attorney, and even the media were picking us apart, trying to figure us out. After the Lori Vallow Daybell trial was over, I had the opportunity to talk to Detective Ray Hermosillo. He told me about each juror and where he thought they would stand. Same with the prosecution team. They put a lot of time into selecting jurors who they thought would be able to keep up with all of the information they would present. I have to say that was a challenge.

A huge difference between this jury and mine is that mine was not confronted with the death penalty. This jury will be. If the jury comes to a guilty verdict, the penalty stage of the trial will begin. Chad will have the opportunity to plead for his life, and the jury will have to go back to their impossibly small jury room and decide whether the state will or will not put him to death. I do not envy them.

I know that jury room well. If the courtroom felt small, that room in comparison was like a closet with a bathroom attached to it.

The Honorable Steven Boyce presides over this trial. He is the same judge who presided over the Lori Vallow Daybell trial. He faced many challenges in her trial, and he handled them all well. I have a feeling this trial will not be quite as civilized as Lori's, and it will be interesting to see how he keeps order in the court and keeps the trial on track.

During the Lori Vallow Daybell trial I was, of course, isolated from Judge Boyce. I have gotten to know him since my jury duty ended. The contrast between his demeanor in court and his demeanor outside of court is striking. Outside of court he is as comfortable and relaxed as anyone can be. We have motorcycle riding in common, and he likes to talk about the rides he has been on and the country he has seen. I do too.

My sketch of Judge Steven W. Boyce.

The Defense

Chad has only one attorney representing him: John Prior. Prior argued in a pretrial hearing that he couldn't keep up with the case on his own and wanted to withdraw. This happened just a few months before the trial was scheduled to begin after he had represented Chad Daybell since May 2021. He also argued that Chad was no longer able to pay him.

I was a little confused listening to Prior explain to Judge Boyce why he felt he should be excused in one sentence and then saying he wanted to stick with the case in the next. What I realized listening to him go around and around was that it was just a ploy to get the death penalty taken off the table. He was trying to make it look like Chad was unfairly represented. I think that he thought he had nothing to lose. If Judge Boyce excused him, the trial would at the very least have been delayed for a long time while a new attorney got himself or herself acquainted with the mountain of evidence against Daybell.

If Judge Boyce did not excuse him, he would at least have an argument he could use in an appeal, saying that Daybell was underrepresented.

It is true that Daybell is out of money. He used up all of the money he wrongly received from Tammy's life insurance, and when that was all gone, he handed over the title to his house. Who would want the house where Tammy, Tylee, and JJ had been murdered? I can't see Prior gaining much from that. Especially since, knowing what I know about Chad, he probably had it mortgaged to the hilt. Anyway, to his credit Judge Boyce denied Prior's appeal to be excused, saying he knew what he was getting himself into

Prior was able to sell the house not long after the trial ended. There is a group who purchased it intending to remove the house and turn the property into a memorial. I personally like the idea. I think it would be nice if it could be kind of a low-key memorial to the victims. I don't think it would be appropriate to make it into a park, but maybe a wild yet neat area with a monument to the victims. A place where people could go and contemplate the lives of Tylee, JJ, and Tammy.

Apparently though, the group that bought the property didn't ask the families of the victims if they supported the idea. I don't think Kay and Larry like the idea of anything happening on that property. When I think about it, I understand how they feel. The family's feelings should be paramount, and I hope the people who bought the property will consider that before moving on with their plans.

John Prior is not a death penalty–qualified attorney. He doesn't have to be. If the court were to appoint an attorney for Daybell, that attorney would have to be, but since Daybell picked Prior, he does not.

Prior is expected to pull out all the stops in his defense strategy. He has already been doing that. Just a few days ago he went on TV and talked about the case. He knows very well that in doing that he is making it harder for the court to find untainted jurors. It's hard enough already in such a high-profile case. Judge Boyce quickly filed a gag order, but the damage was done. That gag order has since been extended for the duration of the trial, which means that people who may have been willing to talk to me during the trial will now have to be very careful not to say anything more than pleasantries.

In 2011 John Prior was embroiled in a sexual assault case. He was accused by a twenty-one-year-old woman. She claimed that when she came to his office, he offered to assist her in a legal case if she would have sex with him. When she refused, he allegedly attempted to force himself on her. He ended up pleading guilty to the lesser charge of misdemeanor battery and was sentenced to 120 days in jail and fined $137.50, with 100 days of his sentence suspended.

Prior has his own law firm in Meridian, Idaho, just outside of Boise. He has been practicing law since 1997.

I would like to tell you more about him. When I researched all of the other attorneys in Lori's and in Chad's cases, I was able to read about them. Not so with John Prior. I can't talk to him because of the gag order. Maybe when the trial is over. (I did try to contact John Prior when the trial ended but got no response.)

Since I don't know John Prior personally, all I can tell you is my impressions of him in court. I find him to be a sad character. Maybe if I knew him personally, I would have a different opinion, but my opinion of him is that his attempt at a smile comes off as a sneer. He seems uncomfortable in the suit he wears and uncomfortable with himself. He seemed out of place and overwhelmed to me. I don't know, maybe anyone in his shoes defending Chad Daybell would be uncomfortable.

Prior has said he plans a vigorous defense. In the Lori Vallow Daybell trial, Lori tied the hands of her attorneys, Jim Archibald and John Thomas. She wouldn't allow them to use anything that might reflect poorly on Chad or Alex. Archibald told me after her sentencing that Judge Boyce would not even let him bring up in court the idea that Lori might be insane. That part I would think will be the same in Chad's trial.

I do expect Prior to go after Lori and blame it all on her. Why wouldn't he? She has already been convicted and she has nothing to lose. Alex is dead so he has nothing to lose either. This could cause some fireworks. Lori has already refused to say anything that might hurt Chad. What if the prosecution calls her in to testify? Will she refuse? Will she take the blame since she has nothing to lose? If given the opportunity to save Chad, will she do it? I wonder if John Prior is talking to her. She is in jail awaiting trial for conspiring to murder her then husband Charles in Arizona, but I don't think that would keep her from coming to Boise to testify.

The possibilities here are endless, and if you can't tell, I'm excited to see how it all goes.

The Prosecution

The prosecution is mostly the same as for Lori Vallow Daybell's trial, and I wrote a lot about them in *Money, Power and Sex*. Lindsey Blake, lead prosecutor for Fremont County, and Rob

Wood, lead prosecutor for Madison County, are the two main attorneys for the state.

I didn't realize the first time I saw these two when I first walked into courtroom #400 as a juror how much time I would end up spending with them and how well I would get to know them. I have spent around seventy days in court listening to and watching them, interviewed them, been interviewed by them, shared meals with them, and had conversations with them. They didn't have to spend this time with me, and I am appreciative beyond measure that they have always taken that time. Lindsey Blake will take the lead role in this trial, and Rob Wood will give the opening statement.

They do have two new attorneys on their team: Idaho Assistant District Attorney Ingrid Beatty and Fremont County Deputy Prosecuting Attorney Rocky Wixom.

I find myself having very little bad to say about the prosecution team, law enforcement, witnesses, and family of the victims and very little good to say about the defense and their witnesses. I assure you, this is not because of any bias on my part. It's because it's simply true. What's also true is that no one on the defense side spent any time whatsoever talking to me or anyone involved in this trial.

The team's background is pretty much the same as it was for Lori's trial, so I won't go into that, but I wonder what will be different in their attempt to convict Chad. They did tell me after the Lori Vallow Daybell trial that this won't be the same trial and that they have new evidence to present. I think there is a lot of evidence that we didn't see in the Lori Vallow Daybell trial. They can't repeat what they said in her trial because they were accusing her of the same crimes they are accusing Chad of committing.

What witnesses will they call who we didn't see in her trial? Will they call Lori? Will they call any of Chad's kids?

Remember, Chad's son Garth was with Chad when he called 911 to report Tammy's death. Will we hear more information about Chad's relationships with other women in the inner circle? Will we hear where Tylee was murdered and dismembered? I have wondered if that happened in the shed or in the backyard. Tools with her DNA were found in the shed, but what was left of her was found in the backyard.

I will say that I know Rob Wood and Lindsey Blake take this case personally. Rob Wood can't talk to me about JJ and Tylee without tears coming to his eyes. Lindsey Blake is a mom herself, and as a mom she is a fierce protector of children. These emotions come right to the surface when I talk to them.

Rob Wood told me he attended the autopsies of Tylee and JJ. He would not have had to but considered it his duty to do so. Both Wood and Blake had reservations about showing the autopsy photos and photos of the exhumed bodies to the jury. They were concerned about the effect it would have on the jurors. They went back and forth until they finally decided they had no choice. They had to do everything in their power to get a conviction.

Since I have gotten to know them both, I can feel their compassion for the jurors, and it has helped me deal with my own feelings. I hope they know that their strength and determination has been the best therapy for me. And I hope they feel the respect and admiration we have for them. They won't admit it, but they need that. They need to know they have a community of good people behind them.

I asked them if they believed that Alex Cox had died of natural causes. I have a very hard time believing that he did. It's just way too convenient for Chad and Lori. As soon as they had everyone murdered who they needed murdered, Alex dies? Come on. But investigators could not find any proof that Alex was murdered or that he took his own life. Blake and Wood were shocked and bewildered at the findings of the autopsy, and it was going to make it hard on the prosecution. I wonder what it would have been like hearing Alex testify. I do think that some of the prosecutors and investigators might have been a little relieved, though, when they heard Alex was dead. As long as he was walking around free, he was a threat to their safety and the safety of their families.

I also wonder about the Mormon connection between some of the people involved in this case. Rob Wood is Mormon, and I haven't asked him about his religion, but it is a factor in some way. Wood says religion was not a factor in any of this, and in a legal sense, I understand that. In an emotional sense, however, they are members of the same church, and Chad used the Mormon Church as a tool and did things that hurt his church. In my experience, Mormons do not like people outside of their religion questioning it, and I want to be careful about offending any of the people I have so much admiration for.

If Rob Wood wants to leave the church out of it in our conversations, I respect that. His job as a prosecutor is not to question the Mormon Church. His job is to convict a man of brutal, violent crimes against innocent victims.

On a lighter note, I really had to laugh when I asked Wood about how his life was going after the trial ended, and he replied that he finally had time to fix his broken sprinklers. My own yard has suffered terribly since I got involved in this case. It's just not what it once was.

Anyway, read on and hopefully we'll get some answers. In fact, I bet we get answers to questions we don't even have yet. We'll see.

21

BACK TO COURT

Going back to the courthouse was interesting. It was kind of like going back to work after a long hiatus. I got caught up with bailiffs Ken and Steve, waved to Judge Boyce, and reconnected with people in the media who have helped me make sense of the first trial. They had been covering it for years before I was called in as a juror and had a lot more knowledge than I did after the Lori Vallow Daybell trial ended and I started doing my research for *Money, Power and Sex.*

It's taken me the whole past year to get caught up to them. I think back to when they interviewed me after the sentencing on July 31, 2023. I really didn't know what I didn't know. There is seemingly no end to the layers to be peeled back, and I learn something new every day.

My juror badge for the Lori Vallow Daybell trial.
Personal photo.

Looking back at my jury service, I am humbled by some of the people who I spent time with every day. Our bailiffs, Ken and Steve, were our guides, our drivers, our protectors, our waiters, and whatever else we needed them to be. I remember well the expression of compassion on their faces when we were subjected to the horrors of the trial. I struggle to explain my feelings for these two guys, but I can just say that seeing them in court a year later felt good.

Now Lieutenant Ray Hermosillo (he was promoted from detective earlier this year) is at the courthouse, but tells me he won't be in the courtroom every day like he was for Lori Vallow Daybell's trial. He will be called on to testify about the searches of Lori Vallow Daybell's apartment, garage, and storage unit as well as the search and eventual exhumation of JJ and Tylee. I'm sure he will be on the stand for a day or two at least.

TUESDAY, APRIL 2, 2024,
Chad Has No Shame

How can Chad sit in court and smile? Has he no shame? Even if he were innocent, the charges against him are severe, and I would think he would take them more seriously. He sits in court, facing straight ahead with his hands folded in front of him most of the time. Occasionally I can see him trying to look to his side without moving his head, kind of like giving the gallery the side-eye.

Dr. John Matthias of *Hidden True Crime* podcast says it shows insecurity. I can see that. Anyway, I guess it's all part of the human condition. A few of us are murderers, a few of us are presidents and everything in between, but we are all of us human.

Chad is plain in every way one can be. Every day in court he wore a button-up shirt and tie. It looked to me like the same clothes he would have worn to church. He is slightly overweight, but less so than he was in some of the earlier pictures I have seen. Lori helped him with his weight and his appearance when they began spending time together. There was no craziness in his eyes like Charles Manson or Warren Jeffs. More of a blankness or emptiness I would say. He expressed little emotion, and I had to watch very carefully to pick it up.

I hear a lot of criticism of Chad's attorney, John Prior. It is not without reason that people criticize him, but he is there to do a necessary job, and I feel like I am his defender for two reasons. The one I just stated and also because I want him to stir things up. I also hope he loses spectacularly, but I want him to get some answers while he's doing that. There are too many people involved in this case who, so far, seem to be getting a pass, and I hope he puts them on the spot.

So, what about the jury? It's hard to tell much so far. There are over 2,000 potential jurors called in just like for Lori Vallow Daybell's case. What I have noticed is that a lot of them seem angry. They have reason to be. Not only are their lives possibly going to be disrupted for up to ten weeks, but they probably feel like this trial is unnecessary. Chad seems pretty guilty, so why doesn't he just admit it and we can all go home?

The questions posed to the jurors today are about hardship, what they already know about the case, and how they feel about the death penalty. Could they vote for the death penalty if the jury instructions say that's the penalty for the crimes he committed?

Wednesday, April 3, 2024,
Cheesy Eggs

Sitting in the courtroom listening to the prosecution and defense read from the same script to every group of potential jurors gets boring. The only thing that keeps me from nodding off is that the potential jurors can be entertaining. Some of their answers are great. I will say that with a few exceptions, people seem to be answering honestly. Hey, if you are opposed to the death penalty, that is your right. A lot of people are, and that excludes you from a death penalty case, as it should.

One lady sincerely explained to the judge that serving on this jury would be a hardship for her because she makes lunch every day for her husband, and she wouldn't be able to do that. To you and me that may seem like a small and insignificant thing, but to her it was important. I realized listening to her that hardship is different for everyone, and I really wanted her to be able to make lunch for her husband. Thankfully, her husband is getting his lunches. I'm really not making light of this. I bet the husband would be just fine making his own lunch, but I don't know if his wife would have been okay with it. And the point is, would not making lunch for her husband distract from her ability to perform her duties as a juror? I think she would honestly have been worrying about her husband and not able to focus on the trial.

Anyway, Prosecutor Lindsey Blake talked a lot about cheesy eggs, and Defense Attorney John Prior kept reminding us that all that glitters is not gold, giving us a clue I think that he is going after Lori Vallow Daybell. Their silly little sayings have a serious reason behind them. They are getting clues about individuals who they may or may not want on their jury.

I didn't realize when I sat in the jury box being questioned how much each of us was being scrutinized. I can say now after talking to them, that the prosecution and the court knew a lot about me. Judge Boyce needed to remain as neutral as possible, but his court attorney, Courtney, checked into us all and gathered all of the information about each of us that she could. She used that information to advise Judge Boyce.

As for Chad, he still sits looking straight ahead with his hands folded in front of him. I asked a Mormon person sitting close to me about that, and she said that is his training. Apparently, people are taught in the Mormon Church to do that. Sit quietly and respectfully for hours. I will say that watching him, I did feel as if he looked optimistic at this point.

John Prior is starting to make it clear about who he dislikes in the courtroom and how he feels about the First Amendment to our Constitution. He made several uncalled-for remarks about the media and even took every opportunity to look in their direction and scowl. Maybe a clue that he intends to put the media on trial, but why would he do that? Was it personal or was it part of his strategy? He probably knows he can't beat the evidence and he can't outsmart Lindsey Blake and Rob Wood, so I'm guessing attacking the media will be his fallback position. They can take it, and it won't do any good anyway.

I don't know if he knows who I am or what my role is. He was in court for Lori Vallow Daybell's trial, so my guess is that he knows exactly who I am and what I am doing. During jury selection there were only a few people in the gallery, and he made a point of turning his head 180 degrees and glaring at me for what seemed to me like a long time. Long enough to know he didn't like me for some reason. Prior to that he and I shared an elevator on the first day of jury selection. I very clearly said: "Good morning, Mr. Prior." He and I were the only ones in the elevator, and he had to have heard me, but I got no response. He just stared down at his shoes. Judge Boyce's gag order didn't preclude people from being civil to each other.

Thursday, April 4, 2024,
Groundhog Day

Three no-shows in the jury pool today. Judge Boyce takes that very seriously. He said the no-shows could be subjected to a $500 fine and five days in jail. I think the no-shows may have underestimated Judge Boyce. He comes off as soft spoken and kind, and I believe he is, but I have learned that he has absolute control of the courtroom. He has four or five clerks and six armed guards in the courtroom, and because of Judge Boyce's ability to lead those people, things go off without a hitch and he seldom has to raise his voice.

In spite of that I couldn't help but laugh out loud at one point today. John Prior was questioning one of the potential jurors. He asked a simple question of her, and by the time he quit talking she had forgotten the question and she told him so, sincerely saying: "You used so much verbiage, I forgot what the question was. Could you repeat that?" She nailed it for all of us who have been sitting through his diatribes!

At the end of the day, there were fifty-seven potential jurors who had not been released for any of the reasons I mentioned. We needed to get to fifty to move forward. Now it would be turned over to the attorneys to pick the final eighteen.

MONDAY, APRIL 8, 2024,
Peremptory Challenges

The final jury would be twelve jurors and six alternates. As I explained in *Money, Power and Sex*, we wouldn't know who the alternates would be until the trial was over and their numbers were pulled out of a hat just before the jury went into deliberations. Now we had to get from the fifty-seven of the previous day to eighteen. The prosecution and the defense would be given the opportunity to release sixteen each without cause.

Cause as it turns out is important. Cause had to be given for each of the jurors released to this point. One side or the other would be given the opportunity to explain why they wanted to release a juror, and the other side would have the opportunity to object. It's a long and tedious process, and I could see what kind of juror each side was trying to get on the jury. Prior wanted people who were not clear on the death penalty and maybe less able to follow such a convoluted case. The prosecution was looking for people who they thought would support a death penalty verdict and who could follow the case they were about to lay out.

Now any potential juror could be released without cause. The opposing side could not argue to keep a juror. Each side could release sixteen. But the math doesn't add up. They have fifty-seven. If they release sixteen each, that would leave twenty-five. Seven potential jurors would have to be released before they could do peremptory strikes. I thought they would have quit the day before when they got to fifty, but they kept going until they ended up with fifty-seven.

That confused me, but on this day, the first thing that happened is Judge Boyce released some jurors until they got down to fifty. Judge Boyce, with the help of his court attorney, decided which seven would be released. I didn't know sitting in court how that worked. I finally got an answer when I talked to Courtney after the trial was over. Anyway, down to fifty and peremptory strikes begin. When it's over, there are eighteen people whose lives are about to change in ways they can't yet imagine. As for the ones who were released, I actually saw disappointment on some of their faces. I'm glad those people were released. If you want to serve on a jury for a trial like this, you are there for the wrong reasons and I think most likely selfish reasons.

Judge Boyce looks over the jury and declares that no particular profile of juror has been selected or dismissed from the process. He goes on to say that the confidentiality of the jurors will be fiercely protected. I know from my experience as a juror in his court that he means that, and it's important for the integrity of a fair trial, and it's important for the individual jurors.

He tells us court will resume on Wednesday, April 10 at 8:30 a.m. and will begin with jury instructions and opening statements.

Opening Statements and Witnesses for the Prosecution

Opening statements were uneventful. Rob Wood did the opening for the prosecution. He changed Lindsey Blake's opening. In her opening in the Lori Vallow Daybell trial, she famously said, "Money, power, and sex" (obviously where I got the title for my first book). Rob Wood changed it to "sex, money, and power." He did do a good job of laying out the case for the state though. He talked about Chad's books and went on to use chapters like you would in a book to lay out the prosecution's case. I thought it was inventive.

I thought John Prior's opening statement was effective. His plan, of course, is to place doubt in the minds of the jurors. He listed the witnesses he would call. At the time it seemed like an impressive list of qualified people. He did say that four of Chad's kids would testify, but as it turned out, only two did.

I could feel the anticipation in the courtroom as the first witness for the prosecution, Rexburg Police Department Lieutenant Ray Hermosillo was called to the stand. If you read *Money, Power and Sex*, you know who he is and what I think about him. I have gotten to know Lieutenant Hermosillo since that trial ended.

Let's talk about heroes and let me just use Lieutenant Hermosillo as an example. I'm not singling him out because there are many heroes in this case. Is Lieutenant Hermosillo a hero? Here's what I would expect from a hero: He has done his job well. He has stuck to this case like glue doing whatever is required to see it through, in spite of the cost to himself. He is Tylee and JJ's champion. There is no doubt that he regrets not being able to save them. He will never be able to forget that. He has not faltered in that for one second. He has a family and kids of his own.

Rexburg Police Department, Lieutenant Ray Hermosillo
at the microphones during a press statement. Prosecutor
Lindsey Blake to his right and Captain Ron Ball to his left in
background. Photo provided by Ray Hermosillo.

But how is he going to deal with what he has been confronted with? My hope, my deepest desire for him, is that he is
able to live with the horror he experienced and move on with
his life in a positive way. No one could blame him if he has a
hard time in his personal life. Most of us would struggle to move
on after what he has been through. If Lieutenant Hermosillo
struggles, we will excuse him for that. How could he not?

And I have higher expectations for him. I hope he is insulted
by my very idea that he might falter. Good cops, unfortunately,
sometimes struggle in their personal lives. My hope for Lieutenant Hermosillo (and all of the other law enforcement and
prosecutors) is that he is somehow able to put things in perspective, even while others in his position have failed. So, to

achieve hero status, he will have to move forward in a positive way, be a good husband and father first, and continue to be a good cop second. He and others like him have gained the respect and admiration of so many who are following this case. But none of us have been through what he has been through, and none of us have the right to judge him. We do, however, care deeply for him and wish him the best.

We come into this case on November 1, 2019. Then Rexburg Detective (now Lieutenant) Ray Hermosillo gets a call from the Gilbert, Arizona, police department. They are looking for a Jeep registered in Idaho that was used in the attempted shooting of Brandon Boudreaux. Brandon had recognized the Jeep as one belonging to his cousin Tylee and even had the VIN since he was the insurance agent for the company that covered Tylee's Jeep. It seemed cut and dried at this point, and Rexburg police were quickly able to locate the Jeep at Lori's address. Gilbert police seized and impounded the Jeep.

In the meantime, JJ's grandparents were becoming concerned about JJ. They were used to being in constant contact with him by FaceTiming him daily. It had been several weeks since they had been able to do that, and Lori just gave them excuses as to why they couldn't. Kay didn't even know Lori had moved JJ to Idaho until she hacked her now deceased brother Charles's email account and found an email from Lori.

Kay called Rexburg police and asked them to do a welfare check on JJ. Detective Hermosillo and Officer Dave Hope went to Lori's address, apartment 107, to perform the welfare check. They ran into Alex and Chad and asked them about JJ. Alex told them that JJ was with his grandmother. When Detective Hermosillo said that was unlikely since his grandmother was the one asking for the welfare check, Alex and Chad just looked at each other and had no response. Detective Hermosillo knew they were lying and sensed that something was very wrong. He asked for Lori's phone number, and Alex replied that he didn't have it, so the two detectives went to Lori's apartment, where they got no answer to their insistent knocking. Detective Hermosillo called for more detectives and began canvassing the neighborhood. Chad tried to drive off, and Detective Hermosillo stopped him. Chad went on to lie about his relationship with Lori, saying he barely knew her and he didn't know her phone number. When pressed he finally gave Detective Hermosillo Lori's number, and he went back to Lori's apartment with Detective Dave Stubbs, who had a bodycam, and Lori finally answered the door. We were shown the bodycam footage of the detectives questioning Lori.

Lori, as we know, is a master manipulator, but to their credit, Stubbs and Hermosillo saw right through her lies. She tried to tell them that JJ was with her friend Melanie Gibb in Arizona probably watching the movie *Frozen.*

The detectives were getting nowhere and finally left, but they weren't giving up. On November 27 they got the search warrant they had been waiting for and immediately went back to Lori's apartment. They didn't hesitate to break down her door and enter the apartment. It had been emptied out and looked to the detectives like Lori left in a hurry. They started searching for clues.

They searched all three apartments: Lori's, her brother Alex's, and her niece Melani Pawlowski's as well as the garages associated with each apartment. What they found left them even more concerned about JJ's whereabouts and his well-being. In the garage they found items belonging to JJ and Tylee. Bikes, skates, winter clothes, and photos. In the apartment in the printer Lori left behind, Detective Chuck Kunsaitis found a receipt for a storage unit under the name of Lori Ryan. They searched the storage unit and found guns, knives, rifles, suppressors, a gillie suit, a pistol, a Halloween mask, duct tape, rope, and Alex's passport.

At the time they didn't know the importance of all of these items, but the detectives were even more concerned and had no idea where Lori, Chad, and Alex had fled to. They held a press conference and announced that Tylee and JJ were missing and that they were searching for Lori and Chad. They soon got a tip that Chad and Lori were in Hawaii. It didn't take long for Detective Hermosillo to join them there and serve a warrant for Lori to produce the kids. They also served a search warrant for her apartment and car in Princeville, Kauai. They found no evidence of the kids being with her, and she could produce no proof of life.

THURSDAY, APRIL 11, 2024,
Judge Boyce's Gag Order

By this time, I was starting to feel like I was becoming the face of this trial, and I was not comfortable with that. I was being interviewed daily. I was happy to have the opportunity to pitch my book and talk about my charity, Hope House, but I felt like it was my face people were seeing more than any other when they watched the news or podcasts about the trial, and that's what was making me uncomfortable. There were people more worthy of that role.

The problem was the gag order Judge Boyce placed on the attorneys and police. Media needed someone to interview, and I was one of the few close to the trial who they could interview. I made a decision to just say no thank you except to a few when they asked for an interview, and I stuck to it until the trial neared its end. I was much more comfortable with that.

In the prosecution's questioning of Lieutenant Hermosillo, we jump forward to June 9, 2020, the day JJ and Tylee's remains were discovered in Chad's backyard. The jury got its first real glimpse into the horror of this case as he jumped right into the search for Tylee and JJ's remains. How they quickly found JJ's grave and Tylee's shortly after.

He described how the team of detectives and FBI agents painstakingly uncovered JJ's body and how they had to trade off because they could only work for a few minutes at a time because of the smell and the horrific nature of what they were finding. He told the jury how JJ's arms had been folded and wrapped in duct tape, how he was still wearing his pull-up diaper, how he had duct tape wrapped around and around his head and mouth, his wrists wrapped in duct tape under the plastic bag.

As Lieutenant Hermosillo was talking, I could plainly see the pictures in my mind that I had been shown a year earlier. Those images will never leave me. It's the saddest, most horrific thing I have ever seen and I hope will ever see. I was again filled with compassion for the people who had to deal with it firsthand and for the families of the victims who were sitting right next to me in court. Thankfully JJ's grandmother, Kay, was not allowed in court because she would be testifying later. When I glanced to my right, I could see JJ's Paw Paw, Larry, his hands folded in front of him rocking back and forth with his eyes clamped shut.

The court had appointed a victim's advocate. I don't know what dictated the times she was there other than she would always be there on days like this. Sitting with Larry holding his shoulders. There was nothing anyone could say or do to lessen his pain, but at least she was there, and I could tell that her compassion was genuine.

Lieutenant Hermosillo went on to describe how he stayed with the bodies of Tylee and JJ from then on anytime they were transported or anything was happening with them. They were his responsibility, and he would make sure they were respected and protected. He rode with them all the way from Rexburg to Meridian where the autopsies were performed and stayed in the room while they were being autopsied. I think this says a lot about him and his dedication to this case. I don't think he was directed to stay with Tylee and JJ. I think he personally felt like it was his responsibility.

Lieutenant Hermosillo with prosecutor Rob Wood in front of the courthouse. Photo provided by Ray Hermosillo.

The prosecution next questioned the lieutenant about the attempted shooting of Tammy on October 2, 2019, and the attempted shooting of Brandon on October 9 of the same year. In Lori's trial the defense team tried to convince the jury that the rifle used in the attempt on Tammy was really just a paintball gun and that it wasn't Alex holding the gun, but a neighborhood teenage prankster.

Defense attorney Prior used that idea in his cross-examination of Lieutenant Hermosillo in this trial. He first tried to say it was a prankster with a paintball gun and then posed the idea that it was Alex trying to kill Tammy, but Chad had no part in it. His idea was that Alex and Lori were the ones conspiring to kill people and Chad was just duped by Lori's good looks. Nice try, but this was the first time I could detect actual eye rolls in the jury.

During John Prior's cross-examination, I could see Judge Boyce losing patience. Prior was asking Lieutenant Hermosillo questions obviously just meant to confuse him. It wasn't working on any level, and I think Judge Boyce just thought it was mean spirited. Prior's idea was to try to make the police look bad. He even accused them of being in some kind of conspiracy to wrongly convict Chad Daybell. He never mentioned what their motive might have been though.

In prosecutor Rob Wood's redirect of Lieutenant Hermosillo, we heard that Alex had looked up drop rates in cold weather the day before for the caliber of rifle the police found in the storage locker. Alex had staged himself in a position to take a shot at Tammy from around 100 yards. His plan fell apart when Tammy used the front driveway instead of the back driveway like she normally did. This put the house in between Alex and his target. He had to revise his plan in a hurry, and I think he faltered not expecting to be in such close range. It would have seemed less personal to take the shot from a long distance, but I don't think Alex could follow through looking her in the eye. Lieutenant Hermosillo reminded the jury that Chad had lied about where the kids were, and if he wasn't involved, why didn't he become suspicious and call the police?

After Lieutenant Hermosillo was done testifying, he disappeared to somewhere in the courthouse. I knew he wouldn't leave even though he was not sitting in court all day like last year. During a break I searched the courthouse until I found him sitting with Detective Kunsaitis in a room on the third floor. I knew I wasn't allowed to talk about the case with him, but I was just overcome with a need to sit with him for a while.

MONDAY, APRIL 15, 2024,
Deputy "K"

Chad sits quietly at his table with John Prior. Judge Boyce admonishes the gallery to keep quiet. He also admonishes the jury as he did every day to not talk about the trial with anyone.

The second witness called by the prosecution is former Fremont County Deputy Sheriff Vince Kaaiakamanu, who was at the time of his testimony in this trial chief deputy for the Madison County Sheriff's Department. He is also the case agent assigned to this trial, which means he not only has to sit through the whole trial, but that he works as a liaison among all of the agencies involved.

He testified about the call between Chad and Lori while Lori was in jail and Chad was sitting in his car in front of his house while the police were searching his backyard and finding Tylee and JJ's burial sites.

In the call Chad sounds pretty hopeless telling Lori the police are searching the backyard. Kaaiakamanu testified that Chad kept looking over his shoulder in the direction of JJ's burial site indicating he thinks that Chad knew what they were looking for. Chad's car was parked in the driveway in front of the house facing the street.

Some of the most comprehensive testimony came from Rexburg PD Detective Eric Wheeler. Wheeler is an eighteen-year veteran and, like all of the police who testified, very professional and believable. He helped exhume Tylee's remains and witnessed the exhumation of JJ's.

He said he actually saw Chad move the car he was sitting in into a position where he could see the gravesites as the police were searching. He also saw Chad looking over his shoulder as they searched. He then watched Chad drive across the street to his daughter Emma's house where he stayed for about one and a half hours before he finally drove away at a high rate of speed. Wheeler testified that the speed limit on the road in front of Chad's house was 55, so it wouldn't be unusual for someone to accelerate like Chad was, but it sounded to him like Chad was attempting a getaway. Chad didn't get far before he was pulled over and detained. Detective Wheeler testified that when pulled over and told that they found JJ, Chad was compliant.

We saw that in the video the jury and gallery were shown by the prosecution. Chad is sitting in the back seat of a police car and the dash cam is rolling. This was something new that we did not see in Lori's trial. The tape was twenty or maybe thirty minutes long and shows Chad talking to his daughter Emma as well as to police. He seems hopeless and even tells Emma he won't be coming back as they make arrangements for Emma and her husband to move into Chad's house. They talk about how she is to make house payments and Chad tells her there is $9,000 in a drawer in Mark's bedroom. All this while they are literally exhuming the bodies of Chad's victims in the backyard.

Emma begins to show her true colors at this point. She laughs as she tells Chad a spirit told her she would be moving soon. She said she didn't understand the spirit at the time, but now it all makes sense. Emma says she will talk to Lori and that she is aware to beware of Lori's son Colby. I think she meant that she knew not to give Colby any money.

Chad went on to say: "It's only a matter of time. Things are starting to come together."

He is still telling Emma that the second coming is imminent.

The next witness called by prosecutor Rocky Wixom was interesting to me. He spoke with a kind of local dialect, which may have made him sound a little less polished than some of the other detectives. I soon found out though that it would be a mistake to underestimate him. He was Lieutenant Joseph Powell of the Rexburg PD.

He testified about seeing Chad and Lori together after they had claimed to police to hardly know each other, indicating that they had been lying to police. He was tasked with following them around in a kind of private-eye style, and he witnessed them holding hands as they walked into Hobby Lobby together. He was asked about Tammy's medical condition and he said: "Tammy don't have any serious medical condition."

She took anxiety and depression medications per her doctor's recommendation. My thought at the time was who wouldn't need those meds being married to Chad.

Prior did his best to tear down Lieutenant Powell's testimony. I think Prior thought he had a soft target, but I don't think you get to be a lieutenant in the Rexburg PD by being soft. Judging by the people I know, I'm guessing the bar is fairly high, even if you have a small-town dialect.

Since Lieutenant Powell was the one who got the search warrant to exhume Tammy's body from the cemetery, Prior questioned him about that. Prior asked why the family had not been notified that Tammy would be exhumed. He asked if Lieutenant Powell had ever looked at the death certificate for Tammy. He asked if Tammy had been taking medication for bruising. In a very loud voice, he reminded Lieutenant Powell that the coroner had declared Tammy's death as being from natural causes.

Prior was doing his best to establish doubt, and I do think he did raise some legitimate questions regarding the police, but I would not go so far as to say he raised doubt.

Anyway, if there was any doubt in any juror's mind at this point, the prosecution quickly cleared it up in their redirect of Lieutenant Powell. It came out that Chad had provided Prior with the information he was using regarding Tammy's physical condition. Lieutenant Powell had witnessed Chad and Lori holding hands shortly after Tammy died. Charles was known to have been shot by Alex. The coroner who declared Tammy's death to be of natural causes had no information about Charles's death or the missing children and no reason to be suspicious.

The next witness was FBI Tactical Specialist Nicole Heideman. She was interesting for two reasons. She first explained burner phones and how she and her team were able to gain access to the texts on those phones. Chad, Lori, and Alex had used at least fifteen burner phones. Chad had nine, and Lori and Alex each had three. Apparently, they thought burner phones were safe. I would have thought the same thing. They are apparently private in the movies. However, the FBI was able to access the information on those phones and find each phone and the information on them through the communications between Chad, Lori, and Alex. They were also able to access email accounts through those phones.

The trio also used aliases. Chad was Raphael, and Chad and Lori were James and Elaina. Chad was Bishop Shumway in Lori's contacts.

The second interesting item came out in Prior's cross-examination of Specialist Heideman. He questioned who might have had access to Chad's email accounts. Could Alex and Lori have set Chad up? Why didn't the FBI do Google searches on Melanie Gibb and David Warwick? I'm guessing they did all the background checking they could on these two, but they weren't bringing any of it up in court.

As I sat there, I wondered why. Why don't we know more about them? They were called in to testify, but their testimony was limited. They were very close to Chad and Lori, and in my mind, I think they had to know more. Are they being protected? Will they be charged with crimes later? Were they given a deal in exchange for their testimony? Questions the prosecution won't answer for me, which of course makes me even more suspicious.

TUESDAY, APRIL 16, 2024,
"All That Glitters Is Not Gold"

John Prior made this point in court today: "It's in the Doctrine [*of*] Covenants." He was talking about all of the religious fundamentalist stuff that Chad espouses and the Doctrine and Covenants of the LDS Church. He meant to say Doctrine *and* Covenants, but he's right. It's all in there to this day just waiting for people like Chad Daybell to use it for their own personal gain.

John Prior can be crass and he is insulting to the family when he says things like "dug up the body" when talking about Tammy's exhumation. He's doing it to make a point, but he could be a little more careful about that. Especially when Tammy's aunt is sitting right there in the courtroom. Even so, some of his points are valid, and I think he will bring out more answers because of it.

He is trying to find a way to get prosecutor Rob Wood on the stand to testify about the text messages between him and Melanie Gibb. Putting the prosecuting attorney on the stand would be unprecedented and I think unfair to the prosecution. Still, there are over 300 text messages between Wood and Gibb and I would love to read them. I've always wondered if the prosecution was protecting Gibb to get her to testify. Surely, she knows more than what she has testified to.

Prior is obviously trying to make a connection with the jury. I think he is kind of a sad character. He seems to not be able to see or sense that he is failing. He seems to me to believe in himself in spite of what I see as his obvious shortcomings. He'll make a statement or ask a question and then turn and glare at the jurors. Instead of making a connection, I think they are repulsed by that. It seems like the only person who can't see it is him. And maybe Chad. He tries to bait the witnesses and even the prosecution, and they seem to outwit him every time.

He makes a point of trying to sound colloquial, like all this is new to him. He's a small-town boy, naive and not sophisticated in the ways of Mormonism or religious fundamentalism. I think he thinks that if he comes off that way to the jury, they will project it onto Chad. It's all Lori's fault and Chad was duped. All that glitters is not gold.

He has a hopeless client, and he is certainly doing what is his best to defend him, and that is what we expect of a defense attorney. I do think there are lines that should not be crossed, even in the attempt to provide the best defense possible. Should a defense attorney lie? Should he refer to things he knows are untrue? Should he twist the truth? Should he raise questions when he knows there is no truth behind them? Where is the line drawn? I think it can only be drawn by the jury. Do they believe him? Which side comes off as more believable?

I watched Chad's face a lot today. I sit about ten feet away from him in court. I thought he would show some embarrassment or humility when they played a tape of his "patriarchal blessing" to Alex Cox. First of all, Chad is in no way authorized by the Mormon Church to give patriarchal blessings. Each stake in the Mormon Church has one patriarch who is supposed to do that.

But Chad seemed to me to have a slight smile or smirk on his face while it was played in court. I struggled to understand that until I talked to Lauren Matthias. She says that she and Dr. John think Chad still believes himself. That's so unbelievable to me at this point that the idea never crossed my mind, but they're right. That's the only thing that makes sense.

Now I have to ask myself: Is he nuts? He would have to be, to be able to sit through all of this and still be able to smile. And then I think about his conversation with his daughter Emma while JJ was being exhumed in his backyard. They talk about finances and who's going to live in the house—the house where Tammy was murdered and the house where JJ and Tylee were probably murdered and buried so disrespectfully in the backyard. And why put us all through this trial? Because he believes it! And believing it means he thinks he's right and we're all wrong. And if he's right, he can't lose. Or if he does lose, it's all beside the point. He's a martyr.

The trial of Lori Vallow Daybell for the murder of Charles Vallow in Arizona has been postponed, but is expected to take place in 2025. There is evidence in that case that also pertains to our trial of Chad Daybell. To bring that evidence to light, the prosecution called Chandler, Arizona, PD Detective Nathan Duncan. Detective Duncan added to what I already knew and wrote about in chapter 10.

According to his testimony he was called to the 5500 block of S. Four Peaks Place on July 11, 2019, to investigate a shooting.

Alex Cox had dialed 911 and claimed he shot his brother-in-law in self-defense. The 911 operator asked Alex if he could perform CPR on Charles, and Alex said he would try. When Detective Duncan arrived at the house, Alex exited the house through the front door, and Detective Duncan had him sit on the curb. Detective Duncan quickly determined that Alex was unarmed and had no serious injuries.

I have to admit I'm a little confused about how I feel about the Chandler and Gilbert, Arizona, police. On one hand, I think they were inept and could have arrested Alex and Lori when they shot Charles. On the other hand, witnesses like Detective Duncan seem very professional and knowledgeable. I guess I'll wait for the trials in Arizona before I make up my mind.

Detective Duncan entered the house and immediately found Charles lying on his back on the living room floor. Duncan went room by room and cleared the house before paramedics showed up and said that Charles was dead. Looking at the body, Detective Duncan determined that Charles had been shot twice. Once while standing and then while lying on the floor. Paramedics said it didn't appear that Alex had performed CPR. They could tell because more blood would have been pumped out of Charles's body than what was apparent.

This would have been the first clue that Alex was not being honest with police. When questioned, Alex explained that his sister Lori had asked him to spend the night because her estranged husband Charles was to come by the next morning and Lori was afraid of him.

The truth was that Charles had not seen his stepson JJ in a long time and was coming to pick him up and take him to school. Charles and JJ had been close. In fact, for a long time the whole family was close and happy. Charles, Lori, Tylee, JJ, and Colby had been a very happy family. Charles loved Lori and the family she brought with her into the marriage.

It was Charles's second marriage and Lori's fourth. Charles had children from his first marriage, but they were grown. Charles had even converted to Mormonism just to please Lori.

Something changed in Lori though. She had always been a little different, but Charles accepted that and even loved that about her. She was a faithful Mormon, a loving mother, and a generally happy, outgoing person. She loved to dance, and remember, Charles even built her a dance studio in the basement of their house where she would dance for hours by herself looking at herself in the mirrors that lined the walls.

Charles could not make sense of what was happening with her, and it just got worse the harder he tried to get through to her. She started accusing him of having affairs, and she was going off the deep end with her religion. She was talking about people's bodies being invaded by zombies. (She denied using the term *zombie* in a phone conversation she had later with her son Colby, but at the very least she claimed that people's bodies had been invaded by some kind of evil spirit or demon.) It got so bad that Charles began to worry about his safety and the safety of the children.

When Charles returned from his business trip and found that his pickup wasn't in the parking lot where he had left it, the locks had been changed on his house, and his business account had been drained of the $35,000, it was enough for Charles, and he called the police, distraught and not knowing what else to do. He hoped that the police would be able to find Lori and get her the mental help she needed.

In Chad's trial we were shown the recording of Charles trying to explain his problem to the police. We could see that he was obviously desperate and afraid. He explained to police what Lori had done and what she was saying about people being invaded by zombies. Charles was a big, strong athletic man in his fifties. It was hard to watch the video of him talking to police. He was obviously in fear. It made me think about what Lori, who probably weighed about 100 pounds less than Charles, would have had to do to instill that kind of fear in Charles. The police agreed to find her and have her committed.

It has never been explained to me how she did it, but Lori was one step ahead of the police and committed herself. She spent a few hours at Community Bridges Mental Health Center and was released, apparently having convinced the people there that she was okay. She claimed that it was Charles who was going off the deep end and who was a danger to her.

Back to Detective Duncan and Alex at the murder scene. He questioned Alex and got his story about how events unfolded. According to Alex, Charles was immediately confrontational when he entered the house. The house by the way was one Charles had rented for Lori and the kids since Lori didn't want to live with him anymore. Lori had grabbed Charles's phone, intending to look at his text messages. This infuriated Charles and precipitated what happened next. Alex got between Charles and Lori, and Charles started yelling at Alex and approaching him in a threatening way.

Tylee was awakened by the yelling and came out of her room with a baseball bat. She didn't play baseball or softball and she didn't share her room with anyone, but according to Alex in his interview with police, Tylee kept a bat in her room for protection.

She confronted Charles with the bat, poking him in the stomach with it. He took it from her and turned on Alex. He hit Alex in the head with the bat, knocking him down. Alex went to his room and got his .45 caliber pistol. He warned Charles, pointing the pistol at him, but Charles refused to back off. He shot Charles twice in the chest, and Charles fell to the floor. Prior to Alex shooting Charles, Lori had sent Tylee out to the car where JJ was fastened in his car seat waiting to be driven to school, so Tylee didn't witness the shooting. Alex called 911 and performed CPR with instructions given by the operator.

I'll pause here and point out a few things wrong with this story. The second shot into Charles's chest was after Charles had fallen to the floor as evidenced by the bullet found embedded in the floor under his body. The cut on Alex's head supposedly caused by Charles hitting him with the bat was very small and barely bleeding, even though Alex was making a show of soaking up the blood with a rag. Remember, Charles was a big, strong man who had been a college baseball player. If he had hit Alex in the head with a baseball bat, I think the wound would have been more severe. The EMTs said no one had performed CPR on Charles, and in fact, Charles had been dead for at least forty-five minutes before Alex even called 911.

So that was Alex's story that he gave to Detective Duncan, but what about Lori and Tylee? We know that right after Alex shot Charles, Lori took Tylee and JJ away in her car. She was taking JJ to school. I can understand that JJ may have been hungry and that would be why she stopped at Burger King on the way. In the surveillance footage of her at the drive-through, she appeared to not have a care in the world.

After dropping JJ off at school, she then took Tylee flip-flop shopping. But I wondered why Tylee needed flip-flops at that moment? Had she been wearing shoes earlier or was she barefoot when she got into the car? Could her shoes have had Charles's blood on them and they had to get rid of them? Or did she simply leave the house in a hurry not, taking the time to get her shoes? According to both Tylee and Lori, Tylee had been sent out of the house before Charles was shot to watch out for JJ.

Anyway, when Lori and Tylee got back to her house, they were asked to stay across the street and were questioned by police. We saw the video of that in court, and it was bizarre to say the least. Lori was laughing with police about being the new neighbor while she gave her version of what happened. Although her story was similar to Alex's, there were enough differences that I would have thought the police would be suspicious. Tylee backed up what Lori said, and I guess that was enough for the police for the moment.

Tylee, Alex, and Lori were asked to go to the police station to give statements. We saw video of that in court, but they did not show the interview of Alex, and I wondered why that was. Hopefully we'll find out in Lori's trial in Arizona.

Detective Duncan testified further about Charles threatening to contact Tammy and tell her about Lori and Chad's affair. In fact, Charles did send an email to Tammy on her school email account. He explained that Lori claimed Charles's body had been invaded by a demon named Ned Snyder. There were many texts between Chad, Alex, and Lori leading up to the alleged murder of Charles. It makes me wonder why Arizona doesn't accuse Chad of conspiring to murder Charles. He was obviously in on it if not the one directing the alleged murder and calling for it.

The prosecution moved on and asked Detective Duncan about Chad's patriarchal blessing to Alex. As I said earlier, a patriarchal blessing is only supposed to be given by the stake patriarch of the Mormon Church, but as we know, Chad saw himself as above the confines of the church.

We listened to Chad's blessing to Alex, and it creeped me out as much as anything else associated with Chad. In his blessing we heard Chad tell Alex that he was sent back to this earth to protect his sister. Alex had walked this earth many times in that role. He told Alex that he had already assisted Chad and Lori and he would continue to do so in his strong, powerful service to the Lord. He told Alex he had to go to great depths to achieve great heights and thy soul is cleansed. He told Alex he was about to enter the terrestrial phase of his existence and he would be known throughout the world. Alex would gather souls through portals.

He would "bring entire families to the gates and they would be allowed to enter on your word. You will be an angel on earth."

This whole thing is creepily interesting and telling, but the most telling thing to me is that Chad said Alex was about to enter the terrestrial phase of his existence, meaning he was about to become immortal. A few days after this blessing, Alex was dead. Did Chad murder Alex? Did Alex commit suicide on Chad's behalf? Or did Alex coincidentally happen to die of natural causes right at that moment?

John Prior continued to lose credibility when he cross-examined Detective Duncan, who was unflappable as Prior tried his best to discredit his testimony. Prior questioned about why Chad hadn't been charged in the murder of Charles, I guess thinking it might make it look like Chad was innocent of everything. Detective Duncan's reply was that Chad might yet be charged in Arizona. I noticed a juror struggling to keep a straight face at that. And I wondered if Prior noticed that.

In her redirect, Lindsey Blake got Detective Duncan to say that he was recommending that Chad be charged in Arizona. She also cleverly insinuated that Alex may have bought drugs to commit suicide when he was in Mexico.

When Detective Duncan was finished testifying, a hearing was held outside of the presence of the jury. John Prior wanted to call Prosecutor Rob Wood to the stand. As I said earlier, this would have been unprecedented and seemed to me unfair to the prosecution. Prior claimed that there were hundreds of texts between Rob Wood and Melanie Gibb.

As much as I wanted to see those texts, I knew Judge Boyce would have to deny the request. Gibb was very close to Chad and Lori. She recorded a call between her and Lori and gave the recording to the police. She also testified for the prosecution. Still, I wonder if she did those things just to protect herself. I wonder if she knew more than she is admitting to. I wonder if the prosecution is protecting her in exchange for her cooperation. She was at Lori's apartment on the night JJ died. She was in constant contact with Chad and Lori. She had originally lied to the police to protect Chad and Lori.

Judge Boyce did end up denying the request so I guess we'll never know. The prosecution won't answer my questions about that, and Melanie Gibb, of course, refuses to talk to me.

The day ended with FBI Special Agent Mark Saari testifying about his investigation into insurance fraud. I won't bore you too much with that other than to say that he concluded that Chad committed fraud by murdering Tammy and collecting the life insurance.

Wednesday, April 17, 2024,
"May I Approach the Witness?"

Rexburg Detective Chuck Kunsaitis testified today. It was the same information I listened to when he was on the witness stand a year ago, mostly about Chad and Lori's flight schedules and insurance fraud. It's integral to this case, so extremely important stuff, and I know Detective Kunsaitis put a lot of work into investigating it all and presenting it in court.

It was hard to watch the 6 foot 6 former linebacker get choked up whenever he talked about Tylee and JJ. It serves to remind me just how much of an impact this case has had on these people. These guys are as tough as they come and battle worn, but the horror of this case is almost too much to bear even for them, but as I keep saying, bear it they will. Whatever it takes. And I could not be prouder of them. I do what I can to support them. All I can do is give them a pat on the back and say good job, but it feels weak when I do it. It can never be enough.

I had been confused about Lori's and others' whereabouts during certain times like when Tammy was murdered. Detective Kunsaitis cleared that up for me and I'm sure a lot of other people. Lori and her niece Melani Boudreaux went to Missouri to see sites sacred to the Mormon Church. She just left JJ with Charles, and this is when Charles reached out to his sister Kay for help and when he switched the beneficiary on his life insurance policy from Lori to Kay.

As a side note, a member of the gallery was slow to stand up when the jury was excused for morning break. If anyone had any doubt about how serious Judge Boyce is about his expectations for the behavior of the people in the gallery, we now know he is very serious. He did not allow that person back into court for the rest of the day. I know this person well, and I have to say that this person was sick that day and not feeling well, and this person was horrified that they did something to offend Judge Boyce. Before court resumed after that break, the bailiff made it clear to the gallery what the expectations are: absolute silence, no nodding of heads or facial expressions and computers and phones are to be kept below the top of the seat in front. And now we knew that the slightest infractions would cost us our privilege of being in the gallery.

It also made me realize that what I had hoped I imagined the day before was not just in my head. When I stood up as the jury was dismissed, I dropped something on the seat behind me, and without thinking, I turned to pick it up. When I turned back around, Judge Boyce was staring at me with what I perceived as a look of disgust on his face. I mentioned this to him in a conversation we had after the trial was over, and he denied it, but I know he had been contemplating removing me from the gallery. I'm so glad he didn't do that and he wouldn't have needed to. Just the idea horrifies me. The last thing I would want to do is disrespect the court I have so much admiration for.

On a lighter note, Prior totally cracked me up asking Judge Boyce: "Your honor, may I approach the witness?" Even I knew with my limited experience in court that that only happens in the movies. It did serve to lighten the mood momentarily albeit at Prior's expense. The way it actually works is the attorney asks the judge if he can hand something to the bailiff to hand to the witness. A copy of whatever it is is also given to the judge and the opposing attorneys and it has to already be admitted as evidence.

Thursday, April 18, 2024,
Is Melanie Gibb Protected?

Melanie Gibb was called to the stand. The prosecution's questioning was generally a repeat of the Lori Vallow Daybell trial. We were all holding our breath for John Prior's cross-examination. At least I was. He's not done with her. She will be back on the stand tomorrow, and Prior will continue his cross-examination. His questioning today was a little disappointing, and I hope there are more fireworks tomorrow. Prior is limited by what Judge Boyce will allow, but my hope is that he gets more truth out of her than we heard in Lori Vallow Daybell's trial. I want to see her text messages with prosecuting attorney Rob Wood. There are about 340 of them, and I want to know if he is protecting her in exchange for her testimony.

On the stand she is stubborn and continues to claim she can't remember things. I can relate to that, but surely being such an important witness, she would have thought it through before testifying in court. She seemed smug to me, and I thought that might be because she knew she was being protected. She was more of a part of Chad and Lori's inner circle than anyone, and I refuse to believe that she has just moved on with her life and matters pertaining to this trial are not important enough for her to recollect. We'll never know for sure unless we get to see those texts.

Court ended a little early today because Judge Boyce needed to hold a hearing. An attorney named Radcliff tried to inject himself into this trial. He claimed to represent Chad Daybell and filed a motion to postpone the trial so he could properly represent his client. No one involved in this trial for several years had even heard of him before he filed his motion. I'm afraid he underestimated Judge Boyce.

By the time the hearing was over, Judge Boyce not only admonished him for trying to inject himself into the trial for selfish reasons, but also charged him with the cost of his actions. He will now have to pay for the cost of the attorneys' time on both sides. Time spent trying to figure out who he is and what he wants out of it. Time preparing for the hearing. It just goes to show that there are people who will do whatever they can to profit from this case and make a name for themselves.

There are many people, including myself, who stand to profit from this case. A lot of people I know whom I see in court every day, mostly people in the media, stand to profit from this case. The difference is we hope to profit by bringing something positive to it. I have personally seen people in the media who only intend to report the truth be criticized for reporting the truth. The First Amendment to our Constitution is as important as any other right given to citizens of our great country. Without it, we are sunk. And I have to say, I thought before my experience in this trial that the media reporting the truth was dead in our country.

In *Money, Power and Sex* I write about how proud I was of the judicial system. I didn't experience the media in that trial because I was a juror. This time, I see the media in action firsthand and I can tell you that truth in the media is not dead. It's just not on mainstream network TV. Technology has given us other platforms. We can be critical of them as we should, but there is real news there.

One thing that is new to me is podcasts and podcasters. I knew next to nothing about that world before the Lori Vallow Daybell trial ended. I have met and been interviewed and even become good friends with several podcasters, and I can tell you that that is where real news is reported. Thanks to that platform, investigative reporting is alive and well.

I'm outside the courthouse with Lauren Matthias of the *Hidden True Crime* podcast. Photo provided by Lauren Matthias.

Something else happened in court today that interested me. There was a hearing not in the presence of the jury about whether the prosecution could use the name Lori Vallow Daybell. The defense's argument was that using Daybell might influence the jury in a negative way for his client, Chad Daybell, since Lori had been convicted. I thought it was only fair for the prosecution to use Lori Vallow Daybell since they are still married and Lori Vallow Daybell *is* her legal name. In fact, I thought it would be unfair for the judge to say they couldn't use her legal name, but he did. He decided that in this trial she would be called Lori Vallow, leaving off Daybell.

If Judge Boyce has made any mistakes in either of these trials, I would say the mistakes have been in favor of the defense. I'm sure he understands this and it's by design. He can give a little here and there without unduly affecting the outcome of the trial.

FRIDAY, APRIL 19, 2024,
Is Melanie Gibb Complicit?

As John Prior's cross-examination of Melanie Gibb continued, I was a little disappointed. I thought Prior would get more out of her. I do think he may call her back as a witness for the defense.

Gibb admitted to lying to police about having JJ with her. Chad and Lori asked her to. She waited two weeks to finally tell the truth. That's when she recorded a phone call with Lori and Chad and gave it to the police. The significance of the phone call for this case is that we hear Chad on the line with Lori lying about the fact that JJ is dead and buried in his backyard. When Gibb asks why they won't tell her where JJ is, they tell her it's for her own protection. That makes no sense to me, and Gibb asked them why she would be in danger.

Prior tried to get Gibb to say that at the time of the phone call Chad didn't know Tylee and JJ had been killed.

Gibb also stated that Chad told her that he had a vision that Tammy would die young. The significance of that is obvious. He said his life would have two parts. The first part with Tammy and the second part after Tammy.

In her redirect of Gibb, Lindsey Blake asked her if a "casting" was successful, would the body of the possessed person die? Gibb answered yes. Another important thing Gibb stated is that Lori got her information about who was light and who was dark and where they stood on the light and dark scale from Chad. She also stated that Chad had appointed Alex to be Lori's protector. She went on to describe how Chad and Lori would discreetly meet at hotels, but that Lori told her it was okay because they had been married in previous lives or probations. Chad had told Melanie that he couldn't divorce Tammy. Mormons don't divorce and maintain their standing in the church.

It got even weirder when she described how Lori claimed to have been married to the angel Moroni and also to the apostle James and that she was Methuselah. Moroni is the angel who revealed the golden plates to Joseph Smith. James was a fisherman and one of Jesus's twelve apostles. Methuselah is an Old Testament character who is said to have lived for 969 years.

When Melanie started to question Lori in the phone call, Lori used her best manipulative skills to throw Melanie off track, telling her she was going off the deep end and that she would be accountable.

Prior had a whole war chest of questions in his cross-examination of Gibb. It felt to me like he was basing most of his defense on this one witness. He meticulously went through the history of when Gibb met Chad at a Preparing a People conference in 2017. He asked her about her relationship with

David Warwick, and we heard that they had married but live in separate states. I'm sure Prior brought that up to discredit Gibb, and I think it does discredit her. I think they are married just so they don't have to testify against each other. I think all of the inner circle is doing whatever they can to protect themselves. One thing Prior tried to get Gibb to say, that she wouldn't say, is that Chad didn't know that Tylee and JJ had been killed.

He asked her if she had taught a class about light and dark theory, and she replied that she didn't remember. Apparently, she has some kind of condition that affects her memory. She said: "I forget" often.

She did admit to writing a book called *Feel the Fire.* She also admitted to the 340 texts between her and prosecutor Rob Wood.

Gibb and her now husband David Warwick are interesting characters to me. Gibb has very selective memory, she is arrogant, she is hard to rattle, and she makes me think she is still a true believer in what Lori and Chad espoused. Warwick is also strangely stubborn on the stand and makes me think he believes things that he thinks we aren't smart enough to understand. Have you ever met someone who is so idealistic and sure of themselves, but you know they are totally wrong? And you just can't get through to them? I have never had a personal conversation with Warwick, but that's how he comes off to me.

People seem to have mixed feelings about Gibb. She did cooperate with police, but it took her two weeks to decide to do that, and during that two weeks, she lied to police. Chad had told her not to talk to the police, and she initially obeyed. My own opinion is that she knew a lot more than she admits to and is guilty of at least knowing that the kids were in danger or maybe even that they were dead. She also most likely knew that Charles was in danger. She could have and certainly should have come forward sooner.

Next former FBI Agent Doug Hart took the stand. Agent Hart became involved in this case in November 2019. Like all of the law enforcement officers who testified, he was extremely knowledgeable and had extensive experience. He said he had testified in over a hundred murder trials and his experience showed in Prior's cross-examination of him.

When the trial was over, I had the opportunity to meet with Hart, now Canyon County chief deputy. His office was exactly what I expected after watching him in court. He is an extremely well put together person. Every part of him is trimmed and ironed to perfection. His hair, his clothes, and his office. I think he is this way for a purpose, but I don't think it has anything to do with vanity or self-awareness. I think he sets an example. He is in a position to be the leader of police officers, and I think the example he wants to set is professionalism and precision.

That's how he came off testifying in court. His answers were thorough and thoughtful. He spoke clearly and had no wiggle room for doubt. You might expect such a person to be cold and demanding, but I found him to be just the opposite. He is warm, interested in who he is talking to, and welcoming of one's views.

I won't go too far into his testimony about the salacious texts between Chad and Lori. I did that when I wrote about Hart's testimony in *Money, Power and Sex,* and I don't feel the need to repeat it other than to add that according to Hart, only three days after Charles was killed, Chad texted Lori: "Good morning my most beautiful Lili."

He also spoke about the idea that Chad and Lori had about the portal in Lori's closet. Chad was able to visit Lori by coming through the portal. Even though he wasn't physically with her, they could take showers together.

Hart quoted Lori saying: "Probably Ned before we got rid of him."

Referring to Ned Snyder, the zombie who they said had taken over Charles's body. We can take that quote one of two ways. Either that they successfully exorcised Ned from Charles's body or that they got rid of Charles. Since we know that Charles was dead and we also know that they had stated that in order to remove the zombie, the body had to be killed, I think it's safe to assume they meant the latter. The question is, did the jury get that? I think they did. I just think that the jury is following very closely and they will pick up on the finer points.

Hart told the jury that Lori had received about $4,000 per month for Tylee and JJ's Social Security benefit, even after they had been murdered. She was convicted of that in her trial.

Something Hart said that I don't remember hearing in the Lori Vallow Daybell trial is that Chad and Lori claimed that Kay Woodcock was possessed by a demon named Rhonda and that she was dark. That would have put her on their hit list. I've wondered how many other people would have been murdered if they hadn't been stopped. They were on a roll, and neither one of them had the slightest remorse for murdering their spouses and Lori's children. I think their list was getting longer.

Lindsey Blake asked Hart if he had seen anything in all of the many text messages and emails with Chad ever saying anything about divorcing Tammy, and he said no. That was interesting because Chad talked a lot about his and Lori's future together without Tammy, and how was that going to happen if Tammy were still alive?

Chad goes on to say permanent change is coming and talking about his future marriage with Lori, he says: "That is the plan and my greatest desire."

That statement alone and certainly all of Chad's statements together, make it clear that Chad was in charge. Everyone was still alive when he said those things. Not long after making those statements, Chad and Lori were married on a beach in Kauai.

We get a better picture of Chad and Lori's relationship through Hart's testimony. We hear Lori actually manipulating Chad to kill Tammy so they can be together. Lori tells Chad she is frustrated being in love with a married man and that he should just move on with his life without her. She said: "I can't take it anymore. I feel so trapped. I'm sorry."

In all of those messages, divorce is never mentioned, and with that fact, in the omission of the idea of divorce, it becomes obvious that Chad and Lori together had a plan to murder Tammy. It was obvious to me what she was doing. Even though they never said the words out loud or in any text that I saw. Chad was taking his time, waiting for just the right moment to murder Tammy, and Lori was getting impatient. This gives us a clear picture of who Lori was and how manipulative and coldhearted she was to get what she wanted.

It was the same with Tylee and JJ. No mention of actual murder, but they alluded to it. When Prior pushed Hart on this issue, Hart replied, "Contextually that's the meaning of those texts. The dark number provided the justification to kill."

I could tell that Hart feels like Melanie Gibb is complicit in some way of the murders of JJ, Tylee, and Tammy. He brought her up while Prior was cross-examining saying she taught classes about light and dark and portals. I was wondering where she taught those classes and he quickly cleared that up saying by "classes" he meant podcasts. So Melanie Gibb was doing podcasts, espousing the same dangerous, supposedly religious garbage Chad was.

Agent Hart turned out to be unflappable in Prior's cross-examination, which gave more credibility to the prosecution and police and less to the defense.

MONDAY, APRIL 22, 2024,
"A Dark Number Provided the Justification for Killing"

Interesting day in court today. We heard the rest of Agent Hart's testimony. He went through more of Chad and Lori's texts. The obvious point the prosecution wanted to get across is that Chad was in love with Lori and had no more use for his wife Tammy. I won't subject you to all of it. There were tens of thousands of texts.

Here is part of the text stream:

CHAD TO LORI: *"I can't take much more. I feel so trapped."*
LORI TO CHAD: *"I can't take it anymore. I'm sorry."*

It goes on like that and the defense made the point that Chad and Lori talk about a time coming soon when all will be resolved and they can be together and they don't mention divorce. How are things going to be resolved then?

In the above text from Lori to Chad, she is telling him that she is done. She can't take the stress of being in love with a married man who doesn't seem to be able to leave his wife. She tells him to move on with his life. I think she is pressuring him to murder Tammy. She knows she has a hold on Chad and that Chad can't live without her, so she is threatening him, saying to move on without her. About two months later Tammy is dead.

It's another layer peeled off the onion or another piece of the puzzle. There are no texts that I have seen that mention murder, but Hart's testimony combined with all of the other evidence brings me to the conclusion that Chad murdered Tammy, and we already know Lori was found guilty of conspiring to murder her. We'll have to wait and see what this jury thinks of it all.

John Prior's cross-examination of Hart was the most interesting part of Hart's testimony. Prior was trying to rattle him, and Hart was obviously one step ahead of Prior the whole time, rattling off dates and quoting text messages off the top of his head.

When asked by Prior if there were any texts that mentioned killing the kids, Hart replied: "There are texts alluding to killing the kids," and "A dark number provided the justification for killing."

The jury may not know yet how important that statement is, but I think they will by the time the trial is over. The whole point of Chad's light and dark scale is that once you hit a certain level of darkness, he said it was 6.0, the only way to save the soul and release the zombie who had inhabited the body was to kill the body. We'll hear more about that in future testimony, and we'll hear Lori asking Chad if each of the victims had reached that level of darkness.

When I was in the jury box, I took that to mean, can we kill them yet? There are some things I think a person would only catch if they were in the courtroom for both trials.

The next witness for the prosecution was JJ's babysitter, Sidney Schenk. She seemed to me to be an innocent young woman with nothing to gain or nothing to lose, and that makes her more credible to me than some other witnesses. She testified that Lori told her that her husband Charles had died of a heart attack and that Tylee was a student at BYU, Idaho. Schenk babysat JJ after Tylee had been murdered. The point the prosecution wanted to make was obvious: Lori was a liar.

Prior upset people in the gallery when he cross-examined Schenk. He tried to make JJ look like a monster. He asked Schenk questions about JJ's behavior. We know JJ's behavior was bad during this time. He had autism, they had done away with his sister who he was extremely attached to and who was his primary caregiver, quit giving him his badly needed medication, and got rid of his dog he loved. All of this of course would serve to move him further down on Chad's dark list. And anyway, does anyone think bad behavior justifies murdering a child?

The next witness for the prosecution was Madison School Principal Dr. David Wilson who testified that Lori also told him that Charles had died of a heart attack. JJ's last day of school was September 21, 2019. When Lori disenrolled JJ, Dr. Wilson offered to forward JJ's records to whatever school he would be attending. She told him that wasn't necessary as JJ would be homeschooled.

Next, we heard from Guen Hill, the records keeper at BYU, Idaho who testified that there was no record of Tylee ever attending BYU, Idaho or even applying for admission.

When Lori's son Colby Ryan took the stand, my heart skipped a beat. His testimony in Lori's trial was extremely emotional and hard to listen to. In Lori's trial they played a recording of his phone call to his mother in jail. By the time of that call, his brother and sister's remains had been found. Lori was brutally unaffected by Colby's obvious anguish. I can't possibly imagine how Colby must feel, but today, a year later, he was still in tears through much of his testimony.

Colby was another person who Lori lied to about how Charles died. I've struggled trying to understand how Lori thought she would get away with telling people Charles died of a heart attack. The only conclusion I can come to is that she has been so manipulative her whole life that she gets some kind of satisfaction telling the lie because she can make people believe it in the moment.

She didn't even tell Colby when she moved to Rexburg. You would think that would have come up since they talked a lot. Colby was also used to texting back and forth with

Tylee almost daily. After Tylee was murdered, he continued to get texts he at first thought were from Tylee. The texts sounded different to Colby, though, and he knew something was wrong.

At first, he thought Tylee was sick or unhappy, but he became suspicious that it wasn't Tylee replying at all. The last actual conversation Colby had with Tylee was on September 8, 2019, when Tylee was in Yellowstone on the last day she was alive. A little over two months later he was contacted by Gilbert police when they were searching for Tylee and JJ.

Colby and Lori's relationship is a little confusing to me. I get the idea that Colby was dependent on his mom, even as an adult. It seems like he was constantly struggling financially and regularly received money, from Lori through Cash App. He testified that Lori sent him money and it turns out that some of that money is from the social security death benefit Tylee and JJ were receiving for the deaths of their respective fathers. Colby must have been shocked to discover later that some of that money came after Tylee and JJ had been murdered.

I'm not sure why Lori didn't bother to tell Colby when she moved to Rexburg. Apparently, she lied a lot to him and avoided confrontation with him. Maybe because he would have been one of the few to hold her to account. She knew he wouldn't fall for any of her crazy religious beliefs and would have pushed back. And I certainly think Colby wouldn't have supported her idea of killing people to save their souls. It wasn't until December 2019 that Colby found out that Lori and Chad were married and the kids were missing. This is when Colby does confront his mom and push back on her beliefs.

The next thing Colby said struck me as odd. He said Lori avoided confrontation and she could be persuaded. He didn't say that in Lori's trial, and I don't think it's true. To me she seems to be very much in charge and manipulative to the point where confrontation is sometimes the result. It's either you go along with Lori, or she will confront you aggressively.

So my guess is that he just threw that in to reinforce the argument that Chad was in charge. I don't think he needed to do that, but who can blame him?

In Prior's cross-examination, he tried to get Colby to say Lori was manipulative and in charge, but Colby countered that argument.

Next to take the stand was David Warwick. Questioning him was prosecutor Rocky Wixom. Prosecutors and defense attorneys all seem to have their own style or flair. Lindsey Blake wears different shoes every day. She questions witnesses with a quiet determination. Rob Wood is thoughtful and thorough and in no way flamboyant. Ingrid Beatty is authoritative yet human. John Prior goes to extremes to relate to the jury and is unafraid to insult people. When Rocky Wixom questions a witness, he appears to be deep in thought, looking down at his notes for what seems like a long time. Then he'll raise his arms as if the question has finally formed in his mind and ask the question. That served to make the question seem terribly important, so by the time he asked it, he had everyone's attention.

David Warwick is presently Melanie Gibb's husband. During the time he was testifying, he was her boyfriend. He was at Lori's apartment along with Gibb on the night JJ was murdered. He and Gibb both claim they had no idea that JJ was murdered, but I am skeptical about that to this day. Maybe it's true, but that wouldn't take all of his guilt away in my mind.

Warwick claims to be a general contractor, but he and Gibb both are part of a circle of people who promote ideas like energy healing, the end of days, prophets, the 144,000, prepping, and visions. He would do "firesides" and give speeches. Chad even tried to get him to cowrite a book, but for reasons I haven't heard, Warwick declined. Chad and Warwick had a plan for Chad's property to be a tent city at the second coming, but were unable for some reason to get others to go along with the idea.

Warwick was associated with other people with dangerous beliefs like John Miller, Julie Rowe, and Thom Harrison. While these people were not part of Chad's inner circle like Warwick was, they were part of the same manipulative belief system and were taking advantage of gullible people for their own personal gain, abusing their agency within the Mormon Church.

For all of the reasons I talk about earlier in this book, that makes them dangerous. The other reason I am suspicious is that Warwick and Gibb got married after all of this happened. Could they have done it so they wouldn't have to testify against each other? The law states that a married person does not have to testify against his or her spouse. And guess what? They live in different states. Gibb lives in Arizona and Warwick lives in Idaho. They hardly ever even see each other.

On the night JJ was murdered they were doing a podcast about prepping and visions and all of that. Warwick says he tried to interact with JJ that evening, but JJ didn't seem to want to have anything to do with him, so he gave up. He made a point of saying that in both trials, and I have to ask myself why he felt the need to throw that in. Was it to make JJ look bad, or was it to make himself seem like a good guy? It could serve either or both purposes, but I didn't think of him as credible enough to take anything he said too seriously.

Another aspect I find telling is that both Warwick and Gibb testified in Lori's trial that they slept in separate bedrooms at Lori's apartment. In this trial they say they shared a bedroom. I'm not sure if anyone else caught that. It matters for two reasons: The obvious one is that it speaks to their honesty, but there were three bedrooms in Lori's apartment—Lori's room,

JJ's room, and Tylee's room. Last year we were told that one of them slept in JJ's room and the other in Tylee's. JJ slept with Lori. If they were sleeping together, was JJ in his own room or Lori's? Gibb already testified that Warwick had a terrible nightmare that night and that she tried to wake Lori so Lori could call Chad over to give Warwick a blessing. Lori's door was locked, and they got no answer, even though they say they pounded on it.

The point I'm making is that it all just adds up to a bunch of confusion, and now we know they lied under oath either in Lori's trial or this one. The inner circle is looking more guilty to me. These people are frauds, and there are more of them out there right now taking advantage of people who are looking for answers where there are no answers, at least none we are meant to have.

Warwick's description of the night JJ was murdered is very bizarre. I already wrote about his nightmare and the fact that Lori told him JJ was off the rails that night. Lori, Melanie Gibb, Zulema Pastenes, Melani Boudreaux, and Warwick were the only people in Lori's apartment that night until Alex showed up with JJ. Tylee had already been murdered and buried in Chad's backyard. Melanie Gibb and Warwick spent the night at Lori's.

They were doing a podcast about the 144,000, past lives, the idea that Zulema had power over the elements and so on. The next morning Lori was talking fast and was nervous. Lori's explanation about JJ's behavior and that Alex had to come get him in the middle of the night was unbelievable, and Warwick claims that he didn't believe her. He gave his reasons. He said there was a crown molding on the top of the cabinets that JJ had supposedly climbed up on and that if JJ had climbed up on the cabinets, that crown molding would have been disturbed. I don't think that's necessarily true. It made me think Warwick was trying to find ways of establishing his credibility. It didn't. When Chad showed up the next morning, he told Warwick that he would assist in gathering the 144,000 and that Tammy would die and Lori would be Chad's wife.

In Prior's cross-examination of Warwick, he tries to expose Warwick. He asks Warwick about his beliefs in visions, prepping, and concepts like energy healing. Warwick claims to believe it all, and I think he has to claim that because he has made a life for himself espousing those things. He also claimed to not have believed Chad.

Tuesday, April 23, 2024,
The Seven Gatherers

Prior continues his cross-examination of David Warwick. Prior asked Warwick for the second time about the "seven gatherers." Warwick claims to have no knowledge of it, but Prior is digging for something. I couldn't find anything referring to the seven gatherers so my guess is that it is the inner circle of Chad, Lori, David Warwick, Melanie Gibb, Melani Boudreaux, Zulema Pastenes, and Alex Cox. No wonder he didn't admit to having any knowledge, but I did get the sense that Warwick was lying about that.

Warwick also said that Chad had told him that Tammy was healthy, but he had a vision that Tammy would pass. Melanie Gibb and David Warwick married in December 2020. They had known each other for six or eight years, so why did they wait until that date to get married? In December 2020 Tylee and JJ's remains had been found and Tammy and Charles were dead. The police had been all over the case looking for the missing children, exhuming Tammy's body, and putting all the pressure the law would allow on Lori and Chad.

Could Gibb and Warwick have been scared about their part in everything? I would certainly think so. Warwick testified that as soon as he and Gibb got married, he took her to a "Call to Zion" camp and that made me think to myself, oh yeah, he's all in on these beliefs that Chad and Lori are espousing. They are frauds through and through.

He went on to testify: "I've never heard of light and dark" and "I've never heard her teach."

Referring to Gibb. If this were a boxing match, I would give this round to the prosecution, and my guess is that it would be unanimous.

Still, Warwick has not been charged with any crimes in this case. Maybe if Prior keeps digging, evidence will rise to the surface that will not be ignored.

When Prior finally gave up on David Warwick, the next witness called by the prosecution was Brandon Boudreaux. Brandon's testimony is super interesting to me because he was lucky enough to survive when no one else did. He's the victim of serial killers who lived to tell the tale. I wrote about Brandon in chapter 11, but I will add to that here because it's important testimony.

At the time of the attempted murder of Brandon, he was married to Melani Boudreaux, who is Lori's niece. Melani's mother, Stacey, who was Lori's older sister, died when Melani was a child, and Melani and Lori were close. Lori was like an older sister to her. Brandon's son, who I won't name, was close to JJ and Tylee. Brandon and Charles were also close. Brandon said Melani went to the temple daily as did Lori, which was excessive, and Brandon was not welcome to join her. When Lori and Melani were off on their trip to Missouri, Charles and JJ came to Brandon's house often.

Brandon and Melani have since divorced, and Melani is now Melani Pawlowski having remarried to Ian Pawlowski.

The divorce was contentious. Melani was right behind Lori going down Lori's path. She was trying to take everything from Brandon, including his rights as a father. She accused Brandon of being gay, which would have hurt him in the Mormon Church and, in that part of Idaho, might have even hurt his ability to keep his children. Brandon was fighting back, at first trying to reason with Melani and save their marriage. When that became hopeless, he fought for custody of their children. Brandon's story is just like Charles's story except when Alex shot at Brandon, he missed.

In chapter 11 I wrote about the night the children were in Brandon's custody, Melani and Alex showed up at Brandon's father's house that night. Melani beat on the door, trying to get to her kids who she claimed were being mistreated by Brandon. Brandon wasn't there, and it scared Brandon's father, and he called the police.

When police arrived, they confronted Melani in the front yard and asked her why she was breaking the judge's order to stay away. She argued with them and tried to manipulate them into thinking her children were in danger and she was a good mom. It appears in the bodycam video I have seen of this event that this was not the first encounter they had with Melani and they weren't buying her story. I don't think Melani was as skillful as Lori at manipulating people, although she was doing her best to follow in her aunt's footsteps.

What the police didn't know at first is that Alex was sitting in his truck a few feet away. When police did see him, they questioned him and asked why he was there. At the time they wouldn't have known Alex was a cold-blooded killer, but it's bone chilling to think what might have happened if Brandon had been home and if the police hadn't been called.

Why was Alex there? Was there a plan to murder Brandon that night? Would they have done that with the kids there?

Were they planning to murder Brandon and kidnap the children? I can't say for sure that they were planning to murder Brandon that night, but I am pretty sure Alex was there to take the children from him using force if necessary.

That opens up other questions for me. What was the plan for the children? Would they have been in danger? Would Chad have eventually decided they were in the way and put them on his dark scale? Would Melani have taken things as far as Lori? She was extremely self-centered and self-serving, but I don't know if she was quite on Lori's level. She did, however, follow Chad and his beliefs to an extreme. More on Melani Boudreaux when she testifies on May 6.

Even more bone chilling is what happened to Brandon a short time later. On October 2, 2019, Brandon had taken his kids to school and stopped off at the gym on his way home. Melani, of course, knew where Brandon had moved to since they shared custody of their children. He had just moved with his kids into a rental house in Gilbert, Arizona. I've thought a lot about what happened that morning, trying to understand how it all happened. It was the event that spurred an investigation that finally led to where we are now. What started out as an investigation into the attempted shooting of Brandon turned into a search for the missing children.

Brandon repeated the testimony I heard in the Lori Vallow Daybell trial and that I wrote about in chapter 11. On the morning of October 2, Brandon slowed his Tesla to a stop before turning left on the street his house was on and then immediately began to turn right into his driveway. As he turned left, he noticed a green Jeep parked directly in front of but across the street from his house facing the wrong direction. As he turned right to pull into his driveway, he noticed a rifle barrel pointing out the back window of the Jeep. Just as he noticed it, the rifle went off and his driver side window exploded.

Thinking quickly Brandon aborted his turn into his driveway and sped off. A few seconds later he could see the Jeep coming up behind him, and a few seconds after that the Jeep thankfully turned off exiting the neighborhood. Brandon pulled off the road shaken and called 911.

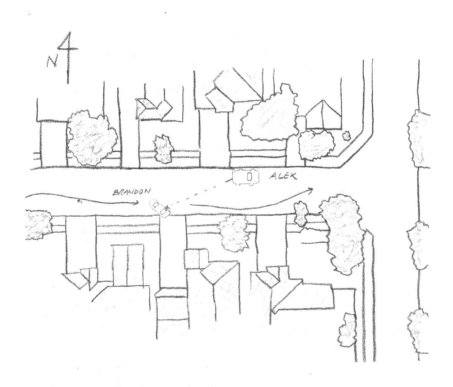

My sketch of how Alex shot at Brandon.

I watched two hours of bodycam footage when the police showed up at Brandon's house. At first Brandon didn't seem to have any idea who the shooter was, but by the time the police were done questioning him, Brandon not only recognized the Jeep, he also identified the lone driver. It was Alex Cox. I think he was putting two and two together and realizing it was his own wife who was trying to have him killed.

Things have changed a lot since the days of John Dillinger, Pretty Boy Floyd, and Bonnie and Clyde Barrow, but I don't think Melani Boudreaux, Alex Cox, Lori Vallow Daybell, and Chad Daybell realized it. The cops now have, among other technology, a license plate reader system or LPR. They were quickly able to use LPR to track Alex's trip to and from Rexburg, and with that they quickly tracked down Tylee's Jeep in Rexburg. Charles Vallow had originally bought the Jeep for Tylee, and she was the person the Jeep was registered to. Brandon had been Charles's insurance agent, so Brandon happened to have the VIN for the Jeep, which he also gave to police. They seized the Jeep and processed it for evidence. They found gunshot residue around the back window and Alex's fingerprints and DNA.

Brandon had something else that ties everything in this case to Chad. He had emails that he got from Charles before Charles was murdered. Remember, Lori had used Charles's computer to send emails to Chad, and Charles found the emails. The emails were between Chad and Lori, and in them Chad declared that Brandon was dark. Everyone who was murdered or who they attempted to murder was on Chad's dark scale.

On June 9, 2020, the police in Rexburg called Brandon to tell him Tylee and JJ's remains had been found in Chad's backyard. They needed Brandon to come identify the remains. On June 11 Brandon made the sad trip and did the identification.

Witnesses never fail to show emotion when testifying about JJ and Tylee, and Brandon was no exception. I think most of the courtroom was in tears at this point. In his cross-examination I thought Prior was uncharacteristically civilized. I guess he thought he had nothing to gain by badgering this particular witness, and it would have been hard to dispute anything Brandon had testified to.

According to Gilbert Police Officer Ryan Pillar's testimony, police were surveilling Alex until he died on December 12, 2019. Officer Pillar had flown to Rexburg to process the Jeep used in the attempted shooting of Brandon. By this time the investigation had changed its priority to finding the missing JJ and Tylee.

Alex was busy screwing everything up before he died. Just a week after his attempted shooting of Brandon, he was back in action going after Tammy in her driveway. Officer Pillar added to what I wrote about the attempt to murder Tammy in chapter 12.

We already know Tammy was coming home from work after stopping at the grocery store, and it was getting dark out as she pulled into her driveway. This would have been after Tylee and JJ had been buried in her backyard and after Charles had been murdered.

Of course, Tammy didn't know about any of this. She stepped out of her car, opened the back door, and grabbed the bag of groceries she was going to prepare for dinner that evening. As she turned away from the car with the groceries in her arms, she was confronted by a man dressed in camo with a black facemask on.

According to Officer Pillar the man was wearing a gillie suit. He explained that a gillie suit is something that would be worn by someone who planned to hide in the bushes. You've probably seen it in the movies. It would look like weeds and leaves. This strengthens the argument that Alex planned to shoot Tammy from a distance. It would have been impossible to identify him in that suit, even from a few feet away. Before she could even comprehend what was happening, the man shot twice.

We now know the man was Alex and he somehow missed from that short distance. Last year in court I remember seeing a text from Lori to Chad saying Alex could f*** up anything.

After shooting, the man ran off around the back of the house and disappeared.

We later listened to Emma's husband Joseph Murray testify for the defense on May 17 that he witnessed the incident from his house across the street and he quickly called 911. Shortly after that Tammy called 911, and we heard the recording of the call in court today. Tammy thought it must have been a paintball gun and she said: "Nothing came out so I don't think it was loaded. They went out and looked and he was long gone."

Both Tammy and her son-in-law gave police a description of the shooter, but they were unable to find him. If they had been able to find him, they would have found Alex Cox with an AR-15 fitted with a silencer. This incident is another one of the times police came close, but they had no idea what they were even looking for yet.

Alex's shot at Brandon came so close to hitting him in the head that I have no doubt that Alex wanted to hit him. Only the trim on the top of the driver's side window saved Brandon and Brandon's car was moving. How he could have missed hitting Tammy from what must have been around six feet is harder to understand. And Tammy was just standing there in shock. Maybe his heart wasn't in it? Maybe he was getting tired of killing. Maybe he was starting to realize what he was doing for Chad and Lori and I also think Melani Boudreaux wasn't right. We'll never know for sure because Alex died shortly after he successfully helped Chad kill Tammy in bed ten days later.

On the morning of October 19, 2019, Fremont County Coroner Brenda Dye was called to 202N 1900E, Rexburg, Idaho. There had been an unattended death, and the coroner was required to declare a cause of death. The legal meaning of an unattended death is a death where no doctor is involved. It could be an accidental death or a sudden heart attack or anything like that where a doctor would not have been present.

I'm going to pause here and tell you about something extremely telling I saw in court today. I said before that I sat about ten feet away from Chad and his attorney, John Prior. When I sat down before court this morning, Chad was sitting by himself looking at pictures on John Prior's computer. I could plainly see they were the coroner's pictures of Tammy's corpse. Some of them were the same horrendous pictures I had to look at in the Lori Vallow Daybell trial, and some of them were pictures that I had not seen before.

I will tell you that these pictures are extremely hard to look at even for a complete stranger. I am very hesitant to describe them to you out of respect for her family, but just like Tylee and JJ, you need to know what was done to poor, unexpecting Tammy at the hands of her murderous husband and Alex Cox.

The pictures Chad was looking at in court showed Tammy's dead body lying on her back on the bed, pink foam coming out of her mouth. They showed Tammy's back side where lividity had set in. Lividity was explained later in court. It is blood settling by the force of gravity after the heart quits pumping. It's important because it tells the position a body is in after death and it gives an indication of how long the body was in that position. Anyway, you get an idea of what Chad was seeing. I watched his face for any sign of emotion, but there was none and I mean absolutely none. He just continued to browse through the pictures. I was shocked that he could even look at them.

Some of those pictures were later shown to the jury while the coroner was on the stand. The monitors were faced away from the gallery so we wouldn't be able to see what was on them. This time as Chad looked at the pictures along with the jury, he couldn't seem to control his emotions. He was visibly crying, although I couldn't see actual tears, and John Prior made a show of handing him a box of Kleenex.

Ever since the conclusion of the Lori Vallow Daybell trial, I have had no doubt about Chad's guilt. If I did have even one molecule of doubt, it was wiped out this morning. I don't think anyone else in that courtroom noticed what I noticed, but I wish the jury could have seen what I saw. That one moment was more telling than any of the evidence the jury will see and would have certainly meant the death penalty for Chad.

But on the morning of Tammy's death, the coroner, Brenda Dye, pronounced Tammy's death as natural causes. She had looked at Tammy's body, the room she died in, and listened to Chad's explanation of what happened. She talked to Chad and Tammy's son Garth who was living with his parents. Garth had been called in by Chad in the morning to help him get Tammy's body back on the bed. Chad claimed that she had slipped out of bed in the morning, waking him. We know her body had lain on its back for hours because of the lividity, and according to Brenda Dye, Tammy had rigor mortis and her body was cold by the time she got there, also indicating that Tammy had been dead for hours.

Chad also claimed that Tammy had been very sick the night before, throwing up in the bathroom. She refused his offer to take her to the doctor.

Still, Dye believed Chad's story. I felt sorry for Dye on the stand. She had only been a coroner for a short time when she was called to Chad and Tammy's house that morning. Chad seemed to her to be distraught, unable to control his sobs. She didn't know anything about the death of Charles, the attempted murder of Brandon, or the missing children. She made a mistake. I wish she would have just said that in those words on the stand.

Given the fact that she didn't know about any of Chad's crimes, I think it was an understandable mistake. I also don't think she was the only one who made that mistake that morning. It was her sole responsibility as coroner to declare that it was a natural death, but there were other police officers at the scene, and surely, they would have argued with her if they felt she was wrong. I think it would have been just too hard to believe that a husband and his cohorts would have murdered her, given the limited knowledge they had.

It did not, however, take long for them to become suspicious. Once the police started gathering more information, they decided to exhume Tammy's body and have an autopsy performed by a medical examiner.

Chad had Tammy's funeral only three days after she died, and she was buried in Utah. The family couldn't understand why it had to happen so fast and why she would be buried in Utah. I think Chad thought her body would be less likely to be exhumed if it were buried in another state. And I think he wanted her buried quickly because he was afraid the coroner would change her mind and call for an autopsy.

Dr. Christensen, the medical examiner, came to a completely different conclusion on cause of death. To Coroner Dye's credit, she attended the autopsy. Dr. Christensen found Tammy's stomach full. How could that be if she had been throwing up the night before? He found that all of her organs were healthy except for her lungs. He found bruises on her chest and arms. He said the bruising was consistent with someone holding her down. He took sections of the bruises and concluded that they happened at the time of her death.

Wednesday, April 24, 2024,
What Really Happened to Tammy?

More cross-examination of Coroner Dye by Prior. She explained more about her decision not to have an autopsy on Tammy's body. Fremont County does not employ their own medical examiner and autopsies are expensive. This is inexcusable to me. If the county budget came into the decision of whether or not to have Tammy's body autopsied, the cost of that budgetary decision is immeasurable.

Tylee and JJ were missing at the time, and Larry and Kay Woodcock, the community of Rexburg, the Rexburg police, the FBI, and many people around the world were looking for them. What trajectory would the investigation have taken if they had known at that time that Tammy had been murdered? Chad would have been the main suspect. Alex would have been quickly implicated. Chad and Alex's association with Lori and the kids would have been discovered.

From there, I'm sure search warrants would have been issued for Chad's home and property. It's likely that the search for JJ and Tylee would have ended much more quickly than it did. The outcome would have been the same, but how many days of just not knowing, how many vigils, how many man hours, and how many candles lit by people who hoped so deeply to find the children alive could have been avoided?

More offensive questioning by Prior as he continued to ask why the family had not been notified when "you were digging their mother out of the ground." The police did the exhumation quietly early in the morning of December 11, 2019. The autopsy was done quickly, and her body was reburied later that day.

There was a lot of questioning about Tammy's homeopathic medications found in her bedroom. The argument was made by Prior that Tammy didn't like going to the doctor, preferring natural remedies. Chad had stated to police on the morning of Tammy's death that he tried to get her to go to the doctor, but Tammy chose to try to cure herself. There were herbal oils and natural medications on her bedside table. I think Chad may have staged those items to strengthen his argument that he tried to get Tammy to go to the doctor.

We then briefly heard from three more witnesses who testified about Tammy's fitness. They all said Tammy was very fit. She was extremely energetic at work, taking on all kinds of extra duties. On the day before Tammy died, no one saw any change in her. She and Emma did a fitness class together called High Fitness, which included burpees, lunges, and other high-intensity movements. Tammy was always able to keep up and was in a great physical condition.

What really did happen to Tammy on the night of October 18, 2019? From all the evidence I have heard in two trials and all of the conversations I have had with people who knew Tammy and the police involved in the investigation, I think most of what happened is clear. Chad hatched a plan to have Alex come to his house late that night after Tammy went to bed. The only other person living in the house was Chad and Tammy's adult son Garth, and he would be working until 1:00 a.m.

From cell phone information gathered by the FBI, we know that Alex was moving toward Chad's house that night and that he turned his phone off just down the street. Chad most likely held Tammy while Alex asphyxiated her. When they were done, Alex left, turning his phone back on on his way home.

I wonder if anyone else helped to hold Tammy down. It was just that simple. Garth came home sometime shortly after 1:00 a.m. and probably went straight to bed. His bedroom was directly across the narrow hallway. Chad waited until morning and called 911 saying Tammy had passed while he was sleeping.

When police became suspicious, they exhumed Tammy and had an autopsy performed on her body. Police had tried to talk to Emma, her husband Joseph, and Garth, but they were uncooperative. The autopsy was performed quickly, and

Tammy's body was back in its grave on the same day. Emma especially doesn't like the fact that the police exhumed Tammy, but Tammy's aunt, sister, and brother understand and support the police and what they felt they had to do.

In his cross-examination, Prior again found a way to insult people, asking if Tammy was really all that fit: "After all, she wasn't petite, was she?"

Eleven days into the trial, it is evident to me that Prior isn't winning. He is throwing darts, hoping to cast some doubt in at least one juror's mind, but he is missing badly and making enemies in the process.

The next witness called by the prosecution was Fremont County Detective Bruce Mattingly. He brought up something we did not hear about in Lori Vallow Daybell's trial. Tammy wore a Fitbit. The Fitbit was conveniently missing the morning Tammy died and has never been recovered. The information gathered by the Fitbit was, however, retrieved by police, and it was active all the way up until the night of Tammy's death. Is a jury supposed to believe the missing fitness tracker is just another of many coincidences? I don't see how they could.

Tammy had two life insurance policies worth $430K through her work, and both have been paid out to Chad Daybell.

Madison County Detective Vince Kaaiakamanu was next up. He testified about the attempted shooting of Tammy on October 9, 2019. There is a debate about whether it was a real rifle or a paintball gun. It's all kind of beside the point to me, but a lot of time was spent on this debate. What difference does it make? Tammy didn't die that night, but she did die ten days later.

After Lori Vallow Daybell's trial when I met with the prosecution, they asked me about my opinion as a juror in that case, what I thought about this particular part of their case. I told them that in Idaho we aren't all that impressed with seeing a rifle. In that trial, they brought the rifle they claimed Alex shot at Tammy with into court and presented it to the jury. My impression was that they thought that would influence the jury to decide it must have been an attempted shooting of Tammy using the rifle they were showing us. This time, in the Chad Daybell case they just showed pictures of the rifle.

Detective Kaaiakamanu testified that Alex Cox's phone was in the area, so we can say it was probably Alex who shot at Tammy.

Thursday, April 25, 2024,
More "Priorisms"

The prosecution continued questioning Detective Kaaiakamanu. He talked about Alex's email account under the name of homerjmaximus. We learned that Alex went to Sportsman's Warehouse and bought clothes and a mask identical to what Tammy described the shooter to be wearing when she was confronted in her driveway the next evening.

Alex also Googled a 2008 Dodge Dakota for info on penetrating the door and the windshield with a bullet. Tammy happened to drive a 2008 Dodge Dakota. In his cross-examination Prior tried to suggest that Chad actually drove that pickup. I can't imagine the jury falling for that since Tammy was the one who Alex shot at, not Chad.

We heard more damning testimony from the detective. On October 18, the night Tammy was murdered, Alex's phone was moving toward her house. It was turned off at around 11:00 p.m. when it was 2.6 miles from her house. It came back on at 7:00 a.m. again at 2.6 miles from her house. Still circumstantial, but we're getting to a point with the jury where they are going to start thinking there is no other conclusion to come to.

Chad was at home that night, Alex was obviously there with him, and Tammy was suffocated. They both went to great lengths to hide those facts. Add the fact that Chad and Lori were married in Hawaii two weeks later, and it becomes even more inevitable that the jury will find Chad guilty of murdering poor Tammy.

In his cross-examination, Prior did his best. I'm getting used to what I call "Priorisms": "W'uld that be fair? Okay, I'm sorry judge, right? I'll slow down."

So far at least, I would say the memories the jury will have about Prior's cross-examination of the prosecution's witnesses will be of those phrases more than any doubt he is trying to instill into their minds.

Next, we learned about Charles's email to Tammy from the Sugar-Salem School District technical director, Spencer Cook. On June 29, 2019, Tammy received an email on her work email from Charles. Cook had access to emails on the school computers and had handed this one from Charles over to police. In the email Charles tells Tammy about Chad and Lori's affair. Prior didn't bother to cross-examine this witness. What would the point have been?

Friday, April 26, 2024,
More Red Flags

The morning started with Steve Schultz on the stand. He was the director of the Springville, Utah, mortuary, and he picked up Tammy's body after the police were done with their investigation on the morning Tammy was murdered.

His testimony came off as a little creepy to me, but I guess that goes with the territory. I'm sure he takes his profession seriously and only has the best intentions. The point of his testimony is that he asked Chad if he wanted an autopsy. He told Chad he thought there should be one. He thought her death was unusual. He also told Chad it would be a good idea to find out what she died of. It could have been some kind of hereditary condition and knowing might help keep his kids from dying of the same thing.

I have a picture of Chad and Garth at Tammy's funeral. I can't use the picture because I don't have permission from the family. Chad and Garth are both standing next to Tammy's casket looking down at it. Behind Chad and Garth is Director Schultz. I'm not a body language expert, but Schultz is standing with his arms folded and an obvious scowl on his face as he looks at Chad's back. I find it very telling.

He went on to testify that the funeral was rushed by Chad, and that seemed to be a red flag to him. He had lived close to Chad before Chad moved his family to Idaho and knew him very well. He said Chad and his family were very good people, but the fact that Chad didn't want an autopsy and wanted a quick burial raised the red flags for him.

When he took Tammy's body to his funeral home and began to prepare her for the funeral, he said he examined her body before he dressed her because of those red flags, but he didn't find anything obviously suspicious.

The prosecution's case is beginning to get more interesting at this point, and I can see the jury paying close attention. They are visibly more attentive. Instead of sitting back and looking like some of them might be falling asleep, I see their heads going back and forth between the questioner and the witness.

It got even more interesting when Ron Arnold took the stand. I honestly wasn't sure what the significance of his testimony was, but he was entertaining. He testified about a piece of property he showed Chad, David Warwick, and Melanie Gibb the morning after JJ was murdered. He also told us that

Chad inquired about the possibility of putting a manufactured home on his current property. Apparently the idea was to pour a big slab of concrete over the area where Tylee was buried.

Prior was doing his typical thing, questioning witnesses, going on and on and asking questions in a circular way. I could see Arnold getting frustrated when Prior was asking him over and over about the property. When he asked more than once about the size of the property, Arnold replied: "You own it, you tell us how many acres it is." He then winked in the direction of prosecutor Ingrid Beatty.

In the gallery we are admonished every morning to keep a straight face. We aren't to show any emotion because that could influence the jury. I have to admit that before I could stop myself, I laughed out loud at that statement. That was the second time I had seen someone stand up to Prior. I described the first time when I was talking about his questioning of potential jurors.

Anyway, my guess would be that the point of this witness for the prosecution was to tie Chad to burying the kids in the backyard and maybe hoping to place a house over the graves. I don't know, but the memorable thing that happened will be Arnold's response. And I sure don't think that will favor the defense. I don't think Prior would want the jury to know that he took Chad's property as payment, and he now owns the house where the kids were buried and Tammy was murdered.

Arnold's wife, Whitney Arnold, was next to take the stand. She provided more circumstantial evidence that will bolster the prosecution's case. She talks about going to Chad's house to console him the morning Tammy was murdered. She found him unaffected and emotionless. She goes on to explain that she and her husband are close friends of Chad and Tammy. She was frustrated when just days later Chad brought Lori to their house to introduce her. She said Chad and Lori were very affectionate and that offended her.

She questioned Lori, and Lori said her husband died of a heart attack and they had seven kids. Seven kids didn't make sense to me. Even adding up her kids and Charles's kids, it doesn't add up to seven. I found out later that what does add up to seven is the seven kids she and Chad had in their prior probation when they were James and Elena. They supposedly had Kenneth, Melani, Jada, Jace, Jenny, Conner, and JJ. All of these supposed kids were above average. One was the high school quarterback and so forth, following the idea that they were all special in their prior probations. No underachievers.

The bishop of Chad and Tammy's ward, Craig Huff, testified that Chad had looked up Tammy's passwords for her church accounts about a week before she died. He also said that Chad told him: "She choked to death."

When Prior cross-examined him, we found out Chad was his executive secretary in the church. He went on to say that Chad was a humble man who loved working with children and that Chad was driven by writing his books. He also says Chad's books were nonfiction. I'm not sure if that means he believes Chad's books are true or if Chad told him his books are nonfiction. Unfortunately, I don't get to question the witnesses.

In Ingrid Beatty's redirect, Huff said he was shocked when he found out Chad remarried, and he is not sure whether or not he believes Chad now.

The last witness of the week would be Richard Garner, the Rexburg elementary school principal and Tammy's boss. We heard more about Tammy's good health. He said she ran a 5k and he was at the finish line when she crossed. She looked exactly like you would expect someone to look. She was a way above average employee, and she took on all kinds of extra duty assignments, always with a lot of energy. He was stunned when he heard about Tammy's death.

The people Tammy worked with were disappointed that she would be buried in Utah and on a workday, so they put a memorial together for her in Rexburg. Chad didn't help at all with that, and Huff thought that was strange.

SATURDAY, APRIL 27, 2024,
Memorial for Tylee and JJ

At 6:00 a.m. my wife and I and a fellow Lori Vallow Daybell juror hopped in our car and drove four hours to Idaho Falls. We had been waiting for this day. For us it would be a time of healing and an opportunity to take a break from the courtroom and visit openly with the people we had become associated with.

I am so thankful to Kay and Larry Woodcock for so selflessly thinking of all of the people who have been affected by these horrible murders. Even people like me who had no idea who any of them were before they were murdered. I am also thankful for people like Chad's brother Matt who attended and Lori's brother Adam and uncle Rex. These people could choose not to expose themselves, but they don't do that.

Rex and Adam even do a podcast about the lives of the victims and the survivors they call *Silver Linings*. Those two men are silver linings for me and a lot of other people, opening themselves up and talking freely about what happened. It was nice for me to meet Matt and have a chance to briefly chat. I'm sure he is hurting in ways I can't begin to comprehend.

Lori and Adam's cousin and Rex's niece Megan sang four songs, and I was moved by her voice. JJ's biological father, Todd, who is serving time in prison on drug charges called in, and we heard him talk about JJ and his desire to be a man worthy of making it to heaven to meet him someday.

Family photos at the memorial service. Photo by Susan Evans.

The reason JJ was cared for by his grandmother Kay and her husband Larry (who is as much of a grandfather to JJ as anyone could be, even though not biological) was that Todd and his wife, Mandy, were struggling with drug addiction and unable to care for him. Mandy passed away shortly after JJ and Tylee's bodies were found. According to her doctor, she died of a broken heart.

Anyway, I have hope for Todd. He has the opportunity in prison to get the drugs out of his system and clean up his act. He needs to be with those of us who are fighting this battle. And it is a battle, not only for justice, but for the future of all of our children. They are all our children. There is no designation of your children or my children. There are only our children, and we need to protect them. They are smaller than we are, weaker than we are, and less worldly than we are. They are totally dependent on adults to care for them and to protect them, and we are letting some of them down in ways that shame me.

Two things brought me to tears at the memorial. If you talk to anyone who knows me, the only time I have ever cried was when our kids were sick and in pain. Not for any reason other than that tears just don't come as easily to me as they do to most people.

When we walked into the Colonial Theatre, there were pictures and mementos of Tylee and JJ. The thing that unexpectedly brought me to tears was JJ's M&Ms jacket. It was a NASCAR jacket given to him by Kay and Larry, and he loved it. I have seen many pictures of him in it.

The next thing that got me was when Larry sat on the stage next to a picture of JJ and told stories. Even before he started to tell the stories, while Megan was singing, I was moved by Larry sitting there. In his face I saw what I have always seen. There is anguish, love, tenacity, and a fierceness that is becoming rare, but it's all there in Larry and he will never know how much I and others admire him for it.

One thing he said in his stories stuck to me. He talked about JJ's lack of fear, and he described it in this way. He said that if you challenged JJ, if you said he couldn't do something, it was like the old Southern saying: "Here, hold my beer and watch me."

I loved hearing him say that. That used to be how we were raised. To not be afraid. To take on challenges without fear. Unfortunately, it's different now. Kids are taught to be afraid. They are taught that there is no hope. They are taught that the opportunities people of my generation had are unavailable to them. That's a bunch of horse shit, but I hear it all the time, and it saddens me and worries me. It's a sham and a shame.

Life is good, our country is good. Nothing is all good, and nothing is all bad, but life is what you make of it. No one is going to do it for you, especially the government that only exists on what they take from you. If you happen to be from this generation and you happen to be reading this, don't let anything keep you from your dreams. Too much has been sacrificed, and you have too much to lose.

Every generation has had its challenges. My parents' generation had poverty as the norm and young men being sent to war without a choice. My generation had high interest rates, gas lines, inflation, poor working conditions, and violent protests. Your generation has high cost of education, inflation, and corrupt media, colleges, and politicians. So what? Work to change those things if you don't like them. Look for the opportunities those negative things might provide for you. They are out there; you just have to let someone hold your beer while you prove it to them and lead by example.

MONDAY, APRIL 29, 2024,
Who Else Was Alex in Contact With?

Most of the testimony today was given by FBI Agent Nicolas Ballance. We heard the same testimony in the Lori Vallow Daybell trial, and I'll just give you a recap here. I had a hard time staying awake through it both times.

The gist of it was that by using cell towers, law enforcement was able to tell where Alex, Chad, and Lori's phones were at given times. They could see that Alex was within three meters of where JJ was buried the day after he was murdered. The damning part for Chad and the part that ties Chad into the murders is that Alex and Lori and Chad were communicating during the time Alex was at Chad's and on his way to or from there. We went through similar evidence in the murder of Tylee and the attempted shooting of Tammy. They were able to access Alex's homerjmaximus@gmail.com account and use that to find communications with Chad and Lori.

One interesting and new piece of information was that Alex was also in contact with someone else at the time of JJ's murder. They didn't say who it was or make too much of it, but I would love to know who that was. Could it have been David Warwick or Melanie Gibb? Did the prosecution hold back that information to protect them? If that's the case, why bring it up at all? Is it a hint into the future? Are they hoping that by bringing it up, people will ask questions? I'm asking.

The prosecution knows Alex was communicating with someone besides Chad and Lori at the time of JJ's murder. They won't tell me who that was, but I think they know. Who was it, and were they aware of what Alex was up to?

The next two witnesses made an interesting point for the prosecution. They were mother and daughter, and both went to Tammy's funeral, walked through the viewing line, and spoke to Chad at different times. Chad told one of them that he and Tammy went to bed at 10:00 p.m., and he woke up at midnight when Tammy fell out of bed and she died right then. The other said Chad told her that he was upstairs, and he came down at 2:00 a.m. and found Tammy dead. She also said that Chad said Tammy was hard to live with and she found that odd.

Witnesses don't hear each other testify unless they have already done all of the testifying they are going to do, so they wouldn't have realized they were contradicting each other unless they were able to anticipate what the questions would be and discuss it beforehand.

In his cross-examination Prior asked if the witness knew the house had only a single story, so how could he have been upstairs? The prosecution didn't question that in their redirect. I found out after court was out for the day, from a friend of Tammy's, that they did have an office upstairs in a loft. I was frustrated with the prosecution in that moment. It seemed like an obvious opportunity to discredit the defense, so why weren't they taking advantage of it? I found out later in the trial that they were just being patient because it came up again in another witness's testimony.

Thursday, May 2, 2024,
Victims Find Their Voice

I have a habit of counting the jurors when they enter the courtroom in the morning. Today I noticed one was missing. That may seem like a small thing since there are six alternates. Yet I found the missing juror disconcerting. What if the missing juror was absent due to illness? What if that illness spread through the other jurors? There is so much at stake at this point.

Judge Boyce explained that the missing juror had to stand down indeed due to illness. I learned later from one of the bailiffs that the juror did everything he could to stick with it. However, he became so ill that the bailiffs finally had to not let him in the van. This points to how seriously the jurors take their duty. They know what is at stake. They have been sitting in court for weeks at this point. They have seen the anguish on the faces of the family members. They have heard most of the evidence against Chad.

I think by now at least a majority of the jurors, if not all of the jurors, think Chad is guilty, is a monster, and is a danger to society. I think by this point they want to make sure Chad doesn't go free.

A few days later a friend of mine came over and told me that it was his dad who was the sick juror. That is something I find strange yet good about Boise. As big as it's getting, it still feels like a small town. I constantly run into people I know or find a connection between people I am somehow associated with.

Kay Woodcock, JJ's grandmother, took the stand today. I have heard Kay speak about JJ in two trials, at one sentencing, and many times outside of court. It's always moving and emotional. She talks about JJ's relationship with his Paw Paw Larry and JJ's will to survive. JJ was drug affected when he was born and had to fight his way into this world and then fight to stay in it. He was also premature. His parents were unable to care for him, and Kay and Larry brought him home from the hospital with them. The story of JJ's short life and how his family came together for him is a story worth telling.

When Lori and Charles adopted JJ, Charles accepted JJ wholeheartedly, even though Lori and JJ were not related by blood. It could not have been easy. It was a huge commitment for Charles, but one he was willing to make. This points to the dichotomy of this story. There are so many good people doing good things. People who are willing to make sacrifices in their own lives to benefit others. That's most of us, right? We are the protector of children. Not many of us could look at a baby and not want to do whatever that baby needs. What JJ needed when he was a baby was a good, solid family to grow up in. He needed a mom, a dad, and siblings to watch out for him and help him thrive.

It certainly looked to Kay and Larry like that was the kind of family they were handing JJ off to. Lori was a caring, doting mother; Charles was a great provider and excellent role model. Tylee loved JJ and would be the best big sister anyone could hope for. It seemed to be the American ideal, but as we now know, something went horribly wrong, and some in JJ's family turned into monsters.

What was it that went wrong? We could say it was Chad. JJ's life was what we would hope it would be until Chad entered the picture. Chad had the crazy, dangerous, fanatical ideas. Something also had to be wrong with Lori though. Something no one detected until she started to believe the things Chad believed.

We know Lori was a little nuts before Chad came along, but not so nuts that she crossed lines that concerned people. Yeah, she was pushy, maybe a little overzealous in her religious beliefs, but still very capable of being a good mom. We've all known people like that. Something clicked in her. Something snapped in her mind. She became susceptible to the people who were using over-the-top religious beliefs for their own personal gain. It's the most unfortunate circumstance imaginable that Chad stepped in right at that moment when Lori was so susceptible.

Chad entering into Lori's world set in motion a chain of events that we couldn't imagine. Even the dangerous people who were using religion for their own selfish purposes would never have intended for Chad and Lori to take things as far as they did.

But that's what can happen, right? We have the benefit of looking back and seeing what religious zealotry can come to. And now that we know, we know who the dangerous people are. *They* know who they are too. I would think at least one of them would now come forward and loudly exclaim what the dangers are. But that's not who these people are. They will never make any sacrifice, no matter how small.

Fortunately, some of the victims are starting to find their voice. Some of the people who have been taken advantage of are coming forward, writing books of their own, speaking on podcasts and generally bringing light to the darkness.

In the process of writing this book, attending the trials, and doing my research, I have personally met four women who grew up in abusive situations and are just recently coming to terms with their situations. Three of them were Mormon, have written their books, and are doing podcasts. One is just beginning the process of writing her book.

Back to Kay's testimony. She explained why Charles felt he needed to change the beneficiary of his life insurance from Lori to Kay and what his directions were to Kay about how she was to use the money. He wanted to make sure that JJ was taken care of, and he wanted some of the money to go to his adult sons—the sons Lori treated so thoughtlessly after Charles died.

She went on to explain how she hacked Charles's computer and shared the information she found with police and how that instigated the search for the children.

After a brief cross-examination of Kay, dwelling mostly on where Lori and Charles had lived, the prosecution called Chad's mother to the stand. There are plenty of people who I feel sorry for in this case and Chad's mother, Sheila, is one of them. The poor woman was called to the stand to testify against her son in a triple murder trial. She really didn't have a lot to contribute. I think the point was that she would testify against her son. I'm sure she would rather not have, but what choice did she have? But, no tears, no plea for his life. She just answered the questions she was asked in a straightforward way.

Prosecutor Ingrid Beatty did the questioning. Beatty asked about what Lori had to tell Sheila about her marriage to Chad. Sheila stated that Lori told her she and Chad were married and that Lori's husband had died of a heart attack and that she had a daughter who had died. Lori didn't mention anything about having three children of her own.

In Prior's cross-examination, Sheila stated that Lori was charming and convincing, and that Chad was not gregarious. The most notable thing I got from her testimony was that she kept smiling over at Chad, but Chad would only look back at his mother when she happened to be looking away.

Heather Daybell, Chad's sister-in-law, was just the opposite. She has been called a pot stirrer, and I have to say she earned the moniker. Heather is married to Chad's brother Matt. She was raised Mormon and was a good, believing Mormon for most of her life. I have met Heather two or three times. She's always been nice, but declines when I ask her for an interview.

I do know she has left the Mormon Church for two reasons. Her son is gay. Of course, she loves her son and the fact that the Mormon Church can't find room for her gay son goes against her feelings that God loves everyone no matter their sexual orientation. She has become disillusioned and has come to the realization that nothing she can say or do is going to change the powers that be in the Mormon Church. Her voice as a woman is just not heard. Her husband Matt is still a member of the church.

The second reason is that Heather has known Chad ever since he was a teenager. She felt that she was not listened to when she voiced her concerns to the church about Chad early on when the children were missing. She feels like she wasn't listened to because she is a woman and Chad is a man. Heather is a strong woman, and the fact that men feel superior just because they happen to be men doesn't fly with Heather.

Rexburg PD Detective David Stubbs testified today. He explained to the jury a computer program called Cellebrite. There was so much information on the nine phones. The police couldn't possibly go through it all randomly, so Cellebrite somehow put it in an order that made it easier. It was another of those situations where it was hard to follow in spite of the witness's attempt to explain how it worked. The gist was that Cellebrite somehow boiled down the pertinent information so the police could go through it more quickly.

He went on to repeat what others had previously testified about the welfare check on JJ, which spurred the whole investigation and Lori's lies to police.

THURSDAY, MAY 3, 2024,
The Pursuit for Justice Begins

Continuing with Detective Stubbs. On November 27, 2019, the Rexburg PD obtained a no-knock search warrant for the three apartments and the garages associated with them on Pioneer Road in Rexburg. Detectives Stubbs, Hermosillo, and Kunsaitis showed up first at apartment 107, the apartment rented to Lori. The police were serious as they now had plenty of reason to be suspicious and concerned for Tylee and JJ and wasted no time entering the apartment.

Finding the door locked they immediately kicked the door in and entered the apartment. I described what they found in Lieutenant Hermosillo's testimony in court on April 10. This is when Detective Kunsaitis found the receipt for Lori's storage unit in the printer. They could see Lori had left in haste. Where were Lori, Chad, and Alex, and more importantly, where were Tylee and JJ? Why had Lori left in such a hurry?

The detectives were even more concerned, now fearing that something bad had happened to the children or at least that they might be in danger. Detective Hermosillo began to wonder what might have become of them. Might they already be dead at the hands of their mother, uncle, and Chad, who they now knew to be Lori's husband?

This is when they began to gather evidence that would later tie Chad into the murders of the children, leaving no doubt that he called for the murders and that, finally, over four years later would result in his death-penalty trial.

When they finished with Lori's apartment, they went to Melani Boudreaux's apartment at 175 Pioneer Road. There they found Brandon's credit cards and driver's license. Why Melani isn't being charged with conspiracy to commit murder for the attempted shooting of Brandon is a question I cannot yet answer. I'm hoping to get that answer at Lori's trial in Arizona.

The police now know Lori, Chad, Melani, and Alex had left the apartments in haste. They have evidence from the apartments, garages, and storage locker. What they don't have are the kids. This was the beginning of a search that lasted until June 9, 2020, and a pursuit for justice that lasted until May 2024. Detectives Hermosillo, Kunsaitis, Stubbs, and many others would see it through, relentlessly pursuing justice for JJ, Tylee, Tammy, and those who loved them.

As soon as they got the tip that Chad and Lori were in Hawaii, Detective Hermosillo was there with a search warrant for Lori's apartment and car at Princeville, Kauai. In the car they found a laptop belonging to the kids and email accounts belonging to Lori, which provide more key evidence. The accounts were Lollytimeforever and lori4style, and on them they found messages, searches, and locations. They found that Chad had looked up wind direction the day before Tylee was murdered. This was the search Emma claimed she had made on Chad's computer, saying she was an amateur meteorologist.

MONDAY, MAY 6, 2024,
Another Nail in the Coffin

First Melani and then Ian Pawlowski testified for the prosecution today. Melani walked into the courtroom flanked by two attorneys. I'm sure they were there to protect her, but my impression and I would bet other people's impressions were that it made her look guilty. Why did she feel the need to have attorneys with her? She hasn't been charged with anything.

A year ago, I listened to Melani testify in the Lori Vallow Daybell trial, and I have seen pictures of her since. She looked different to me today. Honestly, she looked kind of like a clown. Was she trying to be incognito? She had on Coke bottle-thick white-framed glasses. People wear all kinds of outlandish glasses these days, but these glasses I had never seen before. I wondered if she could see clearly through them.

She described her relationship with Chad and Lori. Remember Lori is her aunt, and I guess that makes Chad her uncle since he and Lori married, although she didn't meet Chad until November 18, 2019. That describes her biological and legal relationship, but her personal relationship is strange to say the least.

On the stand Melani admitted to being close to Chad and Lori and very much a part of their inner circle. Melani had rented an apartment right next to Lori's in Rexburg, although it doesn't sound like she spent much time there. The police were relentlessly looking for Tylee and JJ, and Melani, Lori, and Chad decided it would be better if Melani got away from Rexburg.

Melani described how Chad was the one with the gift of discernment and the leader of the group. She went on about Chad using a pendant or pendulum to get answers for people. She talked about castings and who would do them. Chad of course. He would lead a group of the inner circle in prayer to cast out demons. Chad was the one who knew where someone stood on his light or dark scale. Chad was the one who declared Charles, Tammy, JJ, and Tylee dark.

She said he got his ideas from the book *Visions of Glory.* She said she visited Lori in Rexburg in September 2019 and she didn't see Tylee or JJ. Seems like she would have wondered where they were since she spent several days there. She said Lori told her JJ was with a nanny and Tylee was attending college at BYU.

Melani went on to describe a trip she and Lori took to Missouri in late October 2019. After that they flew to Hawaii. Obviously, they were avoiding the police, but what's even more incriminating for Lori was that she never once called Tylee or JJ.

Here's where it gets even more sticky for Chad: Alex was supposed to have gone on this trip with them, but at the last minute, Chad said he had something he needed Alex's help with. Was it killing Tammy that Chad needed help with? Sure looks that way to me, and I'm sure to the jurors also.

When Lori and Melani finally returned to Rexburg in November, Melani didn't stay long. She said Detective Hermosillo wouldn't quit harassing her. I'm sure that's true. He was relentless in his search for JJ and Tylee, not knowing they were already dead and buried.

In Prior's cross-examination, he inadvertently added one more nail to Chad's coffin. When questioning Melani, she said the zombie idea came from Chad, meaning the idea that someone's body could be taken over by an evil spirit and that their soul had already moved on.

Ian Pawlowski's testimony was almost as damning for Chad. The prosecution played a recording. Listening to the recording I unbelievably heard Melani call Chad "daddy." Can this case possibly get any creepier? Chad would have been around fifty and Melani would have been in her thirties. That's just weird.

Later in the recording I heard Chad tell Melani: "He's not going to stop until he gets what he wants. You get out of his way."

Referring to Detective Hermosillo. He got that right! This was all new to me. We had not heard this in the Lori Vallow Daybell trial. It all not only ties Chad more into the murders, but it also plays really well for the prosecution. By the time the testimony phase of this trial is over, the jurors will have nothing but pride, respect, and sympathy for police officers like Lieutenant Hermosillo. To have to sit there and listen to people who they are already deciding are nothing, if not flaky, bad mouth the cops will not go over well for the defense.

Later in the recording Chad gives Ian and Melani a blessing. Remember, Ian is not part of Chad and Lori's inner circle and he was just getting to know these people Melani was associated with. In his blessing Chad says you are part of our "overall plan of our Lord and savior and latter days, moving mountains and changing rivers. I see you both all over the world in portals. You have known each other in the past . . . He is very pleased."

Chad goes on to say that Alex and Zulema, Chad and Lori, and Ian and Melani are the beginning of a new terrestrial order. The police are telestial. "The weakened will be possessed and we will have to save their souls."

I could go on, but you get the idea. Ian, I believe, was getting a little freaked out by Melani's aunt and uncle and their associates. He was a great witness because he is a person with firsthand knowledge about Chad, but never a part of his inner circle. He just happened to be in love with someone who was, and that gave him a firsthand view of what they were like. He's really the only one we get that from.

My Dilemma

"I'm going to ramble for a minute. Would that be fair?"

If you followed this trial, you get the full meaning of those two sentences. Even if you didn't follow the trial, you may have guessed that those words were spoken by John Prior. We're about halfway through this trial.

As a juror in the Lori Vallow Daybell trial, this is where it started to get to me. I didn't know it was happening at the time, but I was slowly losing my ability to control my thoughts. There are some differences for me comparing my experience in that trial to my experience in this trial. In the Lori Vallow Daybell trial, I had to spend about nine and a half hours a day getting to trial, being at the trial, and getting home from the trial. Typically, when I got home, I would have a short conversation with my wife about my day without going into specifics. As soon as we were done with that, we would do anything not having to do with Lori Vallow Daybell and her victims. Hikes, bike riding, catching up on work, games, whatever.

This time it's different. This time when the trial is over for the day, I usually do one of three things. I am interviewed by someone, I interview someone, or I come home and rehash what I heard in court and write about it.

What is the same is my lack of ability to control my thoughts. I go to sleep at night and wake up an hour or so later, either because of a nightmare that I need to interpret or because my mind is reeling with some thoughts that I need to include in this book.

So far, the nightmares have not been like night terrors I experienced that last year. The difference between what I experienced last year and what I have so far experienced this year is that I wasn't able to fully wake up after a night terror. I mean I wake up and tell myself it's just a dream, but the terror of it refuses to subside for a long while.

Anyway, my dream last night was just a standard nightmare, and all I needed to do was interpret it. Dreams have meanings, and we dream our dreams for a reason. When we sleep, our mind is uninhibited, and it goes where it wants. It seems there is more to it than that. Some people think our dreams are visions, and in a way, I guess they are. What I know for sure is that we dream our dreams for a reason.

When I got home from court yesterday, I had a person associated with the trial over for an interview. I wanted to find out more about Lori's family and her childhood. In this dream we sat in my kitchen having a nice chat, I could see through the open door into my garage. My garage is a mess and what I could see is the pile of tires, parts, and tools in the middle of the garage floor.

As we continued our conversation, I felt like I could see something moving in the pile. After a while I couldn't resist the urge to go see what it was. I went into the garage, pulled a few tires and things aside, and looked into the pile. To my horror what I saw was a slithering mass of extremely venomous snakes. It was a mother snake and her baby snakes. The mother raised up like a cobra right into my face, and I knew she was going to strike to protect her babies. I remember thinking at the time that that was the natural reaction of a mother. In her mind I was a threat to her offspring and she would fight to the death to protect them.

Anyway, I knew that if I backed away, she would strike, sinking her fangs into my face and filling me with her deadly venom. I reached to the side and grabbed what I think was like a salt-shaker full of gunpowder. I felt like it was my only hope of defending myself. I shook the gunpowder in her face. It caused her to back away, but at the same time just made her madder. The more I shook it in her face, the madder she got, but I couldn't stop or I knew she would instantly strike.

So that was my dilemma when I awoke. Whew! It was just a dream. But what was my dream trying to tell me? I could think of two things. One was that a normal mother would die or kill to protect her offspring and Lori Vallow Daybell did the opposite. She flaunted a mother's instincts and did the unthinkable.

The other thought I had was that the message was warning me of some danger I was putting myself into. I don't think it was meant to be like danger for my life, but more like I might be stepping on someone's toes. Hurting someone in some way and they might retaliate against me.

I have reconciled myself with the idea that some of what I write might be hurtful to some and I tell myself I am doing what I am doing because what I am doing is important. I fully believe that, but am I inadvertently hurting someone or am I doing something that must be done and the hurt is caused by Lori Vallow Daybell and Chad Daybell? I sincerely hope it's the latter. If I am hurting any of the people whom I have come to love, I will be devastated when they strike at me. Not by their attack on me, but by the fact that I did something to make them want to do that.

Another thought I had attempting to interpret my dream is that if I quit shaking the gunpowder, I knew I would be attacked. That made me think that I should not back off in what I believe. But then, I'm putting myself in this position by my own choice. That's as far as I got. I would need a psychoanalyst to help me understand more.

One thing I'll say about Mormons is that they don't spend a lot of time talking about hell. Maybe they should. Maybe if Chad contemplated an eternity of fire and brimstone, he would have had second thoughts about committing his crimes.

Mormons talk about the telestial (pertaining to earth), terrestrial (closer to God and not a real existence; the word and the idea were made up by Joseph Smith), and celestial (heavenly) kingdoms.

Is it a more optimistic way of thinking or is it a more arrogant way of thinking? Do Mormons focus on more positive concepts than hell or are they so arrogant that they think they are the chosen ones destined for heaven simply because they are Mormon? I bet your average Mormon hasn't thought about it.

Anyway, I guess you can tell it wasn't a very interesting day in court. My mind had time to wander and contemplate.

WEDNESDAY, MAY 8, 2024,
Another Hard Day in Court

Today more than made up for yesterday. We started with Dr. Garth Warren on the stand for the prosecution. Dr. Warren is the forensic pathologist who performed the autopsies on Tylee and JJ's remains. There is a lot for me to tell about his testimony, but I want to start with the fact that listening to his testimony for the second time is one of the primary things that convinced me that poor Tylee and JJ didn't die in any kind of peaceful way.

When questioned by Rob Wood about the toxicology test Dr. Warren had done on Tylee's remains, he testified that Tylee had a small amount of ibuprofen and a small amount of caffeine in her system and nothing that would have contributed to her death.

Remember, in Lori's trial, I had convinced myself that Tylee had been drugged. I heard the same testimony from Dr. Warren as a juror in Lori's trial, but like I said, my mind was playing tricks on me. Even though I had to have clearly heard Dr. Warren testify that there was nothing unusual in Tylee's blood, I had convinced myself that she had been drugged.

He determined her death to be homicide by unspecified means. "Unspecified" didn't mean it could have been anything that killed her though. It wasn't drugs. He was able to determine that much. He just couldn't tell which of the wounds she suffered at the hands of her uncle and possibly Chad had killed her.

Through Dr. Warren's testimony the prosecution provided more information than we had in Lori's trial about Tylee's remains. Dr. Warren thinks they tried to burn her whole body to get rid of it, but finally had to give up. It was harder to do than they realized, so they ended up having to bury what they couldn't burn. My own observation is that Chad and Alex are idiots. It's sad and horrific to think of Alex trying desperately to burn Tylee's remains. I can imagine him giving up as morning was approaching and finally resorting to burying what was left. The next morning Chad was in the "pet cemetery" cleaning it up the best he could.

As he was testifying, pictures of Tylee's remains were being shown to the jury. I knew what they were looking at, and I was filled with emotion that I could barely control. First, I empathized with the jurors, but I was also overcome with anger, feeling like again I was realizing how Tylee actually died. How many times does that realization have to come to me? Even though I know it now, I know she was brutalized, it seems like every time I hear evidence to that fact, I have to realize it over again.

Dr. Warren went on to testify about his autopsy of JJ's body, and again the jury was subjected to horrific pictures. The pictures of JJ's body were even more horrific because JJ was intact. He was still wearing the red pajamas we saw him wearing in Lori's apartment the night he was to die. I describe the pictures in chapter 15, so no reason to revisit that here. You get the point.

Dr. Warren did provide some testimony that interested me though. I don't remember him talking about it in Lori's trial. JJ had scratches and bruises on his neck and face, and he had a smashed thumbnail. Again, in Lori's trial, I was in denial, but I don't think he brought it up. It not only shows that JJ's murder was violent, but it shows that JJ fought back. JJ's Paw Paw Larry told us JJ was a fighter when he gave his soliloquy at the memorial.

The injustice of how JJ was murdered is one of the most unbelievable aspects of this whole case to me, and I have yet to understand how anyone, let alone his uncle, mother, and Chad could be so heartless. One would have to be totally soulless to be able to do it. I'm sure that however Alex's death actually happened, murdering JJ factored into it.

I have heard people close to this case say they want to see Chad and Lori suffer and die. I am always kind of taken aback by that in spite of their crimes, but when I think about it, I do understand how they feel that way. I understand their anger, and who can blame them?

In his cross-examination of Dr. Warren, Defense Attorney Prior threw more darts. Apparently, Tylee's remains had evidence of K-9 bites. Scratches on the bone that would have been done by a dog or possibly a coyote. This would indicate that Tylee's body was left unattended for some period of time. I really don't know what the significance of that is or why Prior brought it up. To me it just adds to the horrific nature of Tylee's murder. It also brings this thought to my mind: Chad, Lori, and Alex claim to be Christians. Christians believe that when a person dies, the soul leaves the body. We treat the body with respect. There are variations depending on customs, but the body is always treated with respect and laid to rest as intact as possible. So even if we believed Chad's ideas about zombies

My sketch of the anguish showing on the faces of the jurors.

invading bodies, I would think it would be important to him to respect Tylee's remains.

I think everyone in the courtroom was relieved when Dr. Warren was finished. His testimony was probably the most important of all of the testimony we heard, but for obvious reasons, it was also the hardest to get through.

I know for myself it was a relief to hear Chandler, Arizona, Detective Ariel Werther's testimony. I could have used a break after Dr. Warren, but Judge Boyce apparently was inclined to push forward.

Detective Werther told the jury that Chad, Lori, and Alex were all in constant contact on the day Charles was shot. Who was where and when and the timeline of events and how they occurred was very important information if Chad was going to be convicted. John Prior had been trying to convince the jury that it was all Alex and Lori's doing and Chad had been duped by a beautiful woman. However, the fact that Chad was talking to Lori and Alex all day that day certainly implicates him in that murder in Arizona also.

I'm hoping there will be charges for Chad in Arizona. Sure, he already is sentenced to six death penalties, but justice is important, and we need justice for Charles and his family.

I went through the whole timeline of Charles's murder in chapter 10, so I won't recount it here except to tell you that according to Detective Werther, Alex had missed calls on the morning of the murder from Melani Boudreaux and Lori's sister Summer. I don't think Summer was involved in any way, so I guess that's just happenstance, but I do wonder about Melani. As I have said, I am very suspicious of her role.

Thursday, May 9, 2024,
Prior Actually Makes a Solid Point

We start the day with forensic biologist Katherine Dace. Like all of the FBI specialists and agents, she was a good witness. Thorough, confident, and to the point. She described how the tools found in Chad's shed, a pick and shovel among other things, were processed and how the samples were sent to a lab and tested for DNA. They tested positive for Tylee's DNA. They also tested the hair they found between the duct tape and plastic on JJ's body and found it was Lori's hair.

Her testimony was pretty clear cut, but Prior would try to instill doubt in his cross-examination. Could Chad have inadvertently used the tools in his yard around the burn pit where Tylee's remains had been buried? I actually thought he made a good point. Sure, it was unlikely at this point that Chad was innocent and had been duped, but Prior's strategy at least made some sense in this instance. Chad had simply done what he always did. He had burned some brush and cleaned up around the burn pit using his tools. In doing so, he picked up Tylee's DNA. How was he to know Alex and Lori had burned and buried Tylee there? I think it would have been impossible for him not to know, and I'm sure by this point the jurors felt the same as I did, but the argument was put out there and at least one could follow the logic.

When Prior was done with Specialist Dace, the prosecution called Kauai Police Officer Colin Nesbitt. He had assisted with the search of Lori and Chad's Princeville condo and car. He stated that he found iPads belonging to Tylee and JJ, their social security cards and birth certificates, and cash, among other things. A mom might be expected to have these items, but where were Tylee and JJ?

FRIDAY, MAY 10, 2024,
There Is an Upstairs in Chad's House

The day started with Fremont County EMT and Deputy Coroner Cammy Willmore on the stand. She gave her feelings about why she initially declared Tammy's death to be of natural causes.

I wrote earlier about Tammy's aunt Vicki and how much I admire her. It was nice on this day to see her surrounded by other family members. Aunt Vicki had been struggling day to day to be in court to represent the family. We all did what we could to support her, but there is nothing like the support of one's family, and I could see that it bolstered her strength to have them there.

Vicki was not able to be in court every day. I could see she was struggling, and on some days it was just too much for her. She was struggling with her health, so I think the emotional toll was the cause. She's one of those people whose face you can easily read, and when I think back on my time with her, it seems like she was always either laughing or crying. She has a beautiful smile and easy laugh, and it was always uplifting to see.

Tammy's brother-in-law Jason Gwilliam took the stand, and he had some insight on Chad's past that I found interesting. Jason and Chad had been close for several years. Chad changed his views when he started writing his books in 2006. He began to be obsessed with visions, last days, the Wasatch wake-up quake, and invading troops. Chad and Jason had grown apart as Jason was unable to reason with Chad or go along with his beliefs. Chad didn't tell Jason when he married Lori. When Jason found out and questioned Chad, Chad replied that his kids were good at keeping secrets and that Tammy had appeared to him in a dream and told him to move on.

That's convenient for Chad, and I don't doubt that Chad's kids are good at keeping secrets. They had been conditioned by Chad their whole lives.

Jason testified that he placed a call to Chad and recorded it while sitting with the police. On the call, Chad tells Jason that Chad's sister-in-law, Heather is behind the rumors of the missing children.

"She is just an evil person."

When Jason asked about the kids' whereabouts Chad replied: "I can't tell you because I don't want to get you involved."

This was new information we didn't hear in Lori's trial. I wondered if Chad didn't know the kids were dead, why would he lie insinuating they were alive and safely hidden away somewhere?

In his cross-examination, Prior tries to show a conspiracy with the police. He tries to tie prosecutor Rob Wood into the conspiracy. He asks Gwilliam if Heather's daughter is married to Detective Hope's son and Gwilliam affirms that. Good try on Prior's part, but it's dishonest. And again, what would the motive be? What would the prosecution and the police gain by conspiring against Chad?

In the prosecution's redirect Gwilliam says the number of people claiming near death experiences is alarming. As I stated before, I agree with him, and it was good for me to hear that from someone who lives in that area. The Mormon Church, in my opinion, shouldn't tolerate their members making such claims. They disassociate themselves with people for all kinds of reasons; why not this one?

Tammy's sister, Samantha Gwilliam, testified next. She said the pet cemetery was important to Tammy and her family. They buried not only pets there, but any dead animal they found. Tammy didn't want to move to Rexburg, but Chad had a vision and she had to follow him. Samantha preemptively contradicted Emma's later testimony, saying Tammy had no aversion to doctors. Just about everything we heard in everyone's testimonies contradicted Emma. Samantha thought it was odd that Chad did not have his name placed on Tammy's headstone as was the custom.

Daybell property looking to the northwest. Notice the Dodge Dakota Tammy drove in the driveway. JJ's remains were found behind the barn. Tylee's remains were found between the slash pile and the driveway. The taller building attached to the house is what the family called the "cozy cone." Nosey neighbor Eldon walked the irrigation ditch daily before he suddenly died. Photo Provided By Jeanine Hansen.

Remember back to April 29 when Prior asked a witness if she realized that Chad's house didn't have an upstairs. Samantha cleared up the stairs controversy saying there were stairs going up to the "cozy cone." Cozy cone comes from the Disney movie *Cars*. Chad and Tammy's son Mark lived up there and played music on his electric keyboard and guitar. Prior had previously tried to get witnesses to say the upstairs was uninhabitable and had no electricity. Samantha said Mark "plugged in" upstairs. I have since seen pictures of the upstairs taken before the house was torn down. It looks very habitable to me, and there are lights and outlets.

I enjoyed sitting in court and in the hallway during breaks with Tammy's family. I found them all to be straightforward, warmhearted people. It's uncannily true of all of the people on the victim's side of this case. They would hang around and visit during breaks, offering support, and showing interest in what I was doing. Not so for the defense. All of the people testifying for the defense bolted from the courthouse as soon as they were done testifying.

Next up was FBI Tactical Specialist Nicole Heideman, and, yes, she lived up to her impressive title. She told about the malachite wedding rings Lori purchased on Charles's credit card after Charles was dead, but Tammy was still alive, indicating premeditation on Chad and Lori's part. She went through some of the James and Elena texts. Remember, James and Elena were Chad and Lori in previous probations on earth. Chad wrote to Lori that they "would save millions and defeat the forces of darkness."

Specialist Heideman went on to tell how on November 18, 2018, Chad and Lori had a sealing ceremony in the temple. That was a farce of course, but Lori claimed Jesus was standing there in the temple with them. After a Preparing a People conference James and Elena shared a room. This was okay, even though at this time they were both married to their living spouses because they had been married in a previous life and they were sealed for eternity now in this one.

MONDAY, MAY 13, 2024,
Was Alex a Sexual Deviant?

FBI Forensic Anthropologist Dr. Angi Christensen testified first today. This is where things take an even darker turn. She had analyzed Tylee's remains and came to some horrifying conclusions about how she was murdered. Exactly how Tylee was murdered is a question I have had for a long time. I wondered if there was a sexual component to her murder. Dr. Christensen filled in some of the blanks.

She stated that Tylee's pelvic area had been struck repeatedly by a sharp object. She couldn't come to any conclusion as to why that was done, but it was done. Was Alex a sexual deviant? Some of his past actions point to that idea. He was known to travel to South America to spend time with prostitutes. He was awkward and struggled in his relationships with normal women he was associated with. He had a, to say the least, weird marriage with Zulema Pastenes, for some reason taking her last name, and his relationship with his sister Lori was weird, to say the least.

People who were close to Alex and Lori growing up say they had a sexual relationship and they expressed it openly. There is some controversy about whether or not it was serious, but I can say for sure that it was abnormal. I wrote in *Money, Power and Sex* about a night he spent in a hotel room with Zulema that terrified her.

Or could Chad have been the sexual deviant? And was he directly involved in murdering Tylee? He had said he would make the kids scream. My guess is that it was Alex at Chad's direction.

The next witness bolstered my idea that Alex was a deviant. It was Ashlyn Rynd, Tylee's best friend. She said she was not comfortable around Tylee's uncle Alex. I found this to be compelling testimony coming from someone who did not hold any of the zealous religious beliefs. It's one of the keys to the mystery of how Tylee died and I think very important. I think it was missed by most people following these trials.

Podcasters Lauren and Dr. John Matthias agree with me. It's not only intriguing, but it also gives us insight about Alex, Chad, and Lori. Some of these less popular witnesses who people paid little attention to actually give answers to those of us who have followed so closely.

It's hard to get straight answers from family members. They contradict each other. One thinks Alex was pretty normal and another thinks he was odd. I think they are just too close. Rynd would only have been around Alex occasionally, and her opinion is probably more objective. Alex made her nervous, and she didn't trust him. In my opinion, Alex was a sexual deviant, and sadly there was a sexual component to the murder of Tylee.

It starts to feel like the prosecution is wrapping up their case as Detective Chuck Kunsaitis testifies for the second time, tying up loose ends. He showed satellite imagery before and after the time Tylee is known to have been murdered. In it I could clearly see a burned area right over her burial site in the image taken after she was murdered.

FBI Firearms Specialist Douglas Halepasca testified briefly, giving more information about the tool marks on Tylee's bones. More evidence about how Tylee was brutally murdered. He described the difference between a chopping action that would be consistent with an ax or cleaver and a stabbing action consistent with a knife. He found both when examining Tylee's bones.

As soon as he was finished, FBI Agent Nick Ballance testified about the night Alex attempted to shoot Tammy. It was interesting and filled in more of the blanks for me. Agent Ballance used cell phone location to place Alex at Sportsman's Warehouse the day before he missed killing Tammy by mere inches. We had seen the receipts for the camo gear he bought earlier. He pinpointed Alex's location on the evening of his encounter with Tammy. He had been setting up for a shot, assuming Tammy would park where she normally parked behind the house. Alex, Chad, and Lori again were in constant contact the whole time. By now we know they were in constant contact every time someone was murdered or attempted to be murdered. This further debunks Prior's attempt to say Chad had been duped by Lori and Alex.

TUESDAY, MAY 14, 2024,
Prior Missed an Opportunity

We are beginning our twenty-third day of testimony with Utah Medical Examiner Department Chief Dr. Lily Marsden who is being questioned by Lindsey Blake. It was more gruesome testimony about her autopsy of Tammy's body. I can say that what medical examiners do is extremely interesting, but I could not do what they do.

I had the opportunity to meet and speak with Dr. Michael Baden. You may have heard of him. He is ninety years old now, but still sharp as a tack. He is probably the most famous medical examiner in America. He has been involved in many high-profile cases including O. J. Simpson, Jeffrey Epstein, and George Floyd. He was fascinating to talk to and had answers to all of my questions. He was not involved in our case but was very familiar with it and basically reinforced everything I heard in court. He told me he knows Dr. Marsden well and she is one of the best.

Dr. Marsden performed Tammy's autopsy along with Dr. Christensen. She described the process of removing the skull cap and brain and all of the organs and putting it all back when they were done. She said Tammy died of pulmonary edema and that there can be several causes. Drug overdose is one cause, but they found no lethal drugs in her organs and her organs were all in good shape.

She declared the cause of Tammy's death to be asphyxia and the manner of her death to be homicide. She said she found bruising on Tammy's chest, which would have been caused by a heavy weight. She didn't say it, but my thought was knees. In the prosecution's redirect they asked her if it could have been caused by knees, and she replied yes.

FBI Special Investigator Rick Wright testified next. You're beginning to get the idea that the FBI was all over this case. Before these two trials I had not thought a lot about the FBI. I thought of them as investigators of crime, but I hadn't thought a lot about all of the specialties they could bring to bear on an investigation. These are extremely qualified, extremely specialized agents. Every one of them is perfectly professional, confident, and knowledgeable about their area of expertise.

The most interesting part of Investigator Wright's testimony was when he described Tylee, Lori, Alex, and JJ's trip through Yellowstone National Park. They originally suspected Tylee had been murdered there, and they searched for her body along with park rangers. I know Yellowstone well, and I can picture the route he described. They could easily have found a secluded area to murder her and bury her body. I wondered why they didn't do that. It would have made a lot more sense than burying her in Chad's backyard. I think the reason they didn't do it there is that Lori was along for the ride and she would not have wanted to witness the cruel murder of Tylee. She was fine with having it done though.

Investigator Wright went on to reiterate the previous witness's testimony about Alex's trip to Sportsman's Warehouse and to the rifle range. I expected that in his cross-examination

Prior would bring up the fact that hunting season was about to start. Hunting season is a big deal in Idaho, and most of us spend time at Sportsman's Warehouse and the rifle range that time of year.

He could have poked holes in at least that part of the witness's testimony, and my thought was that Prior must be one of the few Idahoans who doesn't hunt. He missed a good opportunity to at least somewhat discount the witness's testimony. He should have known to use this. He does question Investigator Wright about cellphone "bings." More Priorisms.

WEDNESDAY, MAY 15, 2024,
"A Marvelous Plan"

Now I'm sure we're getting close to the end. The trial started with Lieutenant Ray Hermosillo, and he is back on the stand this morning. He testifies that Lori and Chad call each other eight to ten times a day while Lori is in jail for not producing the children and Chad is still a free man. Of course, all calls from or to prisoners are recorded. In more than one of the calls Lori asks Chad for information, and Chad replies, "It's a marvelous plan." This definitely makes Chad look like the leader. It's his plan they are following.

Lieutenant Hermosillo says that found in Alex's possession were duct tape, torch, striker, knife, hacksaw, tarp, blue bucket, gloves, bag of concrete, guns, ammo, and knives. All items used in the murders. He goes on to reiterate that the evidence shows it was all Chad's plan. He's the one who has been communicating with Alex, he has the ideas, he would have been the one to say when and how the murders would take place.

Agent Douglas Hart retakes the stand. I see that the prosecution listened to us jurors from the Lori Vallow Daybell trial and are doing their best to reiterate the facts and fill in some holes.

The most interesting thing about Agent Hart's second trip to the witness stand is the texts between Chad and Lori and Blake. Blake is Melani Boudreaux's son, and I think this further ties Melani to the murders.

CHAD: *"I turned up the pain"*

LORI: *"Find out her percentage and JJ's"*

BLAKE: *"Chad Daybell is the source for the death percentages"*

CHAD: *"give them a reason to scream"*

Chad and Lori actually want to cause Tylee and JJ pain. This is something else I couldn't just immediately comprehend. I simply wasn't able to understand, and I had to contemplate a lot. Another of those times when I was overcome with the enormity of Chad and Lori's selfishness and ruthlessness.

CHAD: *"big news about Tammy!"* (four days later Tammy is dead)

Hart said, (This is) "the clearest and most specific plan to kill the children."

This coming from a man who had dedicated his professional life to investigating the murders of children.

22

THE PROSECUTION RESTS!

A motion is immediately filed by Prior stating that the prosecution failed to meet their burden of proof. Of course, it's an empty accusation and went nowhere.

The prosecution made a sad clerical error at this point. It was a simple clerical error, but could have had a huge impact on the trial. Not only that, but it caused a lot of anguish for all of the people wanting and working for justice. It could have caused the trial to be thrown out. It could have caused us to have to go through this all over again. I was beside myself as I knew many others were. We would have to wait and see what Judge Boyce decided. If he could find a way to make it go away.

On the indictment the prosecution got the date of JJ's murder wrong. They superimposed the date of when his body was found with the date he was murdered. How could they make such a monumental error? It was surreal that the prosecution just rested their case and someone at this moment found the error. Judge Boyce's court attorney told me later that she was the one who finally noticed the error, and she was distraught about not having found it sooner.

Larry Woodcock left the courtroom in shock. I was concerned about him and followed him out of the courthouse along with others. I could see he was angry and in distress, and I tried to say something to make him feel better, but what could anyone say? Larry knew what to say. He said, "Why don't we pray?" And we did. Eight or ten of us, whether we were religious or not, stood with Larry in prayer. It was a moment I will never forget.

Unfortunately, the only media person I had already learned not to like or trust broke into our obvious prayer circle and insisted Larry allow her to interview him at that moment. Looking back, I wish I had interrupted her and told her to go **** herself, but for some reason I did not. Larry being Larry, he went and allowed her to interview him.

A little later one of the media people who I have learned to love and respect did just the opposite gesture. We were all gathered in the hall waiting for Judge Boyce to call us back into court. I won't name the media person I don't trust, but I will name this one. She is Lauren Matthias and is an amazing journalist and an amazing person. She brings a lot to this trial. She has selflessly supported the families of the victims, and she has selflessly supported my efforts to write my books. Anyway, she ordered us all food. It was just a simple gesture, and she said it was a Mormon thing, to order food in times of crisis. It meant a lot to all of us.

23

THE DEFENSE

John Prior's Turn

J udge Boyce thankfully starts out the day by saying that his instructions to the jury will clarify the mistake of the dates. What a relief. Court documents, like everything about court in a trial of this magnitude, are extremely important. A simple clerical error can mean a case being thrown out. So much and so many emotions are riding on the correct conclusion to this trial. If it were to have been thrown out at this point, well, I can't begin to describe the consequences.

When I showed up at the courthouse in the mornings, there would be a line of people waiting to get in. In the Lori Vallow Daybell trial, the number of people in line was always more than could fit in the courtroom. Since in Chad's trial court cameras televised it, there weren't as many people coming in person. But today was different. People were lined up down the street to get in, and I could see that most of them wouldn't get in. People were excited to see what the defense would come up with. It would be entertaining. I have to admit that I was interested in what John Prior and Chad Daybell had cooked up.

In that regard, I was not immediately disappointed as Prior's first witness was Emma Daybell Murray, Chad's daughter. Emma and her husband, Joseph Murray, had moved into Chad's house immediately after he was arrested. Emma is the vision of a young Mormon woman. She is very pretty, with big eyes and long blond hair. Dress below her knees and shoulders covered.

She is a teacher and still holds her position in spite of her father's crimes and her blatant lies on his behalf. There is some controversy about that of course. For reasons beyond my understanding, Emma's testimony is the highlight and biggest draw of this trial for a lot of the people who have been following it. I guess it's the Hollywood-like aspect of Emma. For sure she will provide some drama.

My eyes were opened further by her testimony. I had not fully recognized the extent of Chad's influence over people in his sphere. I found Emma's testimony to be disgusting, yet sad. Disgusting that she would blatantly lie for the man who murdered her mother, but sad because she had obviously been conditioned by Chad her whole life. Why else would she do what she was doing?

Emma starts out by saying that she talks daily to Chad, who is in jail, but she has not been coached on what to say. First lie. She is unaware of who owns the home she and her husband are living in. Second lie. She goes on to say that Chad was the "patriarch of our home." In other words, Chad was the leader. His word had to be obeyed by everyone in the household unquestioningly. We know it goes even deeper than that in the Mormon world the Daybells lived in. Chad had a higher standing with God. Chad was their key to the kingdom. Chad was their way into the celestial kingdom.

When asked about Tammy, she says her mom was unhealthy, bruised easily, refused doctors, and was an introvert. Okay, I'm losing track of the number of lies.

Emma goes on to say that she was an amateur meteorologist, and she was the one who looked up wind direction on Chad's computer. The lies are getting bigger and more unbelievable. She was the one who increased Tammy's life insurance. She and Tammy had talked and decided to do it together. She claimed Tammy was more of a religious fundamentalist than Chad and that Tammy was the one who had the light and dark rating system. Wait, it gets even weirder: Emma had been invaded by a zombie, and Chad exorcised it!

At this point I can see Judge Boyce losing patience with Emma and her blatant lies. She was showing so much disrespect for the court, this trial, her mother, and her mother's family members who were sitting right there in court. She is trying to make eye contact with her father, smiling at him and obviously trying to get some sign of his approval.

If this is an example of what's to come in John Prior's defense strategy, he is going to lose spectacularly. While Emma did provide some fireworks and did not disappoint the people who came to watch her testify, she had zero credibility. Her lies were as transparent as they could be. If her only goal was to move up on Chad's light scale, I think she might have lost some ground. I'm sure Chad was disappointed that she wasn't a more believable liar. I did not see her get the approval she was looking for from him either. I don't think any amount of approval would have been enough for her anyway.

Garth Daybell, Chad and Tammy's son and Emma's brother, followed Emma on the witness stand. Garth looks like a younger version of Chad and is every bit as unbelievable as his sister. He is also as disrespectful of Tammy and her family. He says Tammy's favorite meal was a Quarter Pounder. I would love to have slapped him for saying that. My thought was that if her favorite meal was a Quarter Pounder, maybe it was because it was a meal she didn't have to prepare for you and clean up after you ate it.

His following testimony was important, and it's too bad he discredited himself so much right before he made it. It turned out to be just more lies anyway. On the night his mother was murdered, Garth worked at the haunted house until 1:00 a.m. He stated that when he came home from work, he walked by his parents' bedroom. He checked on them as he always did by looking into their room on his way by. His room was directly across the narrow hallway. He saw two forms sleeping in bed and could hear his father snoring.

If Garth hadn't totally discredited himself, that testimony may have had some influence on the jury. As it was, though, it appeared to be just more lies to protect his murderous father.

The most interesting thing that happened during Garth's time on the stand happened during a sidebar. A sidebar is when the attorneys for both sides meet with Judge Boyce to discuss a matter without the jury being able to hear. White noise is played just to make sure. Garth kept looking to Chad, obviously hoping to get his attention and I think looking for a sign of approval. Chad refused to look at Garth and made a point of looking at the floor. It was a sad moment and also very telling. Garth, just like Emma, had been conditioned his whole life by his father. That is so cruel and selfish and tells us more about who Chad really is.

Emma's husband, Joseph Murray, was more outwardly disdainful of the court, the prosecution, and the police while he was on the witness stand. He did have some personality, but I wouldn't say it was attractive. I think Emma chose to marry a person like him because of a lifetime of Chad's influence. Joseph immediately struck me as self-centered and small-minded.

Joseph stated that he and Emma lived "kitty corner" to Chad's house and he had called 911 on the evening Tammy was shot at by a "paintball gun." He is a member of Operation Underground Railroad or OUR. (OUR and its founder, Tim Ballard, have their own problems. Tim Ballard is a Mormon in good standing with the church but is accused of using his organization to abuse and take advantage of women.)

Joseph strikes me as being right out of a movie. He has a long beard and looks like the priesthood-holding fundamentalist you might see in a movie. In his appearance he looks older than Emma. He has a long beard and beady eyes hidden behind dark-rimmed glasses. On the stand he wore a white long-sleeved shirt and dark tie. I keep wondering why he would want to live in the house where Tammy was murdered and the kids were buried. He showed obvious disdain for the police involved in this case. Prior was trying to show a conspiracy. Too bad he didn't have a more believable witness.

When asked by Prosecutor Wixom in his cross-examination of Joseph if he liked the police, he replied: "Absolutely not, I would rather choose any other profession."

At this point, I'm becoming embarrassed for Prior. His star witnesses whom he has been touting are a disaster, showing themselves for what they are. They are working much better for the prosecution.

MONDAY, MAY 20, 2024,
Prior Puts His Foot in It

Another disastrous witness in my opinion was forensic pathologist Dr. Cathy Ravin. She had reviewed Tammy's autopsy and reported on it in court. She claimed her conclusion about Tammy's cause of death was "undetermined." She was totally discredited in the prosecution's cross-examination. She is a private contractor paid by the defense. She did none of the background work that Dr. Christensen did. I think I can detect smirks and eyerolls from the jury during her testimony.

Prior made a huge gaff in his redirect of her, and I wondered if anyone else caught it. Talking about Tammy, he said "at the time of the murder" instead of at the time of her death. So, even Chad's own attorney thinks Tammy was murdered. The defense is a total disaster at this point.

TUESDAY, MAY 21, 2024,
The Professor Contributes Nothing

I watched as Dr. Anthony Hampikian walked to the witness stand and immediately thought okay, this guy is different. He will be interesting. He is a professor at Boise State University and looks the part of a professor. Long gray hair, no socks. Looks like a cool guy. He was interesting to listen to, and I thought it would be interesting to sit through one of his classes. He had worked with attorney John Thomas on the Christopher Tapp case, and I thought that was impressive. Thomas worked for ten years to get Tapp's murder conviction overturned. I was disappointed, though, as Hampikian contributed nothing to the trial.

WEDNESDAY, MAY 22, 2024,
"Give Them Something to Scream About"

Prior starts the day with another academic. It's Dr. Eric Bartelink, professor of anthropology at California State University, Chico. Unlike Hampikian, Bartelink's testimony was very interesting and informative. He had unpacked, sorted, and identified Tylee's bones. At least what was left after the smaller of her bones had been burned away. He explained how hard it was to burn a body. Gas and diesel are not enough.

In Rocky Wixom's cross-examination we got more answers, and this is a little of what I was hoping would happen when the defense called witnesses—answers to some of our questions.

There were many missing bones. Some were missing because they had been burned, but some of the bigger bones, which should have been present because they should have survived the burning, were missing. This just raises more questions. Where would the missing bones be? They weren't buried in Chad's backyard. According to Dr. Bartelink they wouldn't have been burned. My thought was possibly dragged off by the same dog or coyote that gnawed on the bones.

He went on to describe the injuries he could identify to the bones. There were many fractured bones, eighteen sharp force injuries to bones and sixteen impact injuries. This is very interesting to me and gives me more insight into how Tylee was murdered. The impact injuries could have been caused while they were hacking her body to pieces, doing their best to dispose of it. The sharp force injuries were around her pelvic bone and would have been caused by striking it with a sharp-pointed tool of some kind. These kinds of injuries would be inconsistent with dismembering a body.

This testimony caused me to go back to the night Tylee was murdered and question again how it happened and wonder whether Chad was directly involved. Could it have been Chad who was the sexual deviant? Whether it was Chad or Alex who caused these wounds, sexual deviant isn't the correct description of the person who did it. I just can't think of another term that would better describe someone who would do such a horrific thing. Monster, maniacal torturer? Whatever I come up with isn't enough, but I'm beginning to think he's sitting right in front of me. Again, Chad was the one who said they would "give them something to scream about."

This information was not provided by the prosecution in the Lori Vallow Daybell trial and I wondered if that was because they wanted to hold it for this trial, to imply that Chad was directly involved in Tylee's murder. The contrast between the mild-mannered man I saw in court and who Chad really is is terrifying. I'm glad he will never get out of jail alive.

24

THE DEFENSE RESTS

That's it? That's all they had? Prior led us to believe there would be more.

Thursday, May 23, 2024,
Outsmarting Mr. Prior

Judge Boyce asks Chad if he would like to testify, and he replies no. He let his kids testify. He made his kids testify, but he wouldn't take the stand himself? He's a coward or as they used to say, "He's yella."

At this point the state is allowed to call rebuttal witnesses. They first call Jason Mackay Veiglan. He was a coworker of Garth's at the haunted mansion. He totally contradicts Garth's testimony about the night Tammy was murdered. He testified that Garth told him he found his mother dead when he came home from work at 1:00 a.m. The point of this witness is obvious. Garth is lying for Chad.

Prior tried to counter in his cross-examination, but Jason was clear about what Garth told him and a very believable witness with no dog in the race. The prosecution outsmarted Prior again.

25

CLOSING ARGUMENTS

There was an impressive group of people in the gallery for closing arguments. Most, if not all, of the police officers and FBI agents involved in the case were there, and the assistant district attorney for Idaho sat next to me. A lot of family of the victims were there. Not one person for Chad. Garth and Emma didn't stick around. In fact, they were only in court on the day they testified.

Lindsey Blake delivers the closing arguments for the prosecution. She reiterates some of what Chad said in his text messages to Lori. These are direct quotes from Chad:

"We'll give them a reason to scream."

"There is a plan being orchestrated for the children."

"How do I know? It was shown to me."

"Just keep resolving the telestial issues, so we can be unencumbered and totally free."

"We're so close to the finish line."

"We are surrounded by telestial obstacles."

"I turned up the pain to ten."

(Remember, telestial means pertaining to earth.)

Blake reminded the jury that Chad had called Alex to his property on the night JJ was buried. She told them Alex believed Chad 100 percent when he said JJ was at zero dark. (Chad went back and forth with the dark scale. Sometimes it was moving up to six on the dark scale that meant you had to die, and sometimes it was moving down to zero.) He called them: "My original death percentages."

She went on quoting Chad saying: "Big news about Tammy. Level three demonic entity named Viola." "Not fully sure about the timing for removal, but I don't want to wait."

She very effectively nailed it down for the jury. Not that they weren't convinced a long while ago, but she reduced it to the damning evidence that couldn't be denied, even if Chad had had a good defense attorney.

I did think Prior was, among other things, brave and masterful in his closing arguments. I got in trouble with one of the key people prosecuting Chad when Prior finished. He walked away and didn't hang around for the rest of what I was trying to say, which was that Prior was also insulting to the families and law enforcement in the gallery. He was dishonest. While he showed no fear, looked people in the gallery in the eye, and held nothing back, he also lost any shred of self-respect he may have harbored up until that time. He claimed there were four reasonable doubts:

1. Motive: Alex had the motive. Tylee could tell on him for killing Charles. JJ was too much of a handful without Tylee there to care for him. Lori wanted Tammy out of her way because she was in love with Chad. These are

interesting points and could have been part of the reason for the murders, but how does it let Chad off the hook?

2. Lori and Alex: "All that glitters is not gold." That was how Prior opened the trial. He tried to claim that Chad fell for Lori, and she wasn't what he thought she was. She was ruthless to get what she wanted, and her brother Alex was the cold-blooded killer. Chad was taken in by her and duped.

3. No DNA: Prior tried in the trial to argue that the police had used the tools in Chad's shed or maybe Chad used them to clean up the yard like he always did and inadvertently picked up Tylee's DNA. He even insinuated that the police planted the DNA on the tools in a conspiracy. What would their motive have been? He also argued that there was no DNA from Chad on the tools. I don't believe that is accurate. I think the prosecution didn't bring up Chad's DNA on the tools because it would be assumed that they were Chad's tools, so it would be obvious that his DNA would be on them.

4. The investigation was a failure: Prior's claim was that the police failed to have open minds. They decided it was Chad early on and closed their minds to any other possibilities.

John Prior failed on every level. His arguments fell flat because they were far-fetched and unrealistic. He showed himself to be dishonest and dishonorable. His witnesses did more to prove the prosecution's case than his client's. His attempts to relate to the jury backfired.

I don't know for sure how much John Prior got paid for defending Chad, but I think he took this case for almost no money because he thought it would elevate his standing as a defense attorney, and he failed there also. In total, he gave it his best shot, and he failed on every level. He is no Johnnie Cochran from O. J. fame. In his defense I have to say I think he had an impossible client. No attorney, not even Cochran, could have saved Chad. I did request a meeting with Prior, but got no response.

As soon as Prior was done with his closing arguments, Lindsey Blake gave her rebuttal. As soon as she was finished, juror numbers were pulled out of a hat, and five jurors were released from their duty.

I remember how I felt in Lori's trial at this moment. Personally, I felt shocked and insulted. I had invested so much time in this, and I felt like it was unfair that I wouldn't be able to see it through. Of course, I knew that was the deal. I knew that was how things were set up, and I knew my personal feelings were beside the point. A fair trial was the point. I had a hard time shaking my feelings though. But I did. I stood up and walked out of court quietly as I was expected to do.

To add insult to injury to these jurors, the ones who were released from their duty were not free to get up and walk out. They would be sequestered until the trial was over. I think at that point, I would have felt like it was unfair. Why would the jurors who wouldn't get to deliberate or even have contact with the twelve who would deliberate have to be sequestered? Was it because the court didn't trust them to keep their mouths shut until there was a verdict? That's the only reason I can think of. If the court trusted them to be fair and impartial, if the court put the life of a man in the hands of the jury, I would think the court could show them the respect of trusting them to go home and not talk to anyone.

Still, there was so much at stake. If one juror did speak out before the verdict was reached, it would have caused all kinds of problems and put everything everyone had worked so hard on at risk. And the other reason that might have been done is in case one of the twelve had to be released for illness or an emergency. Or as it has happened in other high-profile cases, maybe one or more of the twelve would have compromised themselves in some way.

Anyway, that's the way it was. Seventeen would be sequestered until they came to a verdict. Twelve would deliberate, and five would simply wait it out.

The timing of the end of the trial and the reading of the verdict couldn't have been worse, and it couldn't have been better for me and my release of *Money, Power and Sex*. I had made an agreement with the prosecution that I wouldn't release that book until a verdict was reached in Chad's trial. I made that agreement because they were willing to talk to me and share information with me that they felt could compromise Chad's trial. I also made it because I would have been horrified if I had done anything that affected the trial in any way. When I made that agreement, a date wasn't even set for Chad's trial.

I later made an agreement with my publisher that I would release my book at CrimeCon, which was scheduled for Friday, May 31, in Nashville, Tennessee. We agreed that the only reason I would not release it there would be if a verdict hadn't been reached in Chad's trial. Well, the timing was nuts. As it turned out, our flight was scheduled for the day the verdict was reached, and my wife and I actually watched the verdict on my phone as our plane was taking off. What a surreal moment for me. We were struggling to hear over the roar of the jet engines as our plane took to the air.

If I had had a choice, I would not have left Boise. I would have been in that courtroom just as I had for every single day leading up to the verdict. I wanted to be there not just for myself, but for all the people who had so much invested. I wanted to be there to support Kay and Larry and Aunt Vicki and all of the law enforcement whom I had become close to.

I wanted to be there to see Chad sent off to his prison cell to await the fulfillment of his sentence. I wanted to be there to congratulate the prosecution team on a job well done. I missed all of that.

CrimeCon turned out to be interesting. I went there for one reason: to sell my book and support my charity, Hope House. Being so caught up in the trial, I had not thought about what CrimeCon might be like. It was great though. I was able to make contact with a lot of people. I was able to promote my book. Some of the key podcasters and media people who had been interviewing me were there. I met some new media people who were interested in what I was doing, and they promised to interview me later and promote my book. I have to say that the media people I have been associated with in the process of writing my book have been interested, welcoming, and supportive beyond what I could ever have hoped for. I thank them for that.

As my wife and I were walking around the huge room we were selling my book in, a young lady I recognized grabbed me and said they were about to read the sentencing and she wanted me to join her husband, Joel, on their *Surviving the Survivor* podcast. I said I would, and I ended up spending over an hour live with Joel. Another surreal moment for me. When Chad's sentence was read, a cheer came up in the room. I had mixed feelings about that. I wasn't sure if cheering was the correct response, on one hand, and on the other, it made me realize how many people were following this case.

Anyway, the trial of Chad Daybell was over. He was convicted on three counts of first-degree murder, three counts of conspiracy to commit first-degree murder, and two counts of grand theft by deception. He was to be taken straight to death row at the Idaho State Correctional Center in Kuna, Idaho.

Grandparents Kay and Larry Woodcock get some hard-won relief. Photo by Lauren Matthias.

Larry and Kay Woodcock talk to media in front of the Ada County Courthouse. Photo by Lauren Matthias.

26

MORE QUESTIONS

I guess one of the biggest questions I am left with about the fundamentalist undercurrent in places like Rexburg, Idaho, and in Utah and Arizona is this: Is there an organized effort to cover up crimes? Is there undue influence over state and federal government that the rest of us should be concerned about? Are we just sweeping these things under the rug, not wanting to admit to ourselves that they are happening, or is it something even more nefarious? Is there an organized cover up?

We know that crimes have been and are being committed. Terrible crimes like child sexual assault and murder. There are countless crimes that have been committed in Short Creek Arizona/Utah for which for one reason or another, justice has not been served. I'm okay with people having the freedom to live their lives in whatever way they choose. In a perfect world, I'm okay with someone having more than one wife or more than one husband. But should they then get money from the government to support their way of life that is not in the mainstream? Or is that what motivates people to break the laws of our country and go to great lengths to cover it up?

I don't believe at all in things like "the Mormon Mafia." I don't believe there is an organized effort by the Mormon Church to unduly influence our federal government to cover up crimes, although I do think the Mormon Church does do what it can to influence the government. I do, however, believe there is a very unhealthy underworld of influential people in that part of our country. People who are profiting on untrue doctrine and ideas like faith healing, energy healing, near-death experiences, and visions. And I further think that the people profiting in this manner will go to great lengths to protect themselves and the income they get from exploiting weaker people.

If one can convince a cancer patient that they don't need modern medicine and that you can heal them through energy or faith healing, that is a crime. You take away their real chance at being cured or treated by proven science in favor of whatever snake oil you are selling. It's extremely self-serving and dangerous, but also highly profitable.

Another question I have had is this: Is there something about the Mormon Church that encourages or at least enables fundamentalist cults? I don't think it's the fault of the Mormon Church that people will use the church's beliefs to promote their own agenda. David Koresh used his own religion, Charles Manson used race, The Bhagwan used sex. The fact is that these manipulative, self-serving people will use whatever avenue works for them.

Some people are looking for something more than the church can provide them. They seem to believe there are answers out there that the church is not giving them. Unfortunately, they look to people like Chad and Lori Daybell to provide answers where there really are no answers. We see this kind of gullibility especially in people like Zulema Pastenes. Her testimony in both trials shocked me. I had never been exposed firsthand to someone who possesses the ability to believe wholeheartedly in someone as strongly as she believed in Chad and Lori. And she is not the only one. She and Melani Boudreaux are the two who admit to this day that they would have died to protect Chad and Lori. I'm not sure if I believe Melani, I find it hard to believe anything she says, but I do believe Zulema.

I also wonder if people like Chad Daybell are spoiled by their surroundings. Here's what I mean by that: Goodness was all Chad ever knew. Like a child given every toy imaginable, for his whole life, Chad was showered with goodness. They say there is no dark without light, no good without evil. The scales in Chad's life were out of balance. Weighted down on the side of good with no bad to counterbalance it. So much so that Chad had no appreciation for it. Goodness meant nothing to him. He could discard it like day-old coffee. So if goodness means nothing, it means nothing to do away with it, and that's what Chad did. He discarded everything that was good when he started murdering people, but it meant nothing to him. Just like the saying, there is no good without evil, if it's all good, then in the natural world, at some point, the scales will even out.

In places like Provo, Utah, and Rexburg, Idaho, people can be stifled by what they perceive as goodness. It becomes homogeneous and narrow. Living in such a condition can cause people to become petty, too involved in each other's lives. People become judgmental of each other and pick on the slightest flaws. A hierarchy forms and people are expected to remain in their place. More than that, they are forced to stay in their place. Moving up the ladder is, at worst, not an option and, at best, must be done methodically and with patience.

This starts in school and in church and moves up into the business community and what neighborhood you live in, even what church you go to. Mess with the status quo, and there is a price to be paid. It might be subtle, but total control is in the hands of only certain people, and they hold onto it fiercely.

Mormon Temple in Rexburg, Idaho. Personal photo.

What do I think the Mormon Church should do? I only have one answer to that question: Open up and talk. Instead of sweeping things under the rug and acting like they didn't happen or that the church has nothing to do with it, open up and be willing to make some changes. I have met many people who have abandoned the Mormon Church because they have lost faith in it. And I have met many who still think there is hope for the Mormon Church and they are sticking with it. The ones whom I have talked to who are sticking with the church admit to the problems and are the ones who need to step up. I hope they do.

These ideas of prophets and discernment concern me. Mormons look up to their prophets for guidance. The prophets are their portal to God. God speaks through the prophets. Prophets have knowledge the rest of us aren't privy to. They also have the ability to discern. They have a supernatural ability to know when someone is bad or doing bad things.

Why, then, does the church choose to remain silent about the bad people doing bad things in the name of the Mormon religion? Why aren't they willing to talk about these things? The only answer I can come to is that they think it is in the interest of the church to remain silent. So if that's true, are they putting the supposed interest of the church ahead of the safety of the members of their church? Even helpless children, members of the church or not? Do they think the greater good lies in protecting the church? Is this what God is telling them to do?

If God were telling them to do that, well, I don't believe in a God who would do that. Just what is God telling them to do then? Whether we say it's God or not, whether we believe the voice in our head is God or our conscience, there is a voice in their head. So what is their conscience telling them to do?

We know there are dangerous people within the Mormon Church espousing dangerous beliefs or ideas that are putting people in danger. They are being protected by the church. Thom Harrison and Tim Ballard are perfect examples. Is it more in the interest of the church to protect them, or should the church talk about what they are doing? The church only does that when they are forced to. As long as it is giving the church notoriety or money, they protect them and even promote them behind the scenes if not outwardly. The Mormon Church even has a system set up for this purpose. They have the ability to manipulate what information is out there. They spend a lot of money manipulating Google. I have heard that they pay Google to remove content that puts the church in a bad light. When the outside world finally holds people like Ballard and Harrison to account, the church finally denounces what it is they are doing.

What does that say about the Mormon Church? It says to me that the men who claim they are prophets or in some other way above the rest of us are more interested in themselves than in their congregation or any of the rest of us. People in positions of power who feel that way are extremely dangerous.

In this book, I have talked about the groups Preparing a People and AVOW, the book *Visions of Glory*, priesthood holders, visions, light and dark scale, patriarchal blessings, Mormon fundamentalism, and so much more—all of the things that brought Chad and Lori to a place where they could murder their own children in the most brutal way. Charles, Tylee, JJ, and Tammy aren't the only victims, and they won't be the last innocent people to die because of these ideas. Chad and Lori aren't the only people going down the path that led them to a place where they could commit these horrendous crimes. The very fact that Chad and Lori still believe that what they did was right should tell us how dangerous these ideas and the people and institutions that hold them are.

Are we done now that Chad and Lori have been convicted? Do we pat ourselves on the back for a job well done and leave it at that? Or does what Chad and Lori did open our eyes to the danger?

My sincerest hope is that the prosecutors in this case keep prosecuting, the police keep investigating (especially the FBI), the media keep digging, and the church opens up about those who would abuse their position within it. Sooner or later, it's going to come to a head. I don't believe it will be the second coming of Christ like a lot of people within the Mormon Church believe, but it will be a big deal.

Epilogue:

MY FEELINGS ABOUT IT ALL

I've been looking back on the trials of Chad and Lori and my life over the past year and a half. I've gone through a lot of changes in my life, adapting to what it throws at me, but the only other event that changed the direction of my life as much as this was the birth of my children. That's a profound change, and like some of the other big events in my life, I didn't even see it coming. Even as I was living it, sitting in the jury box, I had no idea that my life had changed in ways I couldn't have imagined.

I think a lot about the other players in this sad saga: JJ's grandparents, Larry and Kay, Tammy's aunt Vicki, Lori's son Colby, and many more. How are they doing? How has this tragic story affected them?

With media outside the courthouse. From left, Jennifer (GiGi) McKelvey of the *Pretty Lies and Alibis* podcast, Lauren Matthias of the *Hidden True Crime* podcast, Laura Pietila, my fellow juror in the Lori Vallow Daybell trial, myself, and Nate Eaton from East Idaho News.com. Photo provided by Lauren Matthias.

Kay and Larry will live the rest of their lives without ever really getting over what happened to JJ, Tylee, Charles, and Tammy. Sure, they got some relief with the conclusion of the trials, but can they move on and live out their remaining years in a positive way? When I looked back at the videos of Larry while doing my research, I saw a man declining in health. As strong and as determined as he has been to see this through, it can't help but take a toll on him. Even if they wanted to spend some time not thinking about the tragic events that occurred in 2019, the world will not let them.

Kay and Larry Woodcock in front of the courthouse after the Lori Vallow Daybell verdict. Photo provided by Lauren Matthias.]

As I write this, Chad and Tammy's house is being torn down, and there is a group of citizens building a memorial. Kay and Larry don't support the idea of a memorial there. There are just too many horrendous memories for them.

But what should be done with the property? I can't stomach the idea of the house remaining intact and someone living in it. Chad and Tammy's daughter Emma and her husband seemed to have no problem living there, but I don't think there is another person in the world who would want to. That part of the problem is solved. The excavators are thrashing it as I write. The "cozy cone" is no more. The stairs that were so controversial in the trial are in splinters. The upstairs window looking over the pet cemetery is gone. The shed that held the implements with Tylee's DNA is a pile of rubble being hauled to the dump. The ground that held Tylee and JJ's bodies will be all that remains.

Something has to be done with the property. Should it be a park-like memorial to the victims and those who loved them? Should it be an understated kind of memorial? Should it be left to return to its natural state? Should it be used in some way? Maybe the neighbors could be allowed to let their cows graze on it. I'm for whatever it is that gives Kay and Larry and the families of the victims the most peace.

What do I think the Mormon Church needs to do? I wish they would open up and be more willing to talk about the tenets in their belief system that at least open a door to people like Chad and Lori and many others to use those beliefs in a negative way. I don't think it's going to happen, and it would take a hundred more pages for me to lay out what I think those problems are. I'll leave it at that. At least I know others are questioning the Mormon Church and bringing to light what they think the pitfalls are.

If you've gotten this far in reading my book, you know how I feel about Chad and Lori's inner circle. I can't help but believe they are in some way complicit and still a danger. I know that prosecutors have a very busy docket. I know there are pressing cases pulling them away from people they might like to be prosecuting. Same with law enforcement. I hope there is one of them that doesn't let this drop. I hope we get closer to the bottom of the pit of the inner circle and the harmful belief system that is still out there.

Can at least one of the inner circle step up and ask for forgiveness? All they would have to do is tell us what they know and when they knew it and accept what comes to them. Maybe that's too much for them, but I would think the burden of holding on to their secrets would get to be too much at some point.

I also, however, hope that the people who spent so much of their lives investigating and prosecuting this case, attorneys on both sides, law enforcement, Judge Boyce, jurors, friends and family of the victims, and anyone else who got close to this case, are able to move on and not let it affect their lives in a negative way. They are the best of us and they deserve that.

How do I feel about Chad and Lori and what do I hope happens now? I feel like they are still in total denial. I think that at this point they are totally unable to admit to themselves what they have done. They have to stick to their belief system. If at some point they start to question it, all hell will break loose in their minds. That's what needs to happen. I hope that at some point they realize what they have done and that it was wrong.

I hope Chad's death sentence is carried out quickly. I know it has to go through all of the appeals and that will take years, but I hope it's a few years and not four decades. Maybe when the day of his execution is imminent, he will have a real conversation with God.

Lunch with some of my favorite people. From left, me, Kay Woodcock, Vicki Hoban, Lauren Matthias, and Larry Woodcock. Photo provided by Lauren Matthias.

Lori is hopeless. She will live out her days in misery. Yes, she will most likely manipulate those around her in prison in some way to her favor, and she will never give up her weird religious beliefs. She may even gain a following. She will be surrounded by hopeless people with nothing to lose, so it seems like they would be easy pickings. In her own private mind, though, the mind she will never share with anyone, she will be in hell for the rest of her days. Her beliefs will turn on her, and she will become the one whose body has been invaded by demons. I wonder if she feels it yet.

My life has changed in ways I could never have predicted. I have cried, had night terrors, felt real existing evil for the first time, and looked it in the eye. I have also been blessed. I have been given a gift. My community, my family, the new friends I have made all have come into focus, and I have a new appreciation for them all. I have become more human.

WHO'S WHO

Name	Description
Chad Guy Daybell, 1968–present	Convicted of three counts of murder, three counts of conspiracy to commit murder, and two counts of insurance fraud. Sentenced to death.
Tammy Douglas Daybell, 1970–2019	Chad Daybell's wife until she was murdered by him.
Chad Daybell's children	Garth, Emma, Mark, Leah, Seth
Jack and Sheila Daybell	Chad Daybell's parents
Matt Daybell	Chad Daybell's brother
Heather Daybell	Chad Daybell's sister-in-law, Matt Daybell's wife
Vicki Hoban	Tammy Daybell's aunt
Lori Vallow Daybell, 1973–present	Chad Daybell's current wife. Convicted of two counts of murder, three counts of conspiracy to commit murder and insurance fraud. Serving consecutive life sentences.
Janice and Barry Cox	Lori Vallow Daybell's parents
Charles Vallow, 1956–2019	Lori Vallow's fourth husband until Alex Cox murdered him. Stepfather of JJ, Tylee, and Colby.

Name	Description
JJ Vallow, 2012–2019	Kay and Larry Woodcock's grandson. Lori and Charles Vallow's adopted son. Biological son of Todd Trahan and Mandy Leger. Murdered in 2019.
Tylee Ashlyn Ryan, 2002–2019	Lori Vallow Daybell and Joe Ryan's daughter. Charles Vallow's adopted daughter. Murdered in 2019.
Colby Ryan	Lori Vallow Daybell's son and Joseph Ryan Jr.'s adopted son.
Joseph Ryan Jr., 1959–2018	Lori Vallow Daybell's third husband. Tylee Ryan's father. Colby Ryan's stepfather. Died supposedly of a heart attack, but there is some controversy about whether he may have been murdered by Lori.
Annie Cushing	Joseph Ryan Jr.'s sister
Alex Lamar Cox Pastenes, 1968–2019	Lori Vallow Daybell's brother. Zulema Pastenes's husband. Considered to be the "hitman" in the murders of JJ, Tylee, and probably Tammy. The alleged murderer of Charles. Died supposedly of natural causes, but there is controversy surrounding his death also.
Summer Cox Shiflet	Lori Vallow Daybell's sister
Zulema Pastenes	Wife of Alex Cox. Part of Chad and Lori's inner circle. Testified at both trials.
Melanie Gibb	Close friend of Lori Vallow Daybell. Part of Chad and Lori's inner circle. Testified at both trials.
David Warwick	Melanie Gibb's boyfriend. Part of Chad and Lori's inner circle. Testified at both trials.
Melani Boudreaux Pawlowski	Lori Vallow's niece, former wife of Brandon Boudreaux. Part of Chad and Lori's inner circle. Testified at both trials.
Brandon Boudreaux	Melani Boudreaux Pawlowski's ex-husband. Shot at by Alex Cox. Testified in both trials.
April Raymond	Lori Vallow Daybell's friend from Hawaii. Testified in both trials.

Name	Description
Kay Woodcock	JJ's grandmother. Testified in both trials.
Larry Woodcock	JJ's grandfather. Larry and Kay were instrumental in the investigation into what happened to JJ and Tylee.
Julie Rowe	Wrote the book *A Greater Tomorrow* published by Chad Daybell. Chad Daybell's friend.
John Pontius	Author of *Visions of Glory*. Deceased.
John Prior	Chad Daybell's attorney
Lindsey Blake	Prosecutor
Rob Wood	Prosecutor
Rocky Wixom	Prosecutor
Ingrid Beatty	Prosecutor and Idaho Deputy Attorney General (She has been appointed to the Kohberger case.)
Judge Steven W. Boyce	Presiding judge in both trials
Lieutenant Ray Hermosillo	Rexburg Police Department
Detective Chuck Kunsaitis	Rexburg Police Department

ACKNOWLEDGEMENTS

I have a lot of people to be thankful for and who have contributed to my ability to write this book.

First and foremost is my wife, Susan, who has spent countless hours helping me wend my way through the technology world and putting up with my frustration with that. She has supported me in every way possible, and I am truly thankful for that.

I mentioned Lauren Matthias of the *Hidden True Crime* podcast more than once in my book. There are several media people I am thankful for, but Lauren tops the list. Promoting and selling books is very hard, and I could not do it without the selfless help from her and others in the media.

Kay, Larry, Aunt Vicki, and all of the family members of the victims in this tragedy who have welcomed me and what I am doing. They have trusted me to write this story and supported me in ways I would not have expected.

My thanks to Lieutenant Hermosillo of the Rexburg Police Department for putting up with me singling him out. I did it because he exemplifies the excellence of all of the law enforcement and prosecutors involved in this case.

Judge Boyce and his court attorney Courtney for providing a seat for me in the courtroom and showing their appreciation for their jurors.

It would be impossible for me to name everyone who has supported me and contributed to what I have written, but you know who you are, and I am truly thankful and humbled by your support.

ABOUT THE AUTHOR

This is Tom Evans's second book about the murders of Tylee Ryan, JJ Vallow, and Tammy Daybell. He never thought he would write the first book, much less a second. He is currently working on a third and, he says, last book about the murder of Lori's husband, Charles Vallow in Arizona.

Tom's life took a 180 degree turn when he found himself on the jury for the Lori Vallow Daybell trial. By the time the trial was over, he decided to drop everything he had planned in his life and dedicate himself to getting answers to questions he couldn't get out of his head.

Prior to his jury service, Tom was a contractor designing and building custom homes. In his early years he spent one year attending Santa Rosa Junior College, one year at Humboldt State, and two years at Cal Poly San Luis Obispo. Even though he was at the top of his class in architectural engineering, he became frustrated with the things they were teaching and the time he was spending. He did, however, meet his soon-to-be wife, Susan, in college, and he says that made it all worthwhile.

Tom took what he learned at Cal Poly and in 1987 started a business designing and building custom homes, which he did for about thirty years. During that time Tom and Susan raised their two children. Susan was a teacher in the small town where they lived. Tom was on the school board and coached baseball and basketball. The couple was always busy helping the children of the community in whatever way they were needed.

Because of Tom's experience working with children, spending the last twenty years in Idaho and his interest in Mormon and Native American culture, he came to believe that writing about this case was meant to be for him. He has read everything he can get his eyes on about Western American history and Mormon history. Both are subjects that come into play in this case.

Made in the USA
Monee, IL
13 April 2025

15679243R00194